THE MYTH OF
QUETZALCOATL

The Myth of Quetzalcoatl

ENRIQUE FLORESCANO

Translation by Lysa Hochroth

Illustrations by Raúl Velázquez

The Johns Hopkins University Press
Baltimore and London

Title page illustration: Ehécatl-Quetzalcoatl from Cholula,
based on Durán, 1984

© 1999 The Johns Hopkins University Press
All rights reserved. Published 1999
Printed in the United States of America
on acid-free paper
9 8 7 6 5 4 3 2 1

Originally published as *El mito de Quetzalcóatl,* second
edition © Fondo de Cultura Económica, 1995
Published by arrangement with Fondo de Cultura Económica
and Enrique Florescano.
The Johns Hopkins University Press gratefully acknowledges
the Consejo Nacional para la Cultura y las Artes of the
Secretaría de Educación Pública, México, for its assistance in
funding the translation.

The Johns Hopkins University Press
2715 North Charles Street
Baltimore, Maryland 21218-4363
www.press.jhu.edu

Library of Congress Cataloging-in-Publication Data will be
found at the end of this book.
A catalog record for this book is available from the British
Library.

ISBN 0-8018-5999-9

In memory of Guillermo Bonfil;
for Héctor Aguilar Camín,
Fernando Benítez,
José Joaquín Blanco,
David A. Brading,
Rolando Cordera,
Pablo González Casanova,
Lorenzo Meyer,
José Emilio Pacheco,
Fernando Vilchis,
and Arturo Warman

According to some ethnologists, until a few years ago, in the jungles of Equatorial America, men and women met at nightfall around a hearth to listen in amazement to the stories of the gods and the genealogy of the tribe. Through myths, which are the substance of these poetic tales, each man and each woman of the group felt a part of a totality in natural and supernatural time, since the dead ancestors were also members of the tribe. The recitation by firelight enlivened the poems that recounted the origin of the world and the ethnic group and, in this way, made it real. The tribe was transformed for an hour or two into a true poetic community that included both the living and the dead.

—Octavio Paz, *La otra voz*

Myths are not history, yet . . . they manifest in time and create history and so are clothed in the language of becoming and change.

—Anne Baring and Jules Cashford, *The Myth of the Goddess*

In sum, myths reveal that world, man, and life have a supernatural origin and history, and that this history is meaningful, precious, and exemplary.

—Mircea Eliade, "Toward a Definition of Myth"

CONTENTS

Illustration plates appear following page 62.

PREFACE AND
ACKNOWLEDGMENTS

THIS BOOK was published for the first time in 1993 and became dated after a few months. In the second edition, I incorporate recent facts, I added an abundance of iconographical representations, and I presented three new chapters. The first aims at a "new interpretation of Quetzalcoatl," whereas the two other chapters compare the Mesoamerican god of corn with its Mesopotamian and Mediterranean equivalents.

During the development of this study, I received much encouragement I would like to acknowledge. A grant from the John Simon Guggenheim Foundation and the support of Lic. Rafael Tovar y de Teresa, president of the Consejo Nacional para la Cultura y las Artes, offered resources and time that were essential for researching, investigating, and writing. Anthony Aveni, Johanna Broda, Luz Evelia Campaña, Michael D. Coe, Manuel Fernández Perera, Alfredo López Austin, Joyce Marcus, Arthur G. Miller, and Karl Taube read different versions of this study and gave me valuable suggestions. I owe Manuel Fernández thanks for the careful editing of the draft, advice on bettering the presentation of the themes, and the translation from English into Spanish of the songs dedicated to the Mediterranean gods of vegetation. Raúl Velázquez produced the numerous drawings illustrating this book, the mastery of which will be much appreciated by the reader. I will always be grateful to Patricia Sámano for her patience in typing my drafts. My greatest stimulus has been to conceive of this book and write it amidst the refreshing flow of new ideas, interpretations, and discoveries that have modified our view of ancient Mayan and Mesoamerican history over the past ten years.

E.F.

I WOULD like to thank Dr. Willis Regier of the Johns Hopkins University Press for his generous and considerate collaboration while I translated Professor Florescano's fascinating book on a subject long close to my heart, the amazing Quetzalcoatl. I am indebted to Laura Benali for her excellent research on specific points and translation of tables 1 and 2. Special thanks also go to the "Divine Twins," Hayden and Tristan Draycott.

L.H.

INTRODUCTION

Years ago, when Joseph Campbell set out to document the different manifestations of the cultural hero, he discovered that there were a thousand of them.[1] At least in Mesoamerica, the combination of god and cultural hero produced a source of endless images. Quetzalcoatl is a great mythical figure evoking wisdom and civilization and is also one of the most ubiquitous and changeable of characters. One of his qualities is to be reborn during each period of history, but with a different face each time around. He always retains the halo of the ancestral aura but also possesses new meanings and a psychic charge that intermingles present yearnings with reverberations from the past.

Even the origin of the mysterious figure of Quetzalcoatl is ambiguous. His name comes from the combination of the Nahua word *quetzalli,* which means "precious green feather," thereby alluding to a bird with brilliant feathers, and the word *coatl,* which means "serpent." In Mesoamerica, the bird and the serpent are symbolic representations of two regions significant to religious and cosmological thought: heaven and earth. In Mesoamerican symbolism, this double entity is a synthesis of opposites: it conjugates the destructive and germinal powers of the earth (the serpent) with the fertile and ordering forces of the heavens (the bird). (See fig. I.1.)

The eternal battle between the creative and destructive forces gave birth to the image of the twins: two characters of similar appearance but endowed with contrasting powers. In Mesoamerica this symbolism is represented by the light of day and the darkness of night, the birth of life and the fatality of death, the green season of sprouting plants and the somber days of dryness and sterility. In Izapa, at the dawn of their civilization, the inhabitants of this southern Chiapas town engraved the deeds of the Divine Twins in stelae. Many years later, during the sixteenth century, this saga continued to be narrated by the Maya of Guatemala in books such as the *Popol Vuh.* In the stelae and the sacred book of the Quichés, the adventures of the Divine Twins

1

Fig. I.1. Painting in Olmec style of a man dressed in a cape of feathers and a bird mask, seated on a throne in the form of an earth monster. The image symbolizes the relation between heavenly and earthly forces. Drawing based on Joralemon, 1976, fig. 10, L.

were retold. These celestial emissaries descended into the earth, redeemed the corn god, who was keeping the gods of the netherworld prisoner, and led him to the surface of the earth, where a new era was born. This era was manifested as the corn plant, the precious food of human beings (fig. I.2).[2]

The figure of Quetzalcoatl, perpetuated through cosmogonic myths, the most durable creations of the Mesoamerican peoples, is linked with the region where these marvelous events take place: the netherworld. The Mesoamerican peoples conceived of the inside of the earth as a large, devouring mouth into which human beings, seeds, and heavenly bodies would disappear. In this conception, the netherworld was seen as the antipode to the daytime sky: it was the place of darkness, cold, sacrifice, and death. In contrast to this somber and ominous part of the cosmos, they represented the birth of the sun, the return of light, fruits, and life as opposite phenomena. The main agricultural myths were related to the cycle of the dry and rainy seasons, symbolically represented as seeds falling into the (damp, cold) netherworld and their later rebirth and transformation into the corn god.[3]

Over time, the creative and destructive forces that the Mesoamericans witnessed in the natural world were transformed into supernatural forces, in numens and deities that had to be appeased through ceremonies and religious practices. In turn, the religious ceremonies were converted into the principal activities of those who governed. In celebrating and directing the ceremonies, the governors appeared before their peoples as beings endowed with special powers to tame these terrible forces. In stelae, monuments, paintings, and codices, they are seen driving the germinal powers

Fig. I.2. The Divine Twins from the *Popol Vuh,* Hunahpú and Xbalanqué, observe the frightful figure of Vucub Caquiz descending toward a nance tree, in Izapa's Stele 2. Drawing based on Smith, 1984, fig. 55a.

of the netherworld and the fertile powers of the sky. In some cases, the corn plant sprouts from the governor's head. In other cases, the sovereign is represented as a cosmic tree that contains in its body the basic forces of the various regions of the cosmos.

The Plumed Serpent, an image alluding to the time when the earth was once again adorning itself with feathery, green cornstalks in spring, was also transformed into an emblem of political and religious power. During the classical period, the representation of the Plumed Serpent as a fertility symbol becomes obsessive. The numerous sculptures and paintings that reproduce it allude to the conjunction of the fertile powers of the heavenly world with the germinal powers of the earth. The Plumed Serpent almost always appears within an aquatic medium, surrounded by lilies, sea conches, Mexican emeralds, and seeds, all symbols of fertility.

Among the classical Maya (from the second to the ninth century), one of the most frequently represented symbols of fertility was the corn god's own effigy reborn on the surface of the earth. Another symbol, even more widespread, was one of the netherworld, the region where the miraculous transformation of death into life force occurred. For the Maya, the inside of the earth was the sacred site where the present era of the world originated and the place where everything debilitated or degenerated was transformed into life.

Nevertheless, in order for this process never to be interrupted, it was necessary to offer a sacrifice to the gods of the most terrible and creative regions of the cosmos. In the classical period, the ball game was the symbolic expression of the sacrifice human beings had to make to the gods of the netherworld. The ball game court was a symbolic representation of the underworld region, where the game was an expression of the forces of life and death contained in the place of sacrifice. At the end of the game, the winner decapitated the loser, whose neck spurted with dripping blood that fertilized the dry, thirsty earth. From then on, in Mesoamerica, the ball game is the space of ritual sacrifice, and the underworld the sacred place where that which degenerates or dies is reborn once again.

In the years following the fall of the kingdoms of the classical period, the cults dedicated to fertility changed. New gods appeared, and other symbols were imposed. The figure of the Plumed Serpent, which we see multiplied in Xochicalco, El Tajín, Cacaxtla, Tula, and Chichen Itza, acquires other meanings. Instead of referring to fertility and the renewal of vegetation, as it did during the classical period, it is converted into the emblem of political power. In these and other sites, the figure is surrounded by persons who occupied powerful positions in the world. This image resembles what historical traditions tell us. In these, Gucumatz, Kukulcán, Nácxit, and Quetzalcoatl are names that refer to figures who have military or political power. In the Toltecs' marvelous city of Tula, Quetzalcoatl appears as a conquistador of vast provinces, a founder of kingdoms and model of priestly virtues. He assumes the insignias of the charismatic hero and makes Tula into a powerful kingdom where the arts and knowledge flourish. It is a realm where hunger, the most frightening specter for these populations, has been eradicated. These same traditions relate the saga of the character who had managed to unify the role of supreme priest with that of the highest ruler of the kingdom of Tula. This character was the legendary Ce Acatl Topiltzin Quetzalcoatl. His charismatic image and unsurpassed deeds have ever since been spread throughout the lands of Mesoamerica.

Throughout Mesoamerican history, the symbols of primordial creation, the origin of time, fertility, the birth of human beings, and the appearance of civilization are intimately related to the figure of the corn god. From the earliest agricultural civilizations and cultures, the corn god holds the rank of progenitor of the cosmos and commander of the order of the new era. In the years following the fall of the kingdom of Tula, the Quetzalcoatl figure is multiplied, and its symbolism becomes more complex. From this point on, its ancient meanings are constantly reinterpreted and incorporated into other traditions. His multiple and ubiquitous figure is assimilated with Ehécatl, the wind god, the rich symbolism of Venus, the cults ritualizing the renewal of vegetation, and the myths of royalty and eternal life. Quetzalcoatl is connected to these cults, gods, and myths. He blends into these diverse entities and changes his symbols and representations.

To grasp this proteiform figure who is constantly dissolving into other, more complex forms, throughout this book, the reader will notice that I have utilized a variety of methods and focused my attention in different ways. Basically, I followed the historians' method that suggests examining changes occurring in human objects from traces left within the same historical process. I also made use of anthropological insights to analyze the structure of symbols and the language of myth. With this main focus, I divided the book into four parts. In the first part (Chapters 1 and 2), I present various manifestations of the myth of Quetzalcoatl as they appear in the texts and monuments, from the most ancient times through the Aztecs. In the second part (Chapter 3), I introduce new interpretations of the myths of creation and the cosmogonic accounts that have recently modified our conception of Mesoamerican history. In the third (Chapter 4), I present my own interpretation of the myth of Quetzalcoatl. In the last section (Chapter 5), I compare for the first time the symbolism and meanings of the Mesoamerican corn god with its American, Mesopotamian, and Mediterranean equivalents. This exercise demonstrates that, faced with the common mystery of death and the periodic resurrection of life in nature, human beings from different regions and cultures produce similar symbols.

ONE

The Diverse
Manifestations
of the Divinity

The Plumed Serpent

In Teotihuacan,* the combination of heavenly and earthly forces is expressed in the sculptures of the Temple of the Plumed Serpent and in the splendid mural paintings in which the serpent, its body covered with feathers, marks the walls where ritual acts involving the sacrifice and regeneration of nature were performed (fig. 1.1 and plate 1). The Plumed Serpent—the Mesoamerican dragon whose supernatural figure combines a rattlesnake's body, a quetzal bird's green feathers covering the scales, and a stylized head with ophidian roots—is one of the most prevalent symbolic expressions in early Teotihuacan. The Plumed Serpent is associated with both fertility and the beginning and ordering of time.

From the beginnings of Teotihuacan, the Temple of the Plumed Serpent was built in the center of the Citadel (fig. 1.2), the seat of political power. Alfonso Caso and Ignacio Bernal saw in the sculptures of this pyramid the cycle between the rainy season, represented by the Plumed Serpent, and the dry season, symbolized by the Fire Serpent. Michael Coe believes that the people of Teotihuacan conceived of their city as the center of the cosmos and suggests that it was through a series of dual oppositions that the

---

* To ensure both ease of reading and accuracy, accents will be used for all proper names as they appear in Spanish, with the exception of place names now commonly known in English, Teotihuacan, Yucatan, and Chichen Itza, and the name Quetzalcoatl. *Trans.*

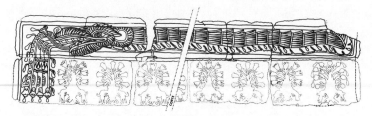

Fig. 1.1. Wall painting of the Plumed Serpent in a Teotihuacan building. Spurts of water from the serpent's mouth water the trees in the lower section. Drawing based on Berrin, 1988, 138 and 143.

Fig. 1.2. The Plumed Serpent sculpted in the main building of the Citadel, the center of political power in Teotihuacan. Drawing based on Séjourné, 1966, fig. 32.

sculptures in this pyramid represented the first creation of the universe. In a recent study, Karl Taube affirms that the curious head on the Plumed Serpent in the Temple of Quetzalcoatl was one of the most important symbols of secular and religious power in Teotihuacan. Following Caso and Bernal, he argues that this entity is a solar or fire serpent, a war symbol. He believes that the alternating heads of Quetzalcoatl and the War Serpent refer to the dual aspects of Teotihuacan's government. The Plumed Serpent is thus connected to fertility and internal matters of state, while the War Serpent is associated with military conquest and the empire.[1] Other researchers observing the ophidian heads in this monument have linked them to Cipactli, the caiman or crocodile whose image was a representation of the first sacred calendar day and a symbol of the beginning of counting time. According to this interpretation, the Temple of the Plumed Serpent is a monument dedicated to time: the place where the inaugural moment in which time was born and began to be accounted for was venerated.[2] What is certain is that the presence of the Plumed Serpent in sculpture, painting, and ceramics is observed in all phases of the great metropolis.

Elsewhere I have noted that one of the characteristics of Teotihuacan is that it is represented as a paradise of fertility. Its principal gods are agricultural deities. The most significant of these is the so-called Goddess of the Cave, a feminine entity invested with powers of fertility (figs. 1.3, 1.4, and 1.5, and plate 2a). She is born from a cave that stores germinal juices and nutritive seeds. Her body is a cosmic axis, and representations show her possessing the power to fecundate, spreading seeds and water. This is a universal goddess: she dominates the reproductive forces of the netherworld and the fertile forces of the heavens. She is a giver of life and death. Tláloc, the deity that follows her in rank, is associated with lightning, thunder, and rainwater (fig. 1.6, plate 2b). The third deity of this agricultural triad is the Plumed Serpent, who symbolizes vegetal renewal. Moreover, these deities are represented in the company of a cortege of characters in priestly garb, walking in a procession, singing hymns and pouring water or planting seeds (fig. 1.7, plate 3).

The symbolism of these agricultural deities dominates Teotihuacan iconography. The paintings, sculptures, ceramic objects, and temples and build-

Fig. 1.3. Wall painting of the Goddess of the Cave, which celebrates an act of fertility of the waters and the fertilization of the plants, in Tepantitla, Teotihuacan. From her ornament of feathers, branches grow out of a cosmic tree blossoming with and surrounded by birds and butterflies. Drawing based on the reproduction of this painting in the National Museum of Anthropology (Mexico).

Fig. 1.4. Reconstruction of a relief sculpture of the Goddess of the Cave found in the Walkway of the Dead, the main avenue in Teotihuacan. The goddess's hands hold symbols of vegetal renewal. Drawing based on Berrin and Pasztory, 1993.

ings transmit the message that in this city the gods had reunited the beneficent powers of earth and heaven to ward off the specter of hunger, creating a paradise where water and the most diverse products of the earth were in abundance. Teotihuacan was an earthly paradise protected by the Goddess of the Cave.[3]

Along with the cult of time and fertility, these societies developed the cults of war and the ball game, also associated with death and the regeneration of nature. Because they were rites involving bloodshed, blood being the supreme food of the gods, it was believed that "the warrior cult and the ball game cult assured the continued cosmic cycle of the sun and the renewal of fertility during the rainy season, and as such overlapped with agricultural fertility cults."[4] The ball game was even more associated with the creation of the present era of the cosmos. Its court was the scene for the great confrontation between the Divine Twins and the Lords of Death as narrated in the *Popol Vuh,* the sacred book of the Quiché people of Guatemala. Hun Hunahpú was decapitated in the netherworld's ball court. He was the First Father who descended into the dark region of Xibalbá, where he was rescued by the Divine Twins, Hunahpú and Xbalanqué, according to the story of one of the most famous myths of the *Popol Vuh.*

Fig. 1.5. **(a)** Mural called the Jade Goddess in Tetitla, Teotihuacan,
A.D. 650–750. From the goddess's hands water runs and precious
objects fall. Drawing based on Berrin and Pasztory, 1993, fig. 2.
(b) The principal deity of Teotihuacan emerges from a cave, which
because of the footprints seems to be a sanctuary that was visited in
a procession. The figure of the Plumed Serpent can be seen above.
Drawing based on Berrin and Pasztory, 1993, fig. 8.

Fig. 1.6. Representation of Tláloc, the god of lightning and rain.
(a) In this painting the Tláloc deity or priest carries the symbol of
lightning in his right hand and in the other an object from which
drops of water run down. He sings a flowery hymn. **(b)** This
beautifully adorned character carries a mask of Tláloc in his right
hand and in his left the powerful lightning, which alludes to this
god's powers. Drawings based on Berrin, 1988.

a

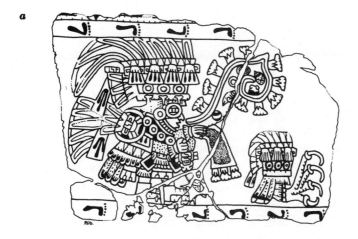

b

Fig. 1.7. Priests singing and sowing seeds in Teotihuacan. **(a)** This profusely adorned character seems to sing and be directed toward a sanctuary, given the footprints. To his side, there is a nondeciphered glyph that identifies him. **(b)** Another Teotihuacan character sings and scatters seeds and precious objects. He moves in the direction of the place where shoots of the American agave plant (*maguey*) are gathered for the bloodletting sacrifice. Drawings based on Berrin, 1988.

Venus

Another divine twin with a strong personality in the Mesoamerican region was Venus. Associated in the classical period with the cults of war and the ball game, the so-called great star played a central role in the cycle of death and resurrection. In the preclassical period, the Morning Star and the Evening Star appeared in association with the solar cycle in the Mayan region. From then on and throughout the classical period, the Maya established the precise synodic cycle of Venus as 584 days. They observed that the cycle was divided into periods during which the star disappeared and others during which it was visible as the Morning Star or Evening Star. They also recorded that one of these phases was equivalent to the sacred calendar of 260 days, which was in turn the lapse of time during which the cycle of planting and harvesting corn took place.

The persistent observation of the firmament and a continual mathematical recording of astronomical phenomena led the Maya to the discovery of five periodic revolutions of Venus coinciding exactly with eight annual revolutions of the earth around the sun. They also discovered that the period of Venus's invisibility, before reappearing as the Morning Star, was equivalent to the eight days' time it took a seed of corn, once planted in the earth, to reappear on the surface with its first sprouts,[5] thus converted into the "precious green plume."

These observations of Venus's movements in the sky, its amazing transformation into two apparently distinct luminous bodies, visible at different times during the year, and its connection with the germination of corn, transformed the great star into the focus of Mayan conceptions of sacrifice, the passage from life to death and regeneration.

As with the sun, the great star was doubled into the Morning Star and the Evening Star.[6] In Mayan mythology, and particularly in the *Popol Vuh,* Xbalanqué, the younger brother of the second pair of twins, seems to be associated with the morning aspect of Venus and with the triumph of light and life over the powers of darkness and death. Hunahpú, the older brother, is connected to the Evening Star and associated with death by decapitation and fertility. Hun Hunahpú, the father of the twins, is decapitated in the netherworld (the Xibalbá region), but his skull is transformed into fertile seeds in a tree laden with fruit (fig. 1.8). Hunahpú, his son, is also decapitated in a confrontation with the Lords of Xibalbá, but Xbalanqué manages

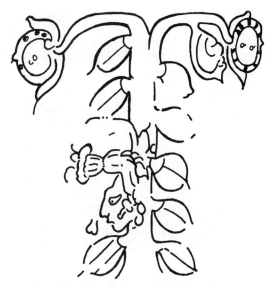

Fig. 1.8. The head of the corn god as the fruit of a cacao tree. This image is similar to the scene in the *Popol Vuh* in which Hun Hunahpú's head is transformed into a tree filled with squashes. Drawing based on Taube, 1985, 176, fig. 4c.

to restore him, and both win in the ball game against the Lords of Xibalbá, sacrifice them, and return in victory to the surface of the earth.[7]

As the Morning Star, Venus is surrounded by a warriorlike symbolism in Teotihuacan and in the Mayan region. In Teotihuacan, we know of representations of the great star associated with warriors, sacrificial scenes, and skulls. Various studies signal a direct connection between Venus and war from the early classical period.

The war waged in the year A.D. 378 by the Tikal kingdom against the kingdom of Uaxactún inaugurates a new type of strategy, armament, and war cult in the Mayan region, whose prototype originated in Teotihuacan. It was not conceived as a war to take captives for sacrifice, as was the ancient custom, but rather it was waged to conquer a kingdom. Its arms, deities, and symbolism came from Teotihuacan. In the monuments that the governors of Tikal erected to celebrate this event, the victors were depicted with clothing that identified the presence of Teotihuacan deities (Tláloc) and with arms characteristic of this region (lances). They made the day of

Fig. 1.9. War scene with signs associated with Venus in the mural of Structure B in Cacaxtla. Drawing based on Baird, 1989, 108.

the battle correspond to a significant moment in the cycle of Venus, in particular, with the first appearance of the Evening Star.[8] From then on, war in the Mayan region assumed the bellicose Teotihuacan symbolism, and Venus adopted a very definite warlike and sacrificial meaning (fig. 1.9).[9]

The various images of Venus represented in the monuments of the late classical period seem to re-create scenes from a myth of sacrifice and regeneration in which Venus is the principal actor. Venus is in combat, suffers a decapitation, becomes invisible for a period of time, and resurfaces transfigured as a god. War and its consequence, the sacrifice of the losers, is one of the dominant themes of this myth, as is the idea that death is a transition to the regeneration of life. In the cult of the warriors and in the cult of the ball game, sacrifice appears as the necessary condition for the preservation of the cosmos and the re-creation of life (figs. 1.10 and 1.11a and b).[10]

The Mesoamerican peoples of the classical period believed in the existence of two suns: the valiant and radiant daytime sun, and the nocturnal sun, which was captured in the netherworld and experienced the sacrifice of death. According to this myth, the appearance of the sun at dawn was the daily portent commemorating the primordial day in which the sun illuminated the earth for the first time. This diurnal life-giving sun was responsible for all the beneficial powers, and its ascendant route, from dawn to noon, was a distance traveled so that the forces of the night would be swept away to impose light, heat, and movement upon the cosmos. Noon signaled the

Fig. 1.10. A warrior with the sign of Venus on the southeast mural of the Higher Temple of the Jaguars in Chichen Itza. Drawing based on V. Miller, 1989, 294.

culminating point of this triumphal ascension. At this moment, when the sun arrived at its zenith, the diurnal sun was finished and the nocturnal sun began its turn.

As opposed to the triumphal route of the first sun, the nocturnal sun's crossing was plagued with dangers, threatened by the fearful forces of the afternoon, and concluded with the star's falling into the netherworld, where

Fig. 1.11. (a) The sign of Venus, in the form of a chest protector, and the stylized figure of the Plumed Serpent accompany these characters on a bench at the northeast colonnade in Chichen Itza. Drawing based on V. Miller, 1989, 298. **(b)** Character decorated with the sign of Venus in a detail of Column 9 from the Temple of the Warriors in Chichen Itza. Drawing based on V. Miller, 1989, 299.

it was decapitated at midnight. Thus, its successor, the new diurnal sun, initiated the arduous task of restoring light, combating the fearful night forces, and finally breaking the barriers of darkness toward its radiant appearance on the east side of the earth.[11]

The Mayan governors converted this astral myth into an image of dynastic power. They made the cycle of diurnal sun and nocturnal sun equate to the succession of royal power.[12] The Maya in the classical period linked this myth of astral and dynastic sacrifice to the ball game, which was transformed into the scene of sacrificial ritual. The death of the sacrificial victim was necessary in the netherworld because blood fed the regeneration of terrestrial and cosmic life. Thus an unbreakable chain was formed alternating between death and regeneration and nourishing the continuous flux of life.

Just as the sun doubled as both a diurnal and nocturnal star, Venus also maintains a double symbolism. In classical Mayan theology, Venus, as the Evening Star, is laden with sacrificial symbolism as part of the malignant forces of the night which, along with the other stars, lead the sun into the monstrous jaws of the earth, consuming their sacrifice at midnight. In addition, the Morning Star appears as a feared warrior who, in the dawn of the new day, anticipates the sun's arrival, combats its apparition by shooting darts at it, and is finally beaten, ceding its place to the resplendent star that in this way comes to dominate as the one and only king of the daytime sky.[13]

The sometimes antagonistic, sometimes collaborative relationship between Venus and the sun has a dramatic astronomical corollary when Venus, after having concluded its periodic distancing from the sun, approaches the sun, penetrates within the fiery halo of the star, and disappears between its rays. This dramatic event was transformed by priests into the portentous birth of the god of the Morning Star. Through their rigorous astronomical calculations, the Mayan sages who composed the Dresden Codex in the twelfth century recorded the precise moment in which, at the end of a synodic return of Venus, its path would converge with that of the sun. Then the fusion of both astral movements would initiate a new Venus's cycle and a new solar year. This spectacular coincidence in the movement of the two stars took shape in the sky in the form of a fire and the disappearance of the Evening Star in the fiery aura of the sun, as if Venus were being transformed into the sun, according to Eduard Seler's terms for it (fig. 1.12).[14]

The Maya, and later the Mixtecs, Toltecs, and Nahuatls, transformed this dramatic disappearance of Venus into a celestial and cosmic climax illuminating the birth of a god. Recently, Dieter Dütting showed that in the seventh century the leaders of Palenque had the birth of King Pakal coincide with the first appearance of Venus as the Evening Star.[15] The Nahuatls believed that after the Evening Star's disappearance into the netherworld, it

Fig. 1.12. Transformation of Topiltzin Quetzalcoatl into the Morning Star, according to the Vatican Codex A. Drawing based on Kingsborough, 1964, 37.

took eight days to return, grand and brilliant, on the day Ce Acatl ("1 Cane"), transformed into the Morning Star:

> It is said that when it burned, at once its ashes arose. . . . When the ashes were finished, at that moment they saw Quetzalcoatl's heart rise. According to those who knew (the ancient sages), he was in the sky and he entered into the sky. The elders used to say that he was transformed into the star that comes out at dawn. . . . They said that when he died, he did not appear for four days, because then he was dwelling amongst the dead (*Mictlan*); and that also by the fourth day he was provided with arrows; so that on the eighth day the great star appeared (Venus, the Morning Star), that they call Quetzalcoatl. And they added that it was then that he was enthroned as Lord.[16]

In the cosmological and religious thought of Mesoamerica, it is clear that, of all the stars, only Venus received the attention that was lavished on the sun. What is important here is to stress the connection between Venus and the beginning of the rainy season, the planting of corn, and the appearance of the first green leaves of the plant on the surface of the earth. The combined study of astronomy, epigraphs, works of art, and myths made possible the discovery in the so-called Temple 22 at Copán of an extraordinary representation of the link between Venus and vegetal renewal. This remarkable edifice was built in the most sacred place of the Copán acropolis. It was situated in such a way as to function as an observatory enabling one to follow the movements of Venus during the days previous to the arrival of the rains. Between April 25 and May 3, the ancient Maya anxiously awaited the first rain, which would initiate the planting of seed, the great inaugural ceremony of the agricultural calendar. Temple 22 was the site where these important events were recorded and the place where vegetal renewal and the appearance of the young corn god were celebrated.[17]

This temple, besides being one of the most beautiful, illustrates the complex symbolism linked to vegetal renewal. Its entrance resembles the mouth of a large serpent or earth monster, receiving the visitor with open jaws. It is a portal that communicates with the inside of the earth, the cold and dark region of the netherworld. The four corners of the temple are decorated with masks that reproduce the First Real Mountain, which arose from the primordial waters on the day of the creation of the cosmos, in such a way that they are a representation of the famous mountain of sustenance spoken of in the creation myths. Its interior is a cave, the humid wall where the waters and primordial seeds are born. Furthermore, in the myths that narrate the creation of the cosmos, there is a crack in the top part of the mountain from which corn plants sprout leaves (fig. 1.13).

Inside this building, there is a room where the kings of Copán invoked their ancestors and protector gods. The entrance to this decorated space is distinguished by another extraordinary portal: a cosmic monster, symbolizing the arch of the Milky Way, extends from one side of the portico to the other, engraved with deep reliefs. On the sides of this powerful representation of the nocturnal sky, there are two *bacabs* (or mares), the Mayan porters in the heavenly sky. The reliefs and sculptures of this part of the temple thus narrate an important episode in the creation: the separation of earth and heaven and the establishment of the distinct regions of the cosmos (fig. 1.14).

Finally, the façade of this building was crowned with beautifully sculpted three-dimensional statues that represented the young corn god being reborn from the depths of the netherworld (fig. 1.15).[18] It may be that this extraordinary building links the rainfall announced by Venus's movements to the first seeds and the birth of the young corn god. The general effect of the building and its symbols is a celebration of the fecundating act constituted

a

b

Fig. 1.13. Representations sculpted in stone of the First Real Mountain, which emerged from the primordial waters the day of the creation of the cosmos and inside which the fundamental necessities for the sustenance of life were hidden. In the upper part of this primordial mountain, there was a crack from which plants hidden in its interior would grow. **(a)** Representation of this mountain in the altar of the Foliated Cross of Palenque. **(b)** Representation of the same mountain in Stele 1 in Bonampak. In this case, one can see the young corn god sprouting from the fissure in the upper part. Drawings based on Freidel, Schele, and Parker, 1993, fig. 3.8.

Fig. 1.14. Cosmic monster representing the Milky Way in the portico of Temple 22 in Copán. This portico gives access to the room to which the kings of this city would summon their ancestors and the protective gods of the kingdom. Photograph of a drawing by Maudslay, 1974.

by the first seeds and the origin of the cosmos, when the First Father created the present order, human beings and the food to ensure the continued reproduction of life.

Nine Wind (9 Wind)

In the representations of Venus we know of from the preclassical and classical periods, there are no vestiges of a link between the great star and Ehécatl, the wind god of the Gulf of Mexico cultures and another of the deities identified with Quetzalcoatl.

The deity Nine Wind,* one of the creator gods of the religions of the postclassical period, appears with these characteristics in cultures different from the Nahuatl tradition. The most ancient record of this deity comes to us from the Mayan region. In texts from the Cross Group Inscriptions that

---

* Like many Mesoamerican deities, the name Nine Wind is associated with a calendar date, in this case, 9 Wind. To underscore the interdependent relationships between sacred characters and the sacred calendar and yet make for easier reading, numbers in the names of deities are written out, whereas numerals are used for calendar dates. See note 23, where a work in English by Nicholson instead uses the term "The Deity 9 Wind." *Trans.*

Fig. 1.15. Hun Nal Ye, the Mayan god of corn, represented as an extraordinarily beautiful youth in a sculpture in Temple 22 at Copán. Drawing based on Maudslay, 1974, vol. 1, plate 17.

King Kan Balam had engraved in Palenque in the year 690, there is a narrative about the origin of the cosmos and the gods. According to the reading that has been given to this text, the First Father and the First Mother lifted the sky and started time on August 13 in the year 3114 B.C.E. (4 Ahau 8 Cumku). They then generated three gods, the famous Triad of Protectors of Palenque. God I was born on the day 9 Ik (or 9 Wind) and is associated with Venus and sacrifice by decapitation. The second son, God III, was born on the day 13 Cimí (13 Death) and is called the Nocturnal Jaguar God. The third god is God II, who was born on the day 1 Ahau (1 Lord) and is the god of lineages, mainly royal lineages. God II is identified with the so-called God K and also has the distinctive feature of having a serpentine leg.[19]

Nevertheless, the first person to specify Nine Wind's characteristics was Alfonso Caso. Examining the Mixtec codices, he discovered the presence of this deity and composed a biography that revealed a deeply rooted cult around Nine Wind outside the Central High Plains area. Relying on the Vienna Codex, Caso discovered the birthdate of this character on the day 9 Wind in the year 10 House of the sacred calendar, thus corresponding exactly to his calendar name. Nine Wind is a god because, as opposed to mortal beings, he is born from a piece of flint (fig. 1.16). From the beginning of his existence, he is a being destined to accomplish extraordinary feats. In his journey to the nocturnal sky, he receives the attributes and functions that would characterize his feats in the earthly world.

In a plate from the Vienna Codex (fig. 1.17), we see Nine Wind in a place in the night sky. He is nude and converses with the two creator gods, who instruct him and make him convey some complicated paraphernalia. They grant him an ancient wooden weapon (*una macana*) with three pieces of inlaid turquoise, a skin wristband, an obsidian knife, a cone-shaped cap in jaguar skin, a bird mouth mask through which he blows air and moves the winds, a tuft of black feathers, lances and a harpoon, shell ornaments, and a snail breastplate—in short, they endow him with the attributes we will later recognize as those of Ehécatl, the wind god in the Mixtec documents and codices and in Nahuatl texts. These gods also assign him four houses, probably those that in Mixtec tradition "are called his houses of prayer."[20]

The exceptional birth of Nine Wind is associated with the beginning of cosmic order and time, the initiation of a new era of the world which, according to the Vienna Codex, occurs on the day 5 Flint of the year 5 Flint (perhaps this is why it is said that Nine Wind was born from a piece of flint). On the day 5 Cane of the year 6 Rabbit, after his meeting with the creator gods, Nine Wind descends from the night sky to earth. He is adorned with all his ornaments and symbols and is accompanied by two characters. One of the characters carries the House of the Sun on his shoulders and the other the House of Xipe. On earth, Nine Wind is received by a divine following,

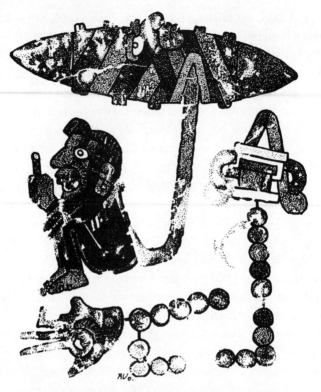

Fig. 1.16. Painting from the Vienna Codex showing the moment when Nine Wind is born from a flint, on the day called 9 Wind, in the year 10 House. Drawing based on the *Codex Vindobonensis Mexicanus I*, plate 49.

and one of his first tasks, which distinguishes him as a creator god of the new era, is to separate the sky from the earth and help to carry the weight of the sky, as can be observed in one of the pages of the aforementioned codex (fig. 1.18).

In the following days and years, the life of Nine Wind is occupied with successive feats. His appearance on earth is associated with the main event narrated in the codex: the emergence of Mixtec land, the appearance of fertile earth, mountains, and rivers. Further on, the codex shows Nine Wind witnessing the birth of a generation of gods and the first Mixtec lineages in the legendary region of Apoala. Later on, he calls an assembly of the gods responsible for ordering the Mixtec universe, and he assigns each god his areas and his tasks. He participates in the discovery and provision of

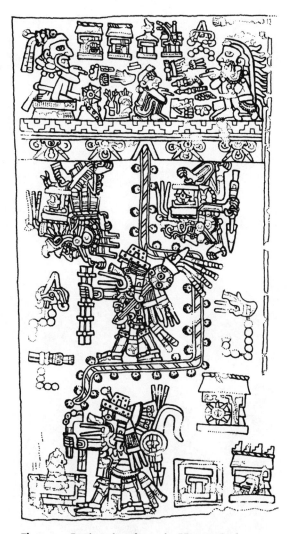

Fig. 1.17. In this plate from the Vienna Codex, Nine Wind is in the night sky embellished with the decorations that identify him as Ehécatl, the wind god. He is then shown on earth, dressed with all his ornaments and symbols. Drawing based on Kingsborough, 1967, plate 5.

Fig. 1.18. Ehécatl, the wind god, carrying the firmament (the sky or heavenly arch), in the Vienna Codex. Drawing based on Kingsborough, 1967, plate 6.

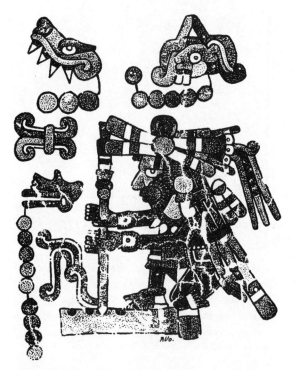

Fig. 1.19. Ceremony of the New Fire. Nine Wind lights the first fire on the day called 3 Lizard, in the year 6 Rabbit.

Fig. 1.20. Nine Wind performs a ritual whereby he grants names and titles to forty-four characters born from the Apoala tree, from which Mixtec beings and their lineages sprouted. Drawing based on the *Codex Vindobonensis Mexicanus I,* plate 30.

plants, arranges matrimonial alliances that establish lineages and dynasties, and participates in various ceremonies, among others the initial kindling of fire (figs. 1.19, 1.20, 1.21, and 1.22).[21] In another part of this codex, there is a portrayal of a group of sixteen masculine characters who share some traits that typify Nine Wind. The traits and qualities of these characters refer to the very arts of the shaman: war, song, writing, sacrifice, and religious ceremonies. These are Ehécatl's attributes. Elsewhere in the codex, he is endowed with the outstanding qualities of singer, poet, and writer. A painting shows him singing and playing a skull-shaped drum (fig. 1.23).[22] In other words, he assumes the characteristics of a cultural hero of divine nature.

Therefore, in Mixtec theogony Nine Wind is the god of air, one of the primordial forces that gave life to the world, the breath that spread wind and rain into the four directions of the cosmos. He is one of the creator gods and thus is present at the time when darkness and chaos reigned in the cosmos. He then helps to separate the sky and water on the surface of the earth and is himself transformed into the support holding up the sky.

Fig. 1.21. Nine Wind perforates Lord Two Dog's ear, in a ceremony whose purpose was to elevate people to powerful positions. Drawing based on the *Codex Vindobonensis Mexicanus I,* plate 30.

Fig. 1.22. Nine Wind sacrifices a quail and scatters wet tobacco, initiation rites of a religious cult. Drawing based on the *Codex Vindobonensis Mexicanus I,* plate 30.

a

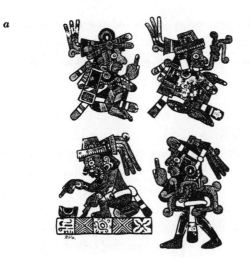

b

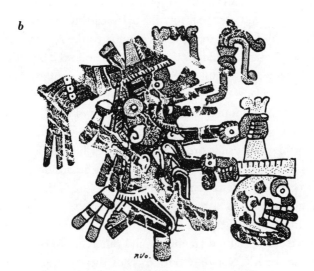

Fig. 1.23. **(a)** Ehécatl represented as a creator
and performer of songs, poems, and paintings.
(b) Ehécatl sings and plays a drum in the form of a
skull. Drawings based on the *Codex Vindobonensis
Mexicanus I,* plates 18 and 24.

Like the Mayan creator gods, Nine Wind appears as a deity who protects the noble lineages and dynasties of the Mixtecs. And like the Mayan deities, Nine Wind appears to be associated with a pair of gods who symbolize respectively the forces of day and night: the deity who bears the House of the Sun and the deity who bears the House of Xipe. Everything indicates that this Mixtec Nine Wind is linked to the cult of Ehécatl, who seems to have his origins in the early classical period among the Huasteca and other groups of the Gulf coast. One of his major religious centers was in Cholula, the famous Tollan, which was the center for the adoration of the wind god and the sacred metropolis where governors of this region were consecrated.[23]

The new interpretations of the Vienna Codex illuminate the meaning that unifies the different parts of this document. According to this new reading, we would have the following sequence of events: the meeting between the pair of creator gods and Nine Wind, who is instructed about his tasks and receives the attributes and the authority to realize them; the appearance on earth of Nine Wind and the revelation of the earthly region of the Mixtec region; the birth of the Mixtec gods belonging to the Apoala tree; the assembly of the gods and goddesses in Mixtec land, followed by the definition of his attributes and the implantation in the Mixtec pantheon; the revelation of the useful plants and their forms of growth and use; the appearance of the sun and the beginning of the incessant flux of time; and finally, the establishment of the rites and ceremonies necessary to ensure the conservation of earthly and cosmic order. The lineage of human beings and their governors begins with these foundations, which, according to the Mixtec codices, is a genealogy descending from the creator gods.[24]

According to available dating, until the end of the classical period, the entities of the Plumed Serpent, Venus, and Ehécatl demonstrate distinct origins, diverse supernatural attributes, and different symbolic and iconological characteristics. Not only does each of these entities have its own personality, but in the different cultures in which they are manifested, there are no identifying ties that connect them to one another. Nevertheless, as of the beginning of the postclassical period (A.D. 900–1000), these three beings begin to mesh until they are melded in the multifaceted character Ce Acatl Topiltzin Quetzalcoatl.

The time period that favors this union is at the end of the classical period and the beginning of the postclassical period, an era characterized by the disintegration of the ancient political organizations created by Maya, Zapotecs, and Teotihuacans, as well as the appearance of new power centers (Chichen Itza, Cholula, Xochicalco, El Tajín, Tula) and new religious practices. The specific place for this transformation is Tula, the city founded by the so-called Toltecs. The protagonist who manages to bring together these diverse entities in his own person is the warrior, cultural hero, and king of Tula, Ce Acatl Topiltzin Quetzalcoatl. The means by which this fusion is transmitted is a Toltec tradition adopted by the Aztecs, who in turn propagated it in various texts and songs that began to appear in the years following the Spanish Conquest. The result of these combinations is a legend, a highly complex myth, which has generated a very mixed bag of interpretations.

TWO

Ce Acatl

Topiltzin

Quetzalcoatl

The Hero of Civilization

In the mythical cosmogonies of Mesoamerica, the genesis of the universe is the work of a pair of gods who are located at the highest level of the heavens. These two gods govern the forces of duality of the three vertical levels and those of the four directions of the cosmos. The creative action of these gods is made present through other pairs of gods whose differences and confrontations produce the cosmic cycle, the beginning and end of the four suns or successive ages. In Nahuatl cosmogony, these ages conclude in a fifth era under which the cosmos is organized, a fifth sun is born, and present humanity emerges. In this cosmogony, Nahuatl, the wind god, is the precursor of the initial pair of gods and the regent who presides over the formation of the second sun, under the calendar name of Four Wind (Nahui Ehécatl). In the creation of the cosmos, four creative powers intervene: earth, wind, fire, and water. These primordial elements and their interrelations imply a history of creation. Nonetheless, once the powers that put the four eras or suns in movement are manifested, the primordial gods cease participating directly in the formation of the cosmos.

The gods who then begin to patronize the creation of the sun and humanity are less cosmic and more connected to the destiny of human beings. The most prominent of these gods is Ehécatl-Quetzalcoatl. According to different traditions, especially Nahuatl tradition, in addition to being one of the creating powers of the cosmological cycle and one of the four

Fig. 2.1. Quetzalcoatl, according to the Telleriano-Remensis Codex. In the text accompanying this figure, it is said: "This Quezalcoatle was the one said to have made the world and so they call him the gentleman of the wind, because they say that this Tonacatecotli (creator god), when he appeared to him, blew into the air and engendered this Quezalcoatle. To him they made round churches, without any corners. It is said that it was he who made the first man." Drawing and text taken from Kingsborough, 1964, vol. 1, plate 2.

supports holding up the sky, this is the deity that directly participates in the creation of the fifth sun and in the generation of the new humanity (fig. 2.1). "Historia de los mexicanos por sus pinturas" (History of the Mexicans through their paintings) narrates that a precursor to Quetzalcoatl, Nanhuatzin, was transformed into a sun by sacrificing his life on the sacred hearth of Teotihuacan. In this way, he began the new world era, a new beginning of time.[1]

The Cultural Hero

The cultural characteristics surrounding the figure of Ehécatl-Quetzal-coatl in the Mixtec and Nahuatl tradition are deified by the Toltecs, whose records were passed down by the Nahuatls. According to this tradition, no other god in the Mesoamerican pantheon joined in his person and in his acts the combination of civilizing qualities that concur in the character of Quetzalcoatl, god and supreme priest of Tollan (Tula), the marvelous place where Quetzalcoatl spread his doctrine and his material and cultural riches. The narratives that relay this tradition recount that

> *Quetzalcoatl* was esteemed and considered a god and they adored him from ancient times in Tulla, and they had a very high *cu* with many very narrow steps a foot could not fit in; and his statue was always cast and covered with shawls, and the face he had was very ugly, his head broad and bearded; and the vassals he had were all artisans and skillful in working green stones that were called *chalchihuites,* and also in melting silver and doing other things, and all these arts had their origin in the one named *Quetzalcoatl.*[2]

These accounts describe Quetzalcoatl as a deity belonging to the Toltecs, who appear in the texts as the people who created civilization and achieved excellence in cultural accomplishments: "First of all the *Toltecs,* who in written language can be called the first artisans . . . , were the first to populate this earth, and the first who came to these parts that they call the lands of Mexico. . . . These *Toltecs* were called *chichimecas* by everyone and they had no other special name for themselves apart from the one they took from the attractiveness and beauty of the works they made."

Together with the god Quetzalcoatl and the civilized Toltecs who populated the marvelous city of Tula, the texts identify the presence of the priest Quetzalcoatl, who is depicted as a model of priestly virtues: "There was also a temple that belonged to their priest called *Quetzalcoatl,* much cleaner and more precious than their houses; the temple had four chambers. . . . The house of this *Quetzalcoatl* was in the middle of a great river that runs through there, through the town of *Tulla,* and there this *Quetzalcoatl* had his bathing place."

Further on the texts enumerate the qualities of the people illuminated by Quetzalcoatl's doctrine: "they were the inventors of the art of making writ-

ten works"; "the first inventors of medicine, and then the first herbalist doc-
tors"; "they knew almost all the mechanical trades, and in all were unique
and excellent tradesmen, because they were painters, lapidarians, carpenters,
masons, tanners, skilled in writing, pottery, spinning and weaving."

> The so-called *Toltecs* were so skillful in Natural Astrology that . . . they
> were the first to keep count of and compute the days in the year. . . . Also,
> they invented the art of interpreting dreams, and were so listened to and
> wise that they knew the stars in the heavens and gave them names and
> knew their influences and qualities. . . .
>
> They were good singers . . . and composed, and arranged unusual
> songs in their head; they were very devout and great orators.
>
> They adored only one master whom they considered a god, the one
> called *Quetzalcoatl*, whose priest had the same name and was also called
> *Quetzalcoatl*, and who was very devout and attached to the things of his
> master and god, and for this was held in great esteem and readily obeyed
> by them . . . ; and as the above-mentioned Toltecs believed them and
> obeyed them in everything, they were no less attached to divine things
> than their priest, and very fearful of their god.[3]

In this exceptional vision of Quetzalcoatl's Tollan, the Aztec authors of
the aforementioned texts attribute the creation of the cultural legacy upon
which Mesoamerican civilization is founded to their Toltec ancestors, and
mainly to their god Quetzalcoatl. The invention of agriculture, the calendar, writing, astronomy, astrology, medicine, the arts, and practical trades
are mentioned. In the Nahuatl and Mixtec myths, Quetzalcoatl is the divine
messiah who brings to the earthly world the benefits of civilization. In
Nahuatl tradition, there is no codex like the Vienna Codex which describes
the descent of Nine Wind from the sky and relates his portentous actions
in the world of human beings, making the land fertile and then populating
this deserted land with gods, lineages, dynasties, kingdoms, and the riches
that favor life. However, the Nahuatl texts and other documents that relate
the origin of the Mesoamerican peoples do carry the same meaning. They
recount, in mythological form, the emergence of the earthly environment
and human beings as well as the gift of the essential things which a divine
emissary makes to them for the development of civilized life.

Another feature emphasized in the texts is the priestly role of Quetzalcoatl. As opposed to the Mayan tradition in the classical period, during

which priestly and ritual functions were obsessively performed by the ruler, in the accounts about Tula, the high priestly qualities of Quetzalcoatl are underscored. His celibacy and chastity are celebrated, as are his retreat in the temple, his strict practice of rites and penitence, his abilities as a sorcerer, and mainly his practice of self-sacrifice. All are archetypal qualities of priestly virtues. Several texts depict him as a religious innovator who introduced self-sacrifice and imposed it as one of the obligatory priestly functions in Tula. In this way, they connect this cult with the Plumed Serpent, a widespread emblem of political power in Tula and Chichen Itza during the ninth to eleventh centuries. The description of his magnificent "four houses" of oration, oriented toward the four corners of the cosmos, is another feature that is repeatedly indicated in the texts:

> One faced the east, and was of gold, and was called the golden room or house, because instead of whitewashed walls, it had gold plates which were cleverly embedded. And the other room faced the west and was called the emerald and turquoise room, because inside it had stonework of all kinds of fine stones, all placed and joined instead of a whitewashed wall, it was like a mosaic, and was greatly admired. And the other room faced the midday, that they call south, and was covered with a variety of seashells. Instead of whitewashing, it had silver, and the shells with which the walls were made were so artfully placed that no junctures appeared. And the fourth room faced north and was very well decorated with colored stone, jasper and shells.[4]

Birth, Youth, and Transfiguration of Ce Acatl Topiltzin Quetzalcoatl

This vision of Quetzalcoatl as god, priest, and cultural hero of Tula was mixed up and confused with the image of a character called Ce Acatl Topiltzin Quetzalcoatl, who had the same name as the god and priest, according to these texts. Ce Acatl Topiltzin performed feats as a warrior, governed Tula at the height of its splendor, lost the throne, and finally abandoned his kingdom, fleeing east with some of his followers.

Even when the sources do not always confuse the god and the legendary character, the identification of one with the other produces a wave of historical interpretation promoting the view that the legendary king of Tula was a flesh-and-bones human being who actually governed this city at a specific point in time. Nevertheless, the facts that make up his biography are more indicative of a mythological figure.

His forefathers, rather than having human features, present supernatural characteristics. The birth of the hero is not recounted as a natural one but rather as something that was accompanied by extraordinary signs. His father, Mixcoatl (Serpent of the Clouds), has the features of a demigod and is a conqueror who accomplishes fabulous feats and founds Toltec power in an imprecise area that falls somewhere in the northwest. Chimalman, his mother, has all the attributes of a goddess of fertility, and the texts describe her as a native of the land conquered both militarily and sexually by Mixcoatl. Topiltzin Quetzalcoatl is born of the union between the legendary foreign conqueror and the native wife with divine attributes. His gestation occurs in an extraordinary form. One of the sources relates that Chimalman swallowed a green stone and died when Topiltzin was born from that precious seed.

Different texts record that the hero was born in the year 1 Acatl (1 Cane), which is also his calendar name. The *Annals of Cuauhtitlan* state precisely: "1 Acatl. It is said that in this year Quetzalcoatl was born, and was therefore called Topiltzin (our prince) and priest Ce Acatl Quetzalcoatl."[5] Although accounts of his childhood and youth are rather vague, some sources indicate that he accompanied his father in military conquest and made sacrifices in order to become a great warrior. The most ancient texts emphasize the youth's qualities as a warrior and conqueror. Likewise, they distinguish a crucial occurrence during these years: his father's death and his bold effort to find the remains of his progenitor. Some texts relate that Mixcoatl was assassinated by his brothers, whereas others attribute this act to his sons. Various sources mention the fervent search for his father's remains and how Ce Acatl Topiltzin buried and honored these and erected the temple (Mixcoatepetl) in order to commemorate his father. These texts underscore how Topiltzin defeated and killed his evil uncles to punish them for the murder of his father.

The texts that narrate Ce Acatl Topiltzin's rise to power are abundant but do not always agree with one another. Even when there are no precise facts that inform us with certainty about how Ce Acatl Topiltzin Quetzalcoatl rises to the highest ranks of supreme political and priestly power, one of the most accepted versions recounts that he leads his people to Tollantzinco

Fig. 2.2. Effigy of Ce Acatl Topiltzin Quetzalcoatl engraved in a ridge in the Malinche, near Tula. Drawing based on Sáenz, 1962, fig. 2.

and later to Tula (the present-day archaeological site of Tula in the state of Hidalgo). Here he established a kingdom and assumed the two offices. Another version narrates that Topiltzin became king of Tula but that Tula had already been founded and built by others before him. In any case, the emphasis during this part of Topiltzin's life is placed on how he led his people, founded a kingdom, and acted as ruler.

In contrast to the plethora of textual references to this character, there is only one image of him, an effigy engraved in the Malinche hillside near Tula (fig. 2.2). The experts indicate that this effigy was not produced during Toltec times but rather during the rise of Mexica power. Although the upper part of the relief is illegible, several details identify it as Topiltzin. On the right side of the figure, the calendar name of King Topiltzin appears, the date Ce Acatl (1 Cane). The emblem of Quetzalcoatl, the Plumed Serpent, is displayed behind his image. Moreover, the character is wearing a *xicolli,* or cape, and has a copal bag, objects that belong to the religious cult. Further, he is presented in the act of self-sacrifice, with a sharpened bone letting blood from his ear. Another image (fig. 2.3), engraved in an altar in a building in Tula, although missing the glyphs that would allow for a clear identification of the individual, does show similarities to the sculpture in the Malinche hillside. It represents an elaborately decorated character wearing a helmet, nose pendant and ear caps. In his left hand, he is holding a circular shield and a bunch of arrows. In his right hand, he is clutching a hook-shaped weapon. These military signs make the character recognizable. Like the figure on the Malinche hillside, there is a Plumed Serpent undulating behind the body and forming a capital "S."[6] During recent excavations in pyramid B in Tula, an engraved column with the image of a bearded warrior was discovered. This appears to be a replica of Topiltzin Quetzalcoatl.

The most extensive literature on Ce Acatl Topiltzin Quetzalcoatl focuses on his kingdom in magnificent Tula. In these accounts, three aspects stand out. First, Topiltzin appears as the founder of a kingdom that subjugated various peoples, although some sources indicate that this dominion was more of a federation, similar to the Aztec Triple Alliance in the sixteenth century. Second, Tula was identified as a flourishing state, a metropolis where material riches were abundant, and as a center of civilization. Finally, the texts that relate Tula's greatness observe that in this marvelous king-

Fig. 2.3. Altar of what is called the "Palace to the East of the Vestibule," in Tula, Hidalgo. The elaborately ornamented central character carries a shield and arms and is surrounded by other individuals who sing or pronounce discourses. His body is distinguished by the emblem of the Plumed Serpent. In the cornice of the altar, there is another undulating Plumed Serpent. Drawing based on Umberger, 1987, 75, fig. 9.

dom political power and religious power were united in the person of Ce Acatl Topiltzin Quetzalcoatl, who had erected sumptuous temples, filled the coffers with riches, and imposed exemplary religious practices. The image spread by these messages is that in Tula political power, agricultural and material prosperity, the fruits of civilization, and religious perfection all came together. Tula was a happy kingdom whose people knew not of hunger. They benefited from a strong, prosperous, and civilized government.

However, this happy kingdom was suddenly undone by internal turbulence that the texts describe as an apocalyptic slaughter. Ce Acatl Topiltzin Quetzalcoatl, the exemplary priest, broke the code of conduct he had himself established, abandoned his duties, violated the norms of abstinence and chastity, and fell into a state of intoxication and lust of the flesh. His downfall is connected to the disturbing presence of Tezcatlipoca, the deity who had been Quetzalcoatl's antagonist since the creation of the cosmos. According to these sources, Tezcatlipoca directly intervened in the fall of Quetzalcoatl and in the destruction of the kingdom of Tula. Both catastrophes are preceded by omens that terrorized Tula's populations. Sahagún and other texts relate that the great necromancer Tezcatlipoca displayed his malevolent arts in order to murder Toltecs in the farmlands, markets, and city streets. He caused plagues, droughts, frosts, food poisoning, starvation, the appearance of monsters, wars, and collective massacres.

Stricken by his own downfall and by a series of disgraceful incidents in his kingdom, Topiltzin Quetzalcoatl decided to abandon Tula. His flight from the magnificent city has become even more widespread a myth than the other tales. It is said in the texts that, before leaving, Topiltzin Quetzalcoatl set his precious sacred houses on fire and ordered his jewels and treasures buried in different places. He said he was leaving for the Tlillan Tlapallan region (the place of red and black, a metaphor alluding to scripture and the dawn, the time of day when the sun's red color melts into the black of night). From there, he left with his faithful followers (fig. 2.4). On the way, some necromancers detained him and made him stay long enough to impart to them "all the mechanical arts of melting silver and working stones and wood, and painting and making plumes and other powers." Despoiled of his riches, Quetzalcoatl went on his way. The texts describe the hero's departure by noting the indelible mark he made on each place through which he passed. Thus the journey of the noble lord adopts the form of an epic odyssey whose geography and memory are sacred.

Fig. 2.4. Quetzalcoatl's Escape. In the text accompanying this plate in the Codex Vaticano Latino 3738, we read: "The two lords of penitence, Quetzalcóhuatl and Tótec, also called Chipe (Xipe), took the people that remained (in Tula), children and innocent people, and left with them going into the world populating it and taking with them other peoples that they encountered, and they say that they went on walking in this way. . . . They arrived at a certain mountain that they were unable to traverse, they thought up a way to bore a hole underneath it, and thus passed through it." Drawing and text taken from Kingsborough, 1964, vol. 3, plate 12.

Quetzalcoatl's escape gives rise to a variety of extraordinary events, from the naming of different places to ceremonies and prolonged visits that can retrospectively be recognized as marking the rise of the Toltecs (Culhuacan, Texcoc, Cholula). As Michel Graulich has noted, Quetzalcoatl's escape can also be seen as a metaphor for a voyage into the netherworld, a passage from death to regeneration. Like the voyage of the Divine Twins through Xibalbá in the *Popol Vuh,* Quetzalcoatl's journey is a passage from west to east through the cold regions of the netherworld. On this trajectory, he crosses over a river and through a dangerous pass in twin colliding mountains. He then builds a ball court in the netherworld and makes some houses under the earth (in a place called Mictlancalco), and his trip is, like that of the first pair of twins in the *Popol Vuh,* a succession of losses.[7]

This interpretation agrees with the end of Ce Acatl Topiltzin Quetzalcoatl's journey. The texts state that, upon arriving at the eastern coast, "after adorning himself, he set himself on fire." In a way that resembles how the twelfth-century Dresden Codex describes the disappearance of the Evening Star between the rays of the sun, Ce Acatl Topiltzin Quetzalcoatl catches fire, disappears into the netherworld, and, finally, is reborn in the east, transformed into the Morning Star or the Lord of the Dawn.[8]

Quetzalcoatl Multiplied

From the rise of Tula and its later disappearance in some place on the coast of the Gulf of Mexico, the character Ce Acatl Topiltzin Quetzalcoatl is reproduced in different parts of Mesoamerica. South of Tula, throughout the valley of Mexico, into the regions of Puebla, Oaxaca, Tabasco, Chiapas, and the Yucatan and throughout Central America (Guatemala, El Salvador, and Nicaragua), there are multiple traces recording the penetration of groups descended from the Toltecs, together with the arrival of a character who reproduces the traits of the legendary king, supreme priest, and cultural hero of Tula.

The transfer of Toltec traditions, and probably Teotihuacan traditions, to other regions of Mesoamerica is manifested forcefully starting with the decline of Teotihuacan and Tula. A first wave of migrations from the center toward the south took place during the eighth and ninth centuries, after the fall of Teotihuacan. Another wave occurred during the thirteenth century, after the dissolution of the kingdom of Tula. Insofar as we know the facts, Tula was the first Mesoamerican state built by a mixture of invading northerners and sedentary populations from the Central High Plains,[9] probably descended from Teotihuacan. Between the years 800 and 1150, this fusion of ancient and new peoples was able to create a strong state, founded on a powerful military organization, that sought to legitimate its political dominance by embracing the ancient values of Mesoamerican tradition, at the same time that it constituted a barrier to the northern invasions. When this state dissolved in turn, it provoked a diaspora of its populations toward the south, opening the door to new invasions from the north. The heirs of this state in their diverse wanderings propagated a political, religious, and cultural tradition of hybrid origins which they presented as the most ancient and original roots of the Mesoamerican peoples.

Among the myths spread by the groups that immigrated to the south, the ones that had the most impact in these regions were those of the god, king, and cultural hero called Quetzalcoatl and his magnificent kingdom in Tollan. In Cholula, for example, the great commercial and religious metropolis that flourished in the present-day region of Puebla, it was said that its founders had come from a place called Tullam, and for this reason they christened their city with the name "Tullam Cholullan Tlachiuh Altepetl": Tullam, in memory of the name of the original city; Cholullan because it was the original name of the site; and Tlachiuh Altepetl because these words mean "hand-built hill."

In the pyramid that dominated the city, which was the largest and tallest built in Mesoamerica, there was a temple where the two rulers of Cholula resided. It was said that the pyramid had been built to honor "a captain who in ancient times brought the people to this city to populate it, from very faraway lands in the west." The name of this captain was Quetzalcoatl, and after his death the temple was erected in his memory. The same text affirms that one of the prerogatives of the two priestly leaders of Cholula was "to ratify in their states all the rulers and kings of this *New Spain*" who, "by inheriting the kingdom or fief, would come to this city to acknowledge obedience to its idol, Quetzalcoatl, to whom they offered rich feathers, cloaks, gold and precious stones." The way in which both priests endorsed the lords in their duties was by "piercing their ears, or their noses or their lower lips, according to the kingdom they held." Likewise, at the end of a cycle of fifty-two years, "they came from all the towns" to confirm their fiefs and "pay tribute to the said temple." The text adds that "the indigenous peoples of all the land came out of a sense of devotion, in pilgrimages, to visit the temple of *Quetzalcoatl*, because this was the metropolis."[10]

There is evidence in the region of Oaxaca showing the presence of traditions from Tula. In the various codices (Vienna, Nuttal, Selden, and others), the deity Nine Wind is the patron of precious knowledge, the protector of dynasties, and the deity most connected to the destiny of the Mixtecs. The myth of the creation of the cosmos and the transmission of the arts of civilization to human beings narrated in the codices are confirmed in a narration that Friar Gregorio García found and included in his *Orígen de los indios del Nuevo Mundo* (Origin of the Indians of the New World). According to this text, which is from Cuilapan, at the beginning of the world, there were two gods of creation who resided in a palace near Mount Apoala. These two produced two brothers who were "very beautiful, discreet and wise in all the arts" and were called Wind of Nine Snakes and Wind of Nine Caverns. The brothers honored their fathers and dispatched their first offerings in their honor. Later, the twins recited prayers and begged their fathers to create heaven, to form the earth, and to favor the development of life. For this, they sacrificed their own blood. After a great flood during which the first human beings perished, the gods created heaven and earth and women and men, and in this way "that Mixtec kingdom was populated."

As has been observed by scholars studying this myth, Wind of Nine Snakes and Wind of Nine Caverns convey a doubling of Nine Wind, the creator god and cultural hero of the Vienna Codex, considered by the Mixtec dynasties and lineages to be the ancestor who founded their people.[11]

The presence of Quetzalcoatl and the Toltec mythology is even more accentuated in the southeast of Mexico. Recent studies show that the Putunes, a Chontal Mayan group located in the lands of Tabasco and Campeche, were the first Maya who came into contact with other peoples from the center of Mexico who spoke Nahuatl. From this ethnic and cultural blend came the Itzáes, a Putun branch of merchants and warriors who dominated the coastal traffic of the Yucatan peninsula and from there penetrated into the interior, invading and founding Chichen Itza in the first years of the ninth century A.D. [12]

Thus, between the founding of Chichen Itza and the year 1250, when it collapsed, the Itzáes, bearers of a culture composed of Mayan and Nahuatl traditions, mixed with the original population from the north of the peninsula, and together they created a city with mixed social, political, and cultural traits that made Chichen Itza a cosmopolitan center diffusing new symbolic messages. With the impetus of the Itzáes and the ancient cultural sediment of the Mayas, Chichen Itza was transformed into a multiethnic metropolis and a political center that surpassed the ancient Mayan kingdoms bound within the limits of the city-state. Like Tula, founded in what is today the state of Hidalgo, Chichen Itza is a city with a hybrid population, mixed with Itzáes from other regions, yet already Mayanized, and original populations imbued with Yucateca traditions.

The urban center of Chichen Itza conserved the architectural heritage of classical Mayan tradition but adapted it to a new social and political order. In place of the predominance of the star representing the king and his deeds, and instead of the hieroglyphic writing that recalled the origins and continuity of royal lineage, in Chichen Itza public art transmits a message alluding to collective symbols and expresses them in the more open language of painting and sculpture. In contrast to classical tradition, in Chichen Itza it is not possible to reconstruct the life and deeds of the rulers because there is no public record of these facts. There are temples and palaces dedicated to the public exercise of power, but in the principal monuments of the city (the Great Ball Court, the Temple of the Warriors, the Patio of the Thousand Columns, the Market, or the pyramid called the Castle) there is not one but many characters portrayed in the rites of the exercise of power. These constructions are of grandiose dimensions. They possess spaces and galleries of immense proportions, and instead of hieroglyphic writing, sculpture, reliefs, and painting dominate. Its architecture and symbolism convey a political and religious message accessible to great audiences, composed of different ethnic groups and ignorant of the secrets of writing.[13]

The presence in Chichen Itza of architectural features similar to those in Tula in Hidalgo, particularly the imposing plumed serpent columns (fig. 2.5), the atlantes, the *chac mool,* and the walls decorated with skulls, leads one to postulate that Chichen Itza is a kind of replica of the Central High Plains metropolis. It may well be a Toltec-founded city on Mayan land, the product of the migration of Ce Acatl Topiltzin Quetzalcoatl and his followers.[14] This impression is based on historical texts that narrate the establishment of Chichen Itza and Mayapan as two events derived from the presence of Quetzalcoatl on Yucateca lands.

The first documentation of the presence of Quetzalcoatl among the Maya was written by the priest Francisco Hernández in 1545. Hernández informed the bishop of Chiapas, Bartolomé de Las Casas, that in Campeche the indigenous peoples affirmed "that in ancient times, there were twenty men . . . with a leader called Cocolcan . . . who came to that land and who was called god of the fevers or of heat." Friar Diego de Landa confirmed this version and added in his *Relación de las cosas de Yucatán* (Report on things from the Yucatan):

> It is the opinion of the Indians that with the Itzaes who founded Chichen Itza, reigned a great lord named Cuculcán. And as proof that this is the truth, the main building [of this city] is called Cuculcán. They say that he came from the west, but they differ as to whether he entered before or after the Itzaes, or with them. They say that he was well disposed, had no wife or children and that after his return he was regarded in Mexico as one of its gods, and called Quetzalcoatl, and that in the Yucatan as well he was considered a god.[15]

Various sources reiterate the foundation of Chichen Itza by Kukulcán. Some narrate the establishment in this city of a political power that subjugated other provinces and record the introduction of new religious practices: "There was a time when all this land was the dominion of one lord, this being the ancient city of Chichen Itza and to whom all the lords of

Fig. 2.5. The imposing columns of plumed serpents at the Temple of the Warriors in Chichen Itza. Drawing based on Gendrop and Heyden, 1975, 290.

this province paid tribute as well as some from outside the area [Mexico, Guatemala and Chiapas]." Further on, the same text adds that "the first to populate Chichen Itza were not believers in idolatry until [Kukulcán], a Mexican captain, came into these parts and taught idolatry." [16]

Other evidence attests to this presence of invaders from central Mexico into Mayan land such as Quetzalcoatl-Kukulcán in Chichen Itza, signaling the profound impact of this figure on the later history of the Yucatan and noting

> that this Cuculcán returned to populate another city, so that he might deal with the natural lords of the land . . . and so that there all manner of things and business might be conducted; and for this they selected a very good site, eight leagues inland, in the land . . . where Mérida is now . . . and that there they enclosed a wide wall of dried stone, a quarter of a league around, leaving only two narrow doors . . . , and in the middle of this circle, they built their temples; and that the greatest one, which is like the one in Chichen Itza, they called Cuculcán. And they built another round [temple] with four doors, different from any other in that land . . . and that Cuculcán gave the city its name, not his own name, as the Itzaes did in Chichen Itza, which means Itzaes' Well, but rather he called it Maya-pan, which means the Mayan Banner, because they call the language of the land Mayan. . . .
>
> That this Cuculcán and the lords lived in that city some years and that he left them in great peace and friendship and returned on the same road to Mexico, and that on the way, he stopped in Champoton, which to honor his memory and his departure, made in the sea a solid building in the style of the one in Chichen Itza, at a good rock's throw from the coastline, and thus, in this way, Cuculcán was forever remembered in the Yucatan.[17]

The invasion of the Toltecs and Quetzalcoatl is also recorded in Mayan land in the highlands of Guatemala. The written records relate that upon his arrival he changed these peoples' ethnic composition, political situation, cosmic vision, and historical memory. From archaeological evidence, we know that the origin of the peoples of this remote region harks back to the beginnings of Mayan civilization in the preclassical era, when El Mirador, Cerros, Uaxactun, and Tikal formed the first Mayan kingdoms in the north of Guatemala. Therefore, it is surprising that the written records concerning the highlands of Guatemala state that the ancestors of the dynasties that had governed these lands from the ninth century on came from the legendary Toltec city of Tollan and that they spoke Nahuatl or "Mexica."

In the *Popol Vuh,* the fundamental text of the Quichés of Guatemala, the creation of the cosmos is the work of the god Gucumatz (a name composed of Guc, green feathers, and Cumatz, serpent). This is a translation of the

Toltec Quetzalcoatl. After the cosmos was ordered and the gods created the first four men, Balam-Quitze, Balam-Acab, Mahucutah, and Iqui-Balam, ancestors of the Quiché dynasties, the first of these began their migrating travels, from the legendary Tollan, which was located toward the east, to the highlands of Guatemala. On the way, his descendants agreed to return to the east, the original place of their forefathers, in order to receive the investiture of royal authority. In this place, Ahau Nácxit, the Lord of the East, endows them with royal emblems and the titles Ahpop and Ahpop-Camha, the two titles of the office of governor, and the "pictures of Tulan," so that with these insignias and traditions they returned to resume their migration toward the lands that would be those of the Quichés. Ah Gucumatz was once again involved in the conquest of lands and the foundation of Quiché power. Ah Gucumatz is the title designating one of the main Quiché chiefs, the head of the Gumarcaah dynasty and one of the most distinguished kings of this lineage, known both as a conqueror and a sorcerer:

> Truly Gucumatz was a prodigious king. Seven days he went up to the sky and seven days he walked to go down to Xibalbá; seven days he was transformed into a snake . . . ; seven days he was transformed into an eagle. . . .
>
> In truth, the nature of this king was marvelous, and all the other lords were filled with fear before Him. . . . And this was the beginning of the greatness of Quiché, when King Gucumatz gave these demonstrations of his power.[18]

Another text relating the migrations and foundations of the Quichés, the *Título de los Señores de Totonicapan* (Title of the Lords of Totonicapan), confirms the *Popol Vuh* version. It recounts that the Quiché lineage came from faraway Tollan, situated where "the Sun comes up," and that its conquests, foundations, and dynasties were favored and legitimated by "the great Nácxit father" Quetzalcoatl.[19]

The *Anales de los Cakchiqueles* (Annals of the Cakchiqueles), a document written in this Mayance language, recounts the migration of the Iximché dynasty from faraway Tollan to Solola, near the Atitlán Lake in Guatemala, where this lineage founded and expanded its power. As in the previous cases, the legitimacy of this dynasty comes from Nácxit, "who was in truth a great king" and the one who granted his ancestors the two highest offices of government, insignias of power, and had them pierce their noses.[20]

The dazzling saga of Nácxit-Quetzalcoatl and the Toltec tradition in the highlands of Guatemala is repeated in other texts. It is mixed in with the migration of the *pipiles,* the Nahuatl group that populated some regions of Guatemala and El Salvador, and it extends to the southern borders of Mesoamerica with the *nicaraos,* the Nahuatl-speaking group of migrants who encountered Spaniards settled in Nicaragua in the years of the Spanish Conquest.

Quetzalcoatl in Tenochtitlan

When Cortés arrived on the beaches of Veracruz, a good many of the multiple images of Quetzalcoatl had been concentrated in Mexico-Tenochtitlan, the city that was then a cosmopolitan hub of multiple traditions. In the Mexican pantheon, Ehécatl—the creator god of the Mixtec codices—occupied a central position, even while he was increasingly disputed by Tezcatlipoca and Huitzilopochtli. As wind god, Ehécatl was the breath that blew life and movement into the cosmos, the deity who made way for the rain gods and traveled to the four corners of the cosmos. His strange, round temple, through which the different winds circulated, occupied a strategic spot in the *sancta sanctorum* of Tenochtitlan, facing the Great Temple (fig. 2.6).

In affirming the imperial dimension of Mexico-Tenochtitlan, its rulers met in a sanctuary in the center of the city dedicated to the gods of the conquered peoples. In this way, the variety of Nahuatl deities combined with the gods, symbols, and theology of other regions. Thus, in addition to their own resemblances and relationships between Quetzalcoatl and other gods of the Nahuatl pantheon, new connections with deities of various pantheons were added. The Mexican Quetzalcoatl received the attributes and meanings of the Quetzalcoatl venerated in Cholula, and particularly the rich symbolic value of the Morning and Evening Star that was part of the tradition in various regions. Thus, Xolotl, Tlahuizcalpantecutli, and other avatars of Venus were assimilated to the Aztecs' Quetzalcoatl (fig. 2.7).[21]

In the Nahuatl cosmogony, Quetzalcoatl is one of the gods who participates in the creation of the cosmos, separating the sky from the earth and helping to support the heavenly vault. Like the Divine Twins in the Quichés' *Popol Vuh,* in Nahuatl tradition, Quetzalcoatl is the divinity sent under the Mictlan, into the netherworld, to gather the bones of ancient humanity in order to forge them into men and women of the new era.[22]

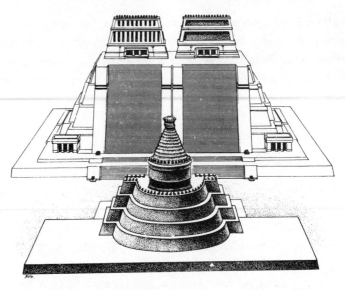

Fig. 2.6. The round temple of Quetzalcoatl, in front of the
Greater Temple in Tenochtitlan-Mexico. Drawing based on
Marquina, 1960, frontispiece.

Quetzalcoatl presides over another foundational act for the Mesoamerican
peoples: the organization of time and space. When the creator gods decide
to found Tonalpohualli, or almanac of their destinies, they consult Quetzalcoatl, and he agrees with them that the first day of the sacred calendar
should be 1 Cipactli (1 Crocodile), the second 2 Ehécatl (2 Wind), the third
3 Calli (3 House). In this way, the three initial days of the calendar represent the three levels of the cosmos (the netherworld, the heavenly sky, and
the earth), and in turn these three levels are linked through the combination of the 20 days of the month and the 13 months (or thirteenths) of the
year with the four corners of the globe. Finally, through the 260 days of this
almanac, the gods ruled the destiny of men and women, imposed order in
the world, and regulated the flux of time throughout cosmic space. Since
Quetzalcoatl was the god that could read the content of the sacred calendar's good and bad signs, he was therefore also the most connected of all
the gods to the destiny of human beings.[23]

In Nahuatl tradition, Quetzalcoatl is thus a divine hero who acquires
sustenance and indispensable worldly goods for flesh-and-bones beings and
the development of civilization. The "Leyenda de los soles" (Legend of the

suns) narrates how Quetzalcoatl, transformed into a black ant, manages to penetrate inside the mountain where all sustenance was kept hidden and extract some precious grains of corn. He carries these corn seeds back to Tamoanchan, where the gods were gathered, and there they decide that corn will become the main sustenance of life for human beings.[24] In a similar fashion, Ehécatl-Quetzalcoatl participates in the liberation of the goddess Mayahuel, prisoner of the monster Tzitzimime. He manages to free her and thereby acquires for human consumption that other indispensable item for infusing happiness into life, *pulque* (fermented agave juice).[25]

According to the Nahuatl texts, Quetzalcoatl is the god who hands down civilization, reveals time, and discerns the movement of the stars and human destiny. The calendar and writing, the two forms of wisdom that ordered

Fig. 2.7. Tlahuizcalpantecutli, according to the Codex Vaticano Latino 3738. In the text accompanying this figure, it is said: "This was the Dawn god or the god of Light when day wants to come in . . . at daybreak. They say that it was created before the sun." Drawing and text taken from Kingsborough, 1964, vol. 3, plate 31.

the Mesoamericans' knowledge of the world, were activities connected to the god Quetzalcoatl. They were also the responsibility of the two highest priests who also bore the title of Quetzalcoatl. These priests presided over religious ceremonies and in accordance with the sacred calendar, they indicated the days that were to correspond with given rites and sacrifices. The priest called Quetzalcoatl Totec Tlamacazqui, "Our Priest and Lord Plumed Serpent," was in the service of the national Mexican god Huitzilopochtli, and the Tlaloc Quetzalcoatl Tlamacazqui, "Plumed Serpent Tlaloc Priest," was dedicated to the god of rain.

In the Nahuatl texts of the sixteenth century and the chronicles spun by the Spanish clergy, Ce Acatl Topiltzin Quetzalcoatl of Tula was the arche-

Fig. 2.8. Ce Acatl Topiltzin Quetzalcoatl, wearing the priest's ornaments, according to the *Códice Borbónico,* plate 22.

Fig. 2.9. Quetzalcoatl in the Codex Vaticano Latino 3738. The text accompanying this plate attributes the following to Quetzalcoatl: "They say this (god) was the one who reformed the world with penitence." Drawing and text taken from Kingsborough, 1964, vol. 3, plate 17.

typal priest. The famous illustrated books, like the Borbonic Codex (fig. 2.8) and the Codex Vaticano Latino 3738 (fig. 2.9), repeat this image. Alfonso Caso relies on this evidence in order to elaborate the following description of Quetzalcoatl as the archetype of the priest:

> The body and face of the god are painted in black, because he is the priest par excellence, and the inventor of the self-sacrifice that consists of blood-letting of the ears and other parts of the body, by puncturing them with maguey spines and with picks made from eagle or jaguar bones. For this reason, we see in his headdress a green sash ending in a blue disk sticking out, indicating the *Chalchiuatl*, the precious liquid of human blood. Also, as priestly attributes, he carries in one hand an incense burner or perfumer with a serpent-shaped handle, and in the other, the copal bag.[26]

By accumulating these characteristics, Quetzalcoatl was the patron god of the *calmecac,* the place where the Mexican nobles studied the high offices of the priesthood and government. His patronage transmitted learning and writing as well as the knowledge of the mysteries of the sky, the earth, and the netherworld.

Besides the images of the god, supreme priest, and hero of civilization, the Mexican texts identify the figure of Ce Acatl Topiltzin Quetzalcoatl as the founder and ruler of the ideal kingdom. In the same way as in the Mexican mythology Tula is the archetype of the ideal city, Topiltzin Quetzalcoatl is the paradigm of the ruler and creator of the royal insignias, investitures, and symbols. He is the first king of the legendary Tollan, the founder of the dynasty and Toltec power.[27] In the *calmecac,* in the illustrated books, in rites and ceremonies, in temples and palaces that adorned Tenochtitlan, songs, stories, and effigies were reproduced which revitalized the memory of the character that the most ancient traditions recognized as the founder of the Toltec state, preceding Mexica power.

While the various manifestations of Ehécatl-Quetzalcoatl were appearing in Tenochtitlan and were combining with its own deities, in Cholula, a cult developed which favored Ehécatl. Friar Diego Durán, much taken with this character, gathered the most significant body of information about him. He says that in "all the villas and places of this New Spain, in their infidelity, the Indians had a particular god . . . who was honored as the advocate of the people with great ceremonies and sacrifices." In Cholula, this patron god was Ehécatl-Quetzalcoatl, who was highly revered by the merchants. Durán thus describes the characteristics of the god in this city:

This idol was in a long, wide room, placed upon an altar, embellished . . . with gold and silver, jewels, feathers and finely embroidered, elegant shawls. This was the wooden idol that had the face we see in the painting (fig. 2.10), and it is well to note: his body was all man and his face, that of a bird, with a colored beak. . . . He had in the same beak some rows of teeth and his tongue was sticking out, and from the beak to the middle of his face, he was yellow and then had a black band that came up to his eye. . . .

This was the decoration of this idol: on his head, he wore a pointed miter, painted black and white and colored. From this miter, some long painted streamers were attached in back. . . . In his ears, he wore drop ear-

Fig. 2.10. Figure of Ehécatl-Quetzalcoatl from Cholula, according to Durán. Drawing based on Durán, 1984, vol. 1, fig. 12.

rings of gold. . . . On his neck, he wore a large jewel in gold fashioned into a butterfly wing.

He wore a very elaborately crafted shawl all made of feathers, in black and white and colors . . . , like the wing of a butterfly. He wore a beautiful truss with the same colors and workmanship. . . . He wore golden stockings on his legs and sandals on his feet. In his right hand, he held a stick made into a sickle, painted black, white and colored. . . . In his left hand, he held a round shield of black and white feathers, all from sea birds.[28]

Around 1519, when Cortés arrived on the coast of Veracruz, Cholula was the second most important city in Mesoamerica. Only Tenochtitlan surpassed it in size and stature. Yet Tenochtitlan was not as ancient, nor did it have the glory of being a kind of holy land founded by the great Quetzalcoatl. The innumerable temples in Cholula created the legend that in this city there was a temple for each and every day of the year. Among the numerous sanctuaries, the greatest and tallest of all was the one dedicated to Quetzalcoatl as Ehécatl. It was also the most frequently visited of the temples.

According to Durán, two dates were celebrated in Cholula with particular devotion: the dates 7 Cane and 1 Cane, the death and rebirth of the god. During these well-attended festivals, this powerful commercial society splendidly and magnificently celebrated its patron god Quetzalcoatl.[29]

⟨⎯⎯⎯⎯⎯⟩
○ ○ ○

THREE

Interpretations

None of the countless known interpretations about the god, cultural hero, supreme priest, and king of Tula has forged a consensus among either experts or the public. The most divergent ones are split into irreconcilable extremes. One current sees in the accounts about Quetzalcoatl a constellation of myths without any relation to true historical occurrences. The opposite version holds that these accounts allow us to discern the historical existence of a royal personage who founded the kingdom of Tula, introduced important religious reforms, and created a civilized political community that was a model of government influencing many different areas of Mesoamerica.[1] The more numerous contingent believes in the historical existence of Quetzalcoatl. This group is also responsible for some of the most subjective, extraordinary, and contradictory interpretations of this figure. Among those who see pure myths in the multiple forms that Quetzalcoatl assumes, there is a current that reduces his disappearances and rebirths to a simple astral myth, to the alternating play between solar light and nocturnal darkness. Lastly, scholars who contend that Quetzalcoatl was a real flesh-and-bones person tend to attribute this figure with the hopes and fears of their own times and thus personalize Quetzalcoatl into some kind of fantasy.

In contrast to these tendencies, this study aims at a new interpretation. Although I have until now limited myself to a summary presentation of Quetzalcoatl's principal attributes, it seems clear that this entity was forged over a prolonged period of time and under the influence of distinct cultural traditions. As the most ancient images of the Plumed Serpent suggest, its first manifestations probably appeared years before the present era, and through a series of fusions, it gradually acquired the complex characteristics presented in archaeological evidence, paintings, and writings from the Mexica era.

Given this extended evolution, recent studies have brought to light the presence of four parts of the myth with distinct origins which later ended up blending together (1) the Plumed Serpent; (2) Venus and the duality of the Divine Twins; (3) Ehécatl, the creator god and wind god; and (4) Ce Acatl Topiltzin Quetzalcoatl, the ruler of historic Tula, which flourished between the ninth and eleventh centuries A.D. From Tula, different versions of Quetzalcoatl spread during the postclassical period to regions as diverse as the valleys of the Central High Plains, the coast of the Gulf of Mexico, the regions of Puebla-Cholula, the Yucatan, and the highlands of Guatemala.[2]

Differentiating the various components of the Quetzalcoatl entity is one of the most useful approaches in attempting to elucidate this fascinating myth. The specific analysis of each one of these components in terms of its iconographical, calendar, linguistic, symbolic, mythical, and theological aspects will permit us to better understand the formation of this extraordinary figure and thereby illuminate the more obscure zones of the Mesoamerican peoples' worship and religion.

For the historian, to study the changeable figure of Quetzalcoatl is to confront the relationships between myth and history. In order to advance our understanding of this relationship, myth must be accepted as such, as an account expressed with its own language and symbols, which can be unwrapped when the structure is penetrated, thereby clarifying the meanings and relationships of mythical language. Such is the case, for example, with the myth of the devouring earth that insatiably engulfs human beings, natural products, and the stars, until such time as the celestial powers impose a limit on this monstrous appetite and oblige it to allow the devoured beings periodically to return.

In this and in other cases, first, the symbolism of the myth must be explained according to its own expressions, and, second, an attempt can be made to explain its meaning. Otherwise, these myths are reduced to simple allegories of death and regeneration of nature or to mere astral myths. They are seen, as has been customary, as strange accounts of mysteries that the peoples who produced them managed to overcome by converting them into the regulatory principles of the cosmos and vital cycles.

Conversely, the obsessive search for historical figures in the numerous appearances of Ce Acatl Topiltzin, Gucumatz, Kukulcán, Nácxit, or Quetzalcoatl, besides creating confusion and inadmissible chronological extrapolations, obscures the symbolic character of this personality in the political development of these peoples. Perhaps a man of flesh and bones did exist in the city of Tula who assumed the double role of priest and supreme ruler of this kingdom. Nonetheless, the facts that shape the archaeological and historical evidence do not support reconstructing his presence in a credible way. Instead, the evidence is invaluable for examining the mythical construction of the archetype of government, which was born in an era troubled by the destruction of ancient political configurations based on the absolute power of the king.

The known historical facts do not allow us to affirm that Topiltzin Quetzalcoatl introduced the practices of priestly sacrifice in Tula or that he provoked a religious schism by being opposed to human sacrifice. Rather, both practices were ancient customs in all the previous kingdoms and cultures and continued to remain so until the Spanish invasion.[3] Perhaps the true innovation was in making the priestly function more relevant within the power structure and in creating the official title of Quetzalcoatl, as can be deduced from the fact that later in Cholula, in the Yucatan, and in Guatemala, the different figures called Quetzalcoatl mentioned in these sites were high priests, rulers, and captains known by this appellation.

Likewise, it is significant that the multiplication of the images of the Plumed Serpent at the end of the classical period and in the postclassical corresponds to the reference, in historical Yucateca, Quiché, and Cakchiquele texts, to invasions coming from the High Central Plains, led by figures that boasted the name of Kukulcán, Gucumatz, or Nácxit. From these invasions, governments and religions were established in these lands that claim a Toltec ascendancy. These connections can be accepted as evidence of Toltec penetration into the southeast but do not prove the presence of Ce Acatl Topiltzin Quetzalcoatl of Tula in these places. The only thing it shows is the diffusion of new political and religious emblems originating in Tula and accepted and reproduced in the southeastern lands.

Just as the ubiquity of Quetzalcoatl in such different times and places corresponds to a symbol and not to a verifiable historical figure, the reference to Tollan as a city ruling over very different and distant peoples from Tula de Hidalgo, such as the Mixtecs, Itzáes, Quichés, or Cakchiqueles, lends credence to the hypothesis not of a single central capital city called Tollan but of various regional capitals. In different times and places, these cities had to assume the function of multiethnic regional political centers. Dependent peoples would pay homage as recognized political intermediaries and support their leaders in order to receive political office, according to the model of Topiltzin Quetzalcoatl in Tollan, the city that thus became the archetype of charismatic power and government.

When the Mixtec codices and texts say that some of the rulers of this region traveled to Tollan in order to receive investiture of their political office; or when the Quichés relate in the *Popol Vuh* that their ancestors proceeded to Tollan to receive the insignias of power; or when the Cakchiqueles recount in their chronicles that the legitimacy of their dynasty was bestowed upon them by Nácxit-Quetzalcoatl, I believe that they are not referring to the city of Tula located in Hidalgo (Tula de Hidalgo) but to Tollan, a region that, like the mythical Tollan, was the magical center of power, the place where military, economic, and religious force was concentrated enough to appropriate these insignias and legitimize the mandate of its regional subordinates.[4]

The ubiquitous Quetzalcoatl and the mythical city where political power was legitimated reveal deeper meanings when the study relies on symbolic analysis and when this examination concentrates, rather than on the supposed historicity of the figure, on the analysis of the mythical structure underlying the account. We will therefore attempt to understand some of the multiple meanings behind the Divine Twins, Ehécatl, Quetzalcoatl, and the Plumed Serpent by delving into the language of the myths themselves.

The Myth of the Creation of a New Cosmic Era

When the sky, the waters, and earth were not yet separated and darkness and silence reigned, the primordial bird residing in the highest point of the heavens decided to create other deities to whom were delegated the tasks of organizing the cosmos, assigning its parts, and originating the plants, animals, men, and women who would populate the earth and venerate the gods.

In this age without order or time, the creator gods wanted to impose an order upon the destructive forces which would sustain the harmonious development of the cosmos and human life. Their great initial tasks were to separate the sky from the earth, to define a center or navel of the world, and to raise the four trees in the corners of the cosmos so that the sky would not

Plate 1. Paintings of the Plumed Serpent in Teotihuacan, in A. Miller, 1973, 165.

Plate 2 (top). A much restored painting of the Goddess of the Cave. The goddess's hands hold flowering plants. Drawing based on Berrin and Pasztory, 1993, catalog 41.

Plate 2 (bottom). Mural painting of the god Tláloc, singing, in Teotihuacan. In one hand he holds a stalk of corn and in the other a lightning bolt that announces the rain. Drawing based on Berrin, 1988.

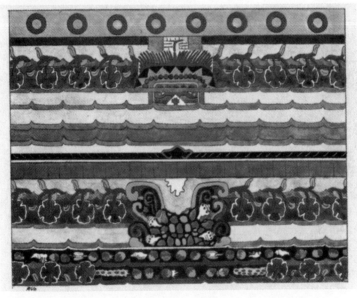

Plate 3. An elaborately decorated Teotihuacan character, seen here singing and moving toward a place of religious worship. Seeds fall from his right hand, while in the left he holds a copal bag. Drawing based on Uriarte, 1992, 132.

Plate 4. Probably a Teotihuacan representation of the primordial waters of the netherworld. In this picture of the so-called Temple of Agriculture, the undulating line on the surface of the netherworld is seen decorated with lilies, conches, and marine animals. In the center of the figure, note that there is also a cave. Drawing based on Gamio, 1979, vol. 2.

Plate 5. Hun Nal Ye celebrates his resurrection with a dance. Drawing based on Robicsek and Hales, 1981, 156, fig. 60.

Plate 6. Painting of the so-called Blom plate which shows another scene of the fight between the Divine Twins and Vucub Caquiz. Using their blowpipes, the twins point at Vucub Caquiz's face. Drawing based on Hellmuth, *Monster und Menschen*, frontispiece.

Plate 7 (top). Hunahpú and Xbalanqué (*left*) greet Itzamná (*right*), a lord of the netherworld, on a Mayan vase from the classical period. Drawing based on *Schatten uit de Nieuwe Wereld,* Brussels, Royal Museum of Art and History, 1992, 243.

Plate 7 (bottom). Scene set in the netherworld prior to the ball game between the twins and the Lords of Xibalbá. In the center, in front of a stepped pyramid standing on one side of the court, two characters greet each other with the game ball in hand. On the left, the Divine Twins can be seen and, on the right, a tree with a great bird Vucub Caquiz. Drawing based on Coe, 1982, 33.

Plate 8. Representation of the decapitated head of Hun Hunahpú, the First Father, on a Mayan plate from the classical period. Drawing based on Reents-Budet, 1994, 326.

Plate 9. Representation of the rain god Tláloc in five different manifestations, sharing attributes with other deities. The five manifestations are related to the east, the north, the west, and the south and the center of the cosmos, regions from which corn stalks sprout. Photograph from *Códice Borgia,* plate 28.

Plate 10. Panel from the southern ball court in El Tajín representing a scene from the primordial creation of human beings. In the central section, below, a kind of sanctuary immersed in water can be seen from which a human figure emerges wearing a headpiece in the form of a fish. On the right side, a seated figure lets blood from his penis. This precious jet wets the face of the character wearing the fish mask. The character performing the self-sacrifice of his blood has fangs that stick out and a kind of mustache, both features associated with Tláloc. Above, a figure of twin bodies with a single face and a bird mouth mask seems to be the creator god Ehécatl, wearing the little net skirts seen on Hun Nal Ye, the Mayan god of corn. Photograph taken by Brüggemann, 1992, 127.

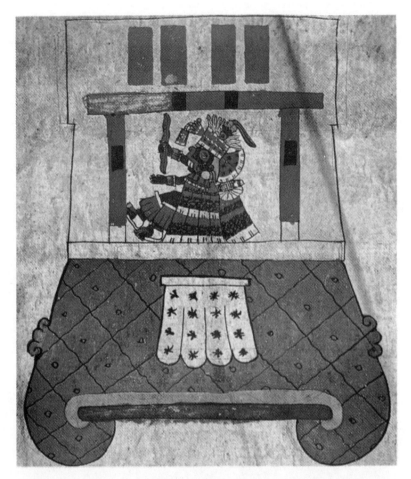

Plate 11. A symbolic representation of Mount Tláloc, the mountain that rose to the south of the Valley of Mexico. This is the classical glyph that in the iconographic tradition of Mesoamerica represents the hillside ridge (*cerro* or *altepetl*), conceived of as full of water with an internal cave housing the basic seeds of life. The lower part of the hill is symbolized by a drawing in the form of a four-sided netting, with a circle in the middle representing the earth. In the upper section, there is a temple with the god Tláloc inside. Photograph from *Códice Borbónico,* plate 24.

Plate 12. Sculpture of Coatlicue, the Mexica Earth Goddess. Museo Nacional de Antropología. Engraving based on Fernández, 1959.

crash into the earth and so that in the open space between them the winds could circulate through the four parts of the world. These were immense and challenging tasks, even for gods. They had to restrict the dominions of the powerful supernatural entities and oblige them to adjust to a new order. For example, in order to separate the sky and earth, the gods had to bore a hole into the body of the monster of the earth and break it in two. To drastically divide the marine waters from the earthly waters, they had to fracture ancient unities and establish new balances to gain the acceptance of the powers that protected these forces. Without this effort, the creator gods could cause uncontrollable catastrophes.

In the ancient cosmogonies, Nine Wind, Ehécatl, or Quetzalcoatl is one of the gods to whom the primordial pair gives the task of creating a new cosmic order. To transform the formless chaos into order and equilibrium, the gods proceeded by dividing, organizing, and placing different parts of the cosmos in relation to one another. The sky, earth, and netherworld were transformed into three levels of vertical space, with different subdivisions and levels, each one presided over by gods and symbols that identified them and expressed their properties. The most frightening of these spaces is the netherworld, the inside of the earth, the great mouth that absorbs human beings, plants, and stars. The dreadful risk of this insatiable mouth is that it can devour the products of the earth and the sky and refuse to return them. This is the danger that the myths attempt to ward off when they refer to the voyage of divine emissaries to the inside of the netherworld. One of the principal themes of the first part of the creation myths, this story is condensed in the accounts that allude to death and resurrection of life in the netherworld.

In the most ancient creation myth we know of, the engraving of Kan Balam in the temples of the Cross of Palenque from the year A.D. 690, it is said that the first god generated by the primordial pair was born on the day 9 Ik, or 9 Wind. We know that this god is the equivalent of the Mixtec or Nahuatl Ehécatl because in Palenque he is the one who undertakes the same action of raising the sky. In addition, for the Maya of the classical period, he was the god of corn, Hun Nal Ye, One Corn. Another deed associates the Palenque myth of creation to later Toltec and Aztec myths: the connection of the First Father with Venus. Hun Hunahpú, the main character of the first bird, who in the *Popol Vuh* travels to the underworld, is also associated with Venus and sacrifice by decapitation. Recently Dieter Dütting has shown that the date marking the birth of Pakal in the monuments of Palenque coincides

Table 1. Names Associated with Quetzalcoatl

Indigenous Name	Spanish Tradition	Attributes	Meaning
Quetzalcoatl	Plumed Serpent, Bird-Serpent, or Precious Twin	Deity associated with fertility	Religious icon representing a deity of fertility; one of its first likenesses is recorded in Teotihuacan (2d–3d centuries A.D.)
Hun Nal Ye	One Corn	God of corn	Mayan god of corn in the classic period (2d–9th centuries)
9 Wind	Nine Wind	God of wind	Mixtec creator god, associated with the discovery of cultivated plants and of corn (9th–13th centuries)
Ce Acatl Topiltzin Quetzalcoatl	One Reed Our Lord Quetzalcoatl	God and Toltec cultural hero	Legendary character whom Aztec sources present as king, god, and hero of the Toltec culture (9th–12th centuries)
Ehécatl		God of wind	Creator god of Cholula, associated with corn (15th–16th centuries)
Ehécatl-Quetzalcoatl	God of Wind, Plumed Serpent	Mexica creator god	According to Mexica sources, he is the creator god of the current era, associated with the beginning of civilization.
Culculcan Cocolcan Kukulcán	Bird-Serpent	Name and emblem of a character of Mexican origin, mentioned in the historical chronicles of Yucatán	Traditional Yucatán name for Quetzalcoatl. The character who appears in Yucatán with this name is a chief and warrior.
Gucumatz	Green-feathered Serpent	Quiché name given in the *Popol Vuh* to a creator god of the cosmos	Deity associated with the first creation of the cosmos

Table 1 (continued)

Indigenous Name	Spanish Tradition	Attributes	Meaning
Nácxit	Four Feet	Quiché name associated with Quetzalcoatl	In the *Popol Vuh*, Nácxit bestows the emblems of nobility upon the Quiché ruling class and is associated with Quetzalcoatl.
Hun Hunahpú	One Lord One Intermediary	The older brother of the first twins of the *Popol Vuh;* his twin is Vucub Hunahpú, Seven Intermediary.	According to the *Popol Vuh,* Hun Hunahpú is the first being to descend to the netherworld and is decapitated there.
Hunahpú	One Ahau One Lord	The older brother of the second twins of the *Popol Vuh*	Hunahpú is also decapitated by the regents of the netherworld, but his brother manages to revive him.
Xbalanqué, or Yax Balam	First or Precious Jaguar	The younger brother of the second twins of the *Popol Vuh*	Xbalanqué and Hunahpú are the heroes of the *Popol Vuh,* the conquerors of the celestial forces (Vucub Caquiz) and of the rulers of the netherworld.

with the first appearance of Venus as the Evening Star.[5] Since the seventh century, the Maya had the birth of their kings coincide with the appearance of the Evening Star, thus transforming them into divine and celestial beings, just as centuries later the Toltecs and Aztecs transformed the earthly disappearance of the legendary king Topiltzin Quetzalcoatl into the portentous birth of the Morning Star.

Hun Nal Ye is the equivalent of Hun Hunahpú, the older brother of the first twins of the *Popol Vuh* who descend to Xibalbá. (See table 1.) In other words, he is the First Father but also the first being who suffers the sacrifice of death and the apotheosis of resurrection. The mysteries of death and rebirth are incarnated in his person, who is transformed into one of the central figures of Mesoamerican theogony. Unlike the primordial bird of the creator gods and the cosmic powers incarnating the fundamental forces (earth, wind, water, and fire), Hun Nal Ye, Hun Hunahpú, and Quetzalcoatl are humanized gods. They suffer persecutions, fears, threats, and losses. Their lives are a drama that goes through death and culminates in resurrection. The three are connected to retrieving corn from the depths of the earth, making human beings from corn dough, and delivering the precious grain to human beings as food. After vanquishing the masters of the netherworld, all three incarnate the corn god and demonstrate the triumph of the forces of life over death.

In the cosmogonies, in addition to the presence of the gods who order the new cosmos, the pair of Divine Twins appears in the most ancient cultures. Recent investigations have discovered the Divine Twins realizing their portentous deeds in the mysterious stelae of the remote culture of Izapa.[6] One characteristic of these myths which unites Nine Wind with Ehécatl and the Divine Twins is that the deeds recounted occur in the years before the foundation of the cosmos and are part of the actions undertaken to establish the ruling order for this new era. Their acts are primordial deeds, and as such, they are exemplary and sacred.

The mysteries of death and resurrection are two central themes of the Mesoamerican creation myths which are intimately linked with the netherworld, astral cycles, the germination of plants, and the relationship with ancestors. From the settling of the first groups in Mesoamerica, these mysteries galvanized the attention of populations and spawned the first myths, rites, and monuments dedicated to commemorate them. What follows is one interpretation of these mysteries, based on my own reading of the cosmogonies, myths, and recent research.

The Netherworld: The Privileged Place of the Creation of the Cosmos

The netherworld, the region of the cosmos whose recent reconsideration led to a new interpretation of cosmological and religious thought of the ancient peoples of Mesoamerica, was previously an unexplored and poorly understood area. Perhaps this lack of understanding was due to the fact that, for years following the conquest of Mexico, the first friars identified this region and its symbols with the Christian hell. As we will see, the Meso-

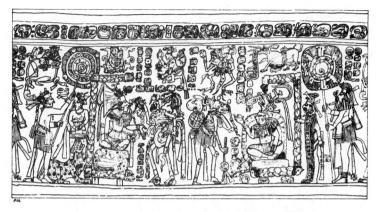

Fig. 3.1. Mayan funereal vase representing scenes, characters, and animals of the netherworld. Drawing based on Kerr, 1992, 446.

american conception of the netherworld is completely different from the Christian view.

In recent years, the netherworld has been the object of very different analyses that revealed a world never before known. The most ancient archaeological evidence depicts an aqueous place, where stagnant waters, rivers, and lakes were abundant. It was inhabited by a diverse and fantastic population: anthropomorphic characters living with dwarves and hunchbacks, half human and half animal beings, or entirely monstrous and zoomorphic ones, vanquished gods and fleshless creatures (figs. 3.1, 3.2, and 3.3). These were the beings who represented illness, physical decay, human sacrifice, and death. Their bodies are therefore painted in black, or represented as skeletons, to indicate the decomposition of the flesh. The Maya called this underworld region Xibalbá. Xibalbá was a cold and dark place that, during the night, rotated over the earth to become the nocturnal sky.[7]

Another discovery enlightened the surface and depths of the netherworld, allowing its crucial importance in the mysterious renewal of nature and its true place in the Mesoamerican cosmos to be determined. In analyzing the funerary vases and other iconographical materials of the Maya of the early classical period, Nicholas Hellmuth discovered the aquatic nature of this region and made an inventory of the beings that populated it.[8] We now know that the surface of the underworld was conceived of as a great reservoir for the primordial waters. In Mesoamerican iconography, this aquatic surface is represented as an undulating line simulating the crests of water in

Fig. 3.2. Scene of the netherworld on a Mayan funereal vase. Drawing based on Kerr, 1992, 451.

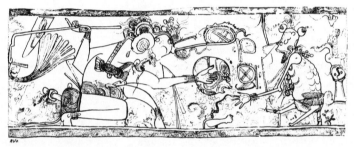

Fig. 3.3. Characters from Xibalbá, the Mayan netherworld, in a decapitation scene. Drawing based on Robicsek and Hales, 1981, 23.

movement in the vicinity of plants and aquatic animals, as well as internal caves. An example is the mural painting from Teotihuacan (fig. 3.4, plate 4).

In the Mayan area, the representation of this aquatic surface of the netherworld takes the shape of a quadriform space, as can be appreciated in an extraordinary vessel cover (fig. 3.5). The representation of this surface in four sections became common in Mayan history, and in the iconography of the classical period, it was identified as a depiction of the netherworld region. The sculpted stones that serve as markers in the magnificent ball game at Copán have the same form and thus indicate that the game described was played in the netherworld (fig. 3.6). Other representations show that the Mayan ball court was a symbolic expression of the geographical space of the netherworld. Moreover, in another vase, the corn god is depicted, frozen in

Other investigators perceived the relationship between the astral and agricultural cycles, since both supposed the alternation between death and regeneration. Esther Pasztory observed that the "essence of the ball game seems to be a contest between opposing forces," a confrontation implying the victory of one of the contenders and the necessary death of the other. In any case, one of the contenders was decapitated within the netherworld (fig. 3.10). In the agricultural cults, one of the most common practices was the blood sacrifice of children or adults in the initial and terminal phases of the agricultural cycles. The cycle of planting seeds in spring and the harvest in fall was connected to the annual cycles of the sun's movement (solstices and equinoxes) and to the great religious ceremonies, like the ball game, which was one form of celebrating these radical changes in nature (fig. 3.11).[13]

Until recently, the most accepted interpretation of the symbolism of the ball game was the following: "The ballgame is associated with the move-

Fig. 3.11. The ritual sacrifice of a ball player in the sculptures that flank one of the main ball courts in El Tajín. On the right, the winner is preparing to sacrifice the loser. Drawing based on Scarborough and Wilcox, 1991, fig. 3.10.

ments of celestial bodies, especially the sun and moon, which are related to seasonal agricultural fertility. The ritual game concluded with a sacrifice of a player symbolizing the death (and eventual rebirth) of the sun or moon which was necessary for the cyclically recurring astral movements to proceed in their usual manner." Today, recent investigations link the ball game to the netherworld and attribute it with the deepest meaning: it is the place of primordial creations, the region where the present era of the world originated. According to this interpretation, the ball court is a representation of this sacred region, the site at which the "First True Mountain" arose and from whose fissure the corn plant sprouted to bear the essential food for beings that from then on populated the earth.[14]

The recognition of these characteristics made the netherworld into one of the most important regions and encouraged the study of its relationships with the other levels of the cosmos. In Mesoamerican thought, the netherworld, the terrestrial surface, and celestial space were clearly distinguishable regions with their own characteristics but not separate worlds. Each one

Fig. 3.12. Monument from Chalcatzingo which represents the great mouth of the netherworld in a quadriform design. Drawing based on Grove, 1987, 125.

Fig. 3.13. Monument in Olmec style from Chalcatzingo showing the inside of a netherworld cave. Drawing based on Gay, 1971, 41, fig. 11.

of them communicated with the others through portals that would open up during the execution of extraordinary acts. One of the most represented sites of the netherworld were caves, which were like umbilical chords linking the netherworld to the surface of the earth. Caves were portals through which forces from the inside of the earth surged and the conduits for beings and terrestrial forces that descended to the underworld. The most famous of these thresholds was the great mouth of the monster of the earth, which was depicted in the form of an open jaw or as a fourfold shape enclosure where scenes and characters of the netherworld were represented. Two noteworthy monuments of Chalcatzingo show the great mouth of the earth monster (figs. 3.12 and 3.13).

In both representations, the allusion to the germinating powers inside the earth is clear. In figure 3.13, a highly narrative scene depicts clouds in the upper section which fall into raindrops irrigating the outside surface of the cave and making corn plants sprout. The human figure, holding a kind of scepter, seated on a throne inside the cave is identified by some as the Master of the Earth. Together, these images communicate the idea that the transcendental act of generating vegetal life was controlled from within the earth and that the cave symbolizing the netherworld was the generator of cosmic energy.[15]

In these first cosmograms, or representations in basic images of the conception of the cosmos, the role that the masters and leaders wanted to represent before the public is also revealed. In the Chalcatzingo monument, one observes a seated personage inside the cave appearing as the being who channels and drives the forces of water and earth to produce the miracle of the corn plant. Later, the corn plant image was used as a symbol of the reproduction of vegetal life and incorporated into the effigies of the rulers, thereby identifying them with the reproductive powers of nature.

In various objects and monuments representing Olmec leaders, the corn plant sprouts from the heads of these personages (fig. 3.14). In addition, the symbols of these plants, the husk, leaves, and kernels of corn, are the basic elements of the frontal band worn by leaders to distinguish themselves from mortal men (fig. 3.15). From then on, the symbols of the flowering of the corn plant, transformed into precious jade objects, adorn the rulers' headband. In other representations, a V-shaped crevice from which a corn plant sprouts splits the figure's head in two (fig. 3.16).[16]

The split in the heads of chieftains and great figures is an iconographical motif designating a prolonged life in representations of the supernatural world. In its most ancient known manifestation, it is the motif that connects the Olmec rulers' heads to the process of the corn plant's germination. As we know, this biological phenomenon occurs inside the earth, but in these representations, vegetal germination is directly associated with the generating power with which Olmec leaders were endowed. The message transmitted by these images is that the reproductive powers of nature and human life were attributes belonging to the person of the governor.

The Olmec monuments from this early period show that the netherworld is the place where the generation of life occurs and the site where the ancestors were transformed into gods. This is why the rulers maintain a direct connection to this environment (fig. 3.17). In the throne Monument 14 from San Lorenzo, a figure emerges from within a cave symbolizing the underworld, in such a way that his earthly power is linked to the domination exercised over the forces of the netherworld and to its relation with the ancestors. Its right hand holds a chord that, just like an umbilical chord, connects it with another figure engraved on the side of the monument who appears to be his ancestor or relative.[17]

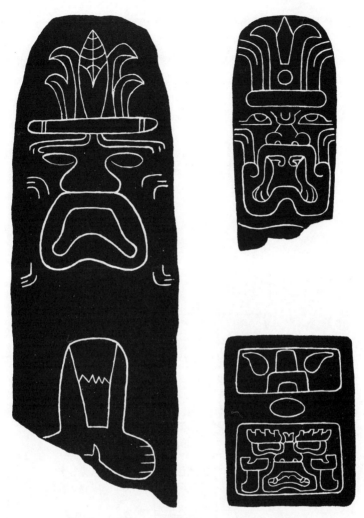

Fig. 3.14. The corn plant sprouts from the head of some characters who are represented on Olmec-style ceremonial hatchets. In the figure on the left, the representation of the ear of corn and corn leaves is very natural, whereas in the others it is much more stylized. Drawings based on Soustelle, 1992, figs. 63 and 69.

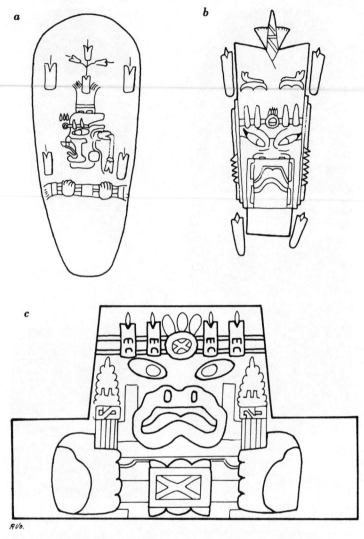

Fig. 3.15. Aspects of the corn plant on a headpiece worn by Olmec figures. Drawings **(a)** and **(b)** based on Joralemon, 1976, 32 and 41, and **(c)** on Martínez Donjuán, 1982.

Fig. 3.16. Olmec characters with a frontal V-shaped fissure.
Drawings **(a)** and **(b)** based on Covarrubias, 1961, 56, fig. 30, and
(c) on Furst, 1981, 149 and 154.

Fig. 3.17. Basalt throne from San Lorenzo (Veracruz) called
Monument 14. Below the effigy of the earth monster, in a niche
resembling the entrance to the netherworld, the figure of a ruler or
powerful ancestor emerges. The secondary character engraved in the
left section has been identified through facial features and the bird
claws on his helmet as the ruler portrayed in the colossal Head 4 in La
Venta. If this interpretation is correct, it means that there was a familial
relationship between the rulers of San Lorenzo and La Venta. The cord
that in this monument links one individual with another would be a
symbol of the union, "a royal tie." Drawing based on Campos,
1988, 29.

These facts and other recent studies suggest that the formative or preclassical period was one in which the culture that flourished in La Venta and in
Chalcatzingo had developed a conception of the corn seed similar to that of
the period several centuries later which is expressed in the Mayan book of
the *Popol Vuh*.

In the agricultural practices that sustained the life of these peoples, each
year the corn seed was introduced into the earth through a pit or crack that
broke the ground's surface. After eight days' time in the underworld, its
fruit rose up from these depths, opening the earth again to allow for the
green corn plant to sprout. This entrance of the seed into the heart of the
earth and its prodigious rebirth in the form of a life-producing plant was
a cycle that also implied sacrifice. In order for the plant and the corn husk
to germinate each year in fall, each spring a part of the previous harvest,

planting seeds, had to be sacrificed to the earth, where they would suffer underground the process of decomposition and transformation which transformed the buried seed into nutritious, revitalized fruit. In this sense, the kernel of corn was a precious seed, the ancestor upon whom the production of the future harvest depended. This vital nucleus ensured the continuity of the cycle of death and the resurrection of nature.

For all the peoples of Mesoamerica, the corn plant's cycle of death and resurrection established the paradigm of the process of creation. In harmony with the process of generating corn, all creation was necessarily implicated in the sacrifice of a part of life, and in the case of the creation of beings or vital materials, this creation was controlled in the netherworld, through the transformation of wasted material into vital energy.[18] This is how, from the earliest times, the inside of the earth, the deep, watery, dark, and frightening region below, was conceived of as the most important place of regeneration in the Mesoamerican cosmos.[19]

Following these interpretations, other authors have found interesting traces of ancient cults dedicated to the death and germination of vegetation through sacrifice. In the iconography of an extraordinary vase from the site of Chalcatzingo (fig. 3.18), Brian Stross discovered one of the earliest manifestations of the corn god and its relationship to the creation of life (vegetal germination) and the blood sacrifice.[20]

According to Stross, the so-called Princeton vase, a vase in Olmec style with Mayan silver, like the first vase, has the corn god as its central image (fig. 3.19). Both vases distinctly define the three levels of the vertical axis of the cosmos: the netherworld, the surface of the earth, and the celestial region. In the silver on the Princeton vase, the spatial orientations of the four corners of the universe are especially clear.

Like its Olmec predecessors from the Gulf of Mexico coast, the dismembered head occupying the central part of the Chalcatzingo vase has in its middle section a deep crevice, from which leaves of corn sprout, and another image of corn vegetation in a tuft of feathers depicted in the upper section. According to Stross's interpretation, the figure of the corn god appearing on these pieces functions like an *axis mundi* linking the netherworld with the surface of the earth and the sky. It therefore represents a place of transformation, mediation, and balance.[21]

In recent years, archaeological explorations in the Olmec area, on the coast of Veracruz, and the iconographical analysis of pieces in the "Olmec

Fig. 3.18. The extraordinary "Chalcatzingo Vase" with one of the most ancient representations of the corn god. Drawing based on Coe, 1985, 53, fig. 46.

style," found in different regions of Mesoamerica, have suggested that the fertility and vegetal renewal cults were related to the corn god, as Peter Joralemon indicated years ago.[22] A small jade figure, with a sumptuous handle decorated with corn symbols, suggests that we are in the presence of one of the most ancient manifestations of this god (fig. 3.20). Another piece, recently brought to light, places us before one of the most ancient representations of Quetzalcoatl as the transporter of corn seeds (fig. 3.21). As mentioned, this Olmec carrier of precious seeds was immortalized in this piece by representing this fundamental action.

New studies that have revolutionized our knowledge of Mayan culture have also drawn attention to the representations of the corn god. Iconographical analysis has illuminated the various components and glyphs associated with the figure of the corn god, personages who accompany it and its link with sacrifice by decapitation and the regeneration of life in the depths of the netherworld. In reconsidering previous studies, Karl Taube showed that a characteristic of the Mayan corn god in the classical period is the representation of its head in an extremely widened fashion—simulating the growth of the plant; its cranium is bulging and thus widens his face, which portrays a youthful appearance. The corn god is the ideal of youth, beauty, regeneration, and vital force in the Mayan world of the classical period. His name is Hun Nal Ye: *Hun* means "one," *Nal* means "corn stalk," and *Ye* is a term with several meanings (fig. 3.22).[23]

The identity of the corn god's head with the spike of the same plant is widespread in various Mayan objects and objects from other cultures, where it is clear that the god's head is the equivalent of the ear of corn (figs. 3.23

Fig. 3.19. The "Princeton Plate" with the representation of the decapitated head of the corn god. The head of the god rests on a plate, which since this period has been presented as the most important offering in religious sacrifices. Drawing based on Schele and Miller, 1986, 207, plate 75.

Fig. 3.20. Jade figure of a young character with an elaborate headpiece. The frontal band has grains of corn as symbols, and the upper part of the headpiece is crowned with an image of the Olmec corn god. Kernels of corn and corn flowerings sprout from its head. Drawing based on Benson and De la Fuente, 1996, 216.

and 3.24). In these and other representations, the head of the god, dismembered from the body, alludes to sacrifice by decapitation. Observing the representation of heads of the corn god on plates and Mayan funerary vases at the end of the classical period (fig. 3.24), Michael Coe suggested that these represented the decapitated head of Hun Hunahpú, the mythical Mayan hero who first descended into the netherworld and was decapitated by the masters of Xibalbá.[24] Taube notes that the decapitated heads with corn foliage undoubtedly symbolize the corn cut from the plant.[25]

Nicholas Hellmuth made more progress by clarifying the symbolism of the corn god and its relationship with the netherworld. Studying Mayan ceramics and monuments, Hellmuth described a figure who is almost always represented with a youthful look and enlarged head in a peculiarly ostentatious fashion that Taube later identified as the Mayan god of corn in the classical period. This figure wears a collar, a breastplate, and a skirt decorated with jade spheres and cylinders. His belt is composed of a series of tubular cylinders that fall vertically and exhibit an underskirt in netting, made of little jade balls and cylinders. Above this skirt, there is a conch medallion (*Spondylus*) with the effigy of the monster Xoc (fig. 3.25). Hellmuth observes that in the altar of the Foliated Cross in Palenque, Kan Balam, the king who succeeds Pakal to the throne of this city, wears an outfit very similar to the corn god's (fig. 3.26).

In this representation, it seems that Kan Balam, dressed in his splendid green suit, personifies the growing corn, since his body emerges from a fissure in the head of the earth monster, from which corn leaves sprout.[26] Likewise, Pakal, the figure facing Kan Balam, represents the corn buried inside the netherworld, since his body is rising up on foliage under his feet, where the decapitated head of the corn god lies, shaped like an ear of corn (fig. 3.26). Thus, in this image of the altar of the Foliated Cross of Palenque, the dynastic succession between the dead king and the live king is made into the equivalent of the cycle of death and resurrection in the corn plant in the

Fig. 3.21. Olmec carrying case for precious corn seeds. Small jade figure with one of the most ancient representations of the transport of alimentary grains. Drawing based on Benson and De la Fuente, 1996, 232.

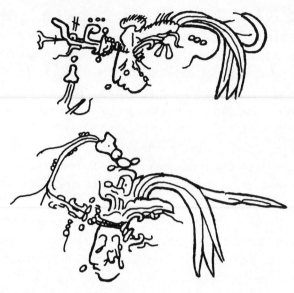

Fig. 3.22. Representations of the Mayan corn god.
Drawings based on Taube, 1985, 12, fig. 1.

netherworld: royal succession is transformed into a metaphor of the eternal cycle of renewal in nature.

Mayan ingenuity connected the cycle of agricultural life that occupied the majority of the population with symbols of the succession of power. So, just as the corn god dies in the husk and is reborn in each seed, royal blood also is interpreted as the precious seed that connected dead kings with their successors. In these images, the kernel or seed, the vital element allowing for the cyclical rebirth of the corn plant, is the equivalent of human blood transmitted from fathers to sons, thus ensuring the continuity of the royal lineage.[27]

In the altars of the Temple of the Cross, engraved in the year 690 to commemorate Kan Balam's ascension to the throne, the version of the origin of the cosmos inscribed in Palenque stated that it was ordered and put into movement by Hun Nal Ye, on the day 4 Ahau 8 Cumku (August 13, 3114 B.C.), the first day the Mayans began the present era of the world.[28]

Following the trail left by Michael Coe's work, Francis Robicsek and Donald M. Hales published a book, *The Maya Book of the Dead: The Ceramic Codex* (1981), containing a collection of extraordinary photographs of Mayan funereal vases. In the first publications dedicated to these vases,

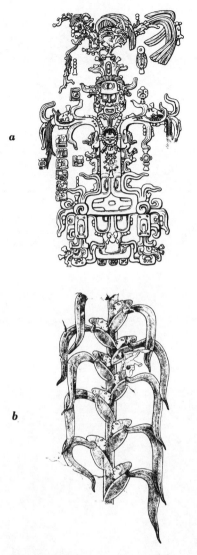

Fig. 3.23. Representations of the ear of corn in the shape of a human head. Drawing **(a)** based on Schele and Miller, 1986, 195, and **(b)** on *Cacaxtla*, 127.

Fig. 3.24. Representation of dismembered heads of the corn god on Mayan plates. Drawings based on Taube, 1985, 176, fig. 5.

Fig. 3.25. Two elaborately decorated characters with symbols of Hun Nal Ye dance the dance that precedes his resurrection, on a Mayan vase. Drawing based on Kerr, 1992, 451.

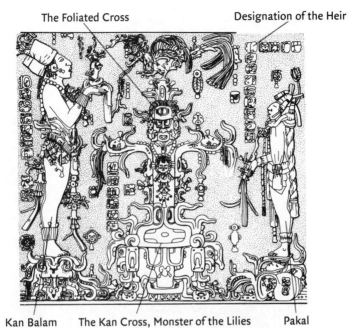

The Foliated Cross   Designation of the Heir

Kan Balam   The Kan Cross, Monster of the Lilies   Pakal

Fig. 3.26. The Foliated Cross panel from Palenque, with figures of the new king of this city, Kan Balam, on the left, and the dead king, Pakal, on the right. Drawing based on Schele and Freidel, 1990, 240.

Michael Coe discovered that a part of these scenes refers to the celebrated voyage of the Divine Twins into the underworld, as recounted in the *Popol Vuh*. Robicsek and Hales, in addition to enriching the saga of the twins with new images, also introduce other vases where the main theme is the corn god's entrance into the netherworld and his rebirth on the surface of the earth.

According to my interpretation of these disparate scenes, the narrative sequence would be as follows: first, the corn god seems to confront other personages who menace him with axes and instruments of decapitation in an aquatic environment (fig. 3.27a). In another episode of this saga, he is seen in another aquatic region with young, beautiful, naked women (fig. 3.27b). In carved bones found in a tomb in Tikal, a figure with corn god decorations is transported in a canoe manned by two gods rowing toward the depths of the underworld, where the canoe ends up capsizing (fig. 3.27c). They are accompanied by an iguana on this trip, as well as a spider monkey,

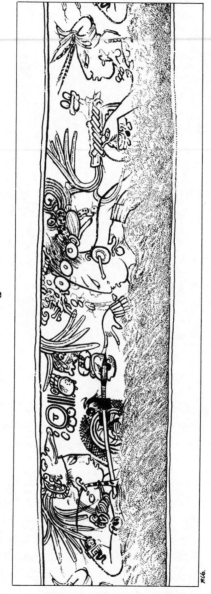

a

b

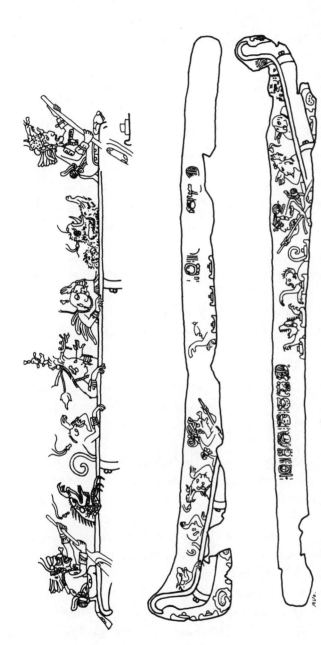

Fig. 3.27. Voyage of the corn gods to the netherworld. **(a)** The corn god encounters menacing characters. Drawing based on Kerr, 1989, 269. **(b)** The corn god converses with nude youths. Drawing based on Robicsek and Hales, 1981, 67. **(c)** The corn god travels by canoe through the netherworld, accompanied by rowing gods, a spider monkey, a parakeet, and a dog, in search of the place where the necessities for the sustenance of life are hidden. Drawing based on Schele and Miller, 1986, 270, fig. 8.1.

Fig. 3.28. Extraordinary Mayan funereal vase showing one of the Divine Twins (Xbalanqué), with a receptacle containing the ornaments and symbols of Hun Nal Ye's garb. On the left, the corn god seems to be performing the self-sacrifice of bloodletting. Drawing based on Kerr, 1989, 178.

a parakeet, and a dog. We recall that in the *Popol Vuh* animals also lead to the site of the hidden mountain of sustenance, the place where the yellow and white ears of corn were kept.[29]

In another plate with an extraordinary painting, on the right side, one of the Divine Twins carries a vessel with symbolic objects related to the corn god, while on the left side, it seems that Hun Nal Ye is performing the ceremony of sacrificing his own blood (fig. 3.28). The scenes that show Hun Nal Ye naked, and then in the process of receiving ornaments and symbols by those recognizing him, are similar to images from the Vienna Codex in which Nine Wind, the Mixtec Ehécatl, receives his garb and symbols from the creator gods. (See fig. 1.17.) If the painted scenes in the Vienna Codex are the same as those represented in the Mayan funereal vases, then it means that these represent a period preceding the creation of the cosmos and that this scene occurs in the netherworld, the place of primordial creations. If this is the case, then the descent of Nine Wind, which has been interpreted as a descent from heaven to earth, should instead be considered as a passage from the nocturnal sky to the earth, that is to say, from the netherworld.

Other vases present Hun Nal Ye preparing himself for his resurrection, assisted by two women who help him get dressed. Before this extraordinary omen, the corn god is seen, already dressed in his green jade costume, performing a dance in anticipation of his glorious rebirth. (See fig. 3.25.) Other vases recording this same scene indicate that performing the dance before resurrection was one of the main parts of this saga (fig. 3.29).[30]

As anticipated in Michael Coe's early studies on the Mayan netherworld, the analysis of funerary objects opened up a new path toward comprehending the cosmos and mythology of the Mesoamerican peoples. The discoveries made to date show that Mayan funerary evidence is equivalent to the famous Egyptian Book of the Dead, a kind of registry of myths, gods, inhabitants, places, and routes within the netherworld.[31] Recent studies have unveiled isolated parts of this fantastic and fearsome world. The most significant finding refers to the theme of the death and resurrection of the corn god and the voyage by the twins into the netherworld in search of the First Father.

The splendid images gathered in iconographical studies suggest that the day that leads the corn god into the netherworld begins with his falling into the aquatic and dark realm of Xibalbá. He then confronts the gods and beings of the netherworld, relating to naked women, lilies, vegetation, and marine animals inhabiting this aquatic medium. He then continues his voyage by canoe, which leads Hun Nal Ye to the place where the essential provisions are kept hidden. He also returns by canoe, with a cargo of precious grains of corn. Before Hun Nal Ye's appearance on earth, he is adorned with his ornaments and symbols. Then, some young women help him to put on his magnificent jade costume, which he wears in performing his festive dance preceding his resurrection. The corn god lives these and other adventures during his journey through the underworld. He is the equivalent of Hun Hunahpú, the character from the *Popol Vuh* who first descends to Xibalbá. However, unlike the mythical account, the graphic narration on the funer-

Fig. 3.29. Mayan funereal vase with a character who represents the corn god, Hun Nal Ye, performing the dance preceding his resurrection. Drawing based on Kerr, 1989, 116.

Fig. 3.30. Hun Nal Ye comes out of a tortoise shell on the day of his resurrection. On the right, the Divine Twins celebrate the event with a dance. Drawing based on Robicsek and Hales, 1981, 155, fig. 58b.

ary vases is much richer in events and characters, more charged with the symbolism of death and sacrifices and a much closer approximation of the natural processes of corn seeds' burial and transformation inside the earth.

The voyage of the corn god into the netherworld is followed by a second phase, which is well known through the *Popol Vuh,* where the Divine Twins, Hunahpú and Xbalanqué, are the main protagonists. The Divine Twins' mission is to voyage to the heart of the netherworld to retrieve from the First Father, Hunahpú, the essential corn seed upon whose reproductive power the generation of life and the cosmic cycle depend. The *Popol Vuh* narrates this deed in mythological and epic language, whereas the classical-period funerary objects offer us an account of this prodigious act in dynamic and beautiful images.[32] In addition to including episodes ignored in the great saga of the Mayan book of the netherworld, whose purpose was, according to Michael Coe, as in ancient Egypt, to gather incantations and supplications to ward off the dangers of this overwhelming region, the painted vessels record the marvelous act of the corn god's resurrection.

The resurrection of the corn god is the climax of the voyage to the world of obscurity and death, one of the outstanding themes depicted on the funerary vessels. The corn god is seen emerging from the V-shaped fissure in a tortoise shell, the symbolic representation of the earth floating in the primordial waters (figs. 3.30 and 3.31a and b). The resurrected god has a youthful appearance—he seems to rise out of the earth dancing (plate 5). He is received by Hunahpú and Xbalanqué, who rush to help him complete his exit out of the netherworld. On one of these vessels, the god clutches a bag full of grains of corn in his right hand. This image seems to refer to the epi-

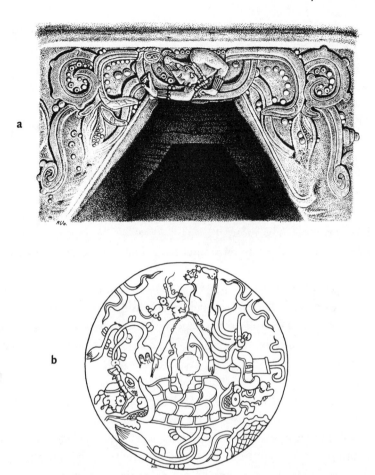

Fig. 3.31. **(a)** The corn god at the moment in which he is being submerged into the netherworld, with half of his body in the form of a corn plant and the upper part in human form. This representation is found in one of the subterranean buildings in the Royal Palace of Palenque. Drawing based on Robertson, 1985, illustrations 119 and 120. **(b)** Surrounded by an aquatic environment, Hun Nal Ye emerges from the crack in a tortoise shell that symbolizes the surface of the earth. Drawing based on Freidel, Schele, and Parker, 1993, fig. 6.20.

sode in the Nahuatl texts which narrates Quetzalcoatl's capture of the corn from the netherworld when he was able to extricate the divine food from the inside of the hidden mountain of sustenance.[33]

These extraordinary representations show that between the years A.D. 600 and 900, one of the most widespread themes in the imagery of the Maya was the theme of the death and resurrection of the corn plant, the birth of the corn god and the association of these mysteries with the creation and ordering of the cosmos by the First Father. Hun Nal Ye is the First Father of the Mayan classical period, the incarnation of life and the regulator of the creative forces of the netherworld, the heavenly sky and earth. The equilibrium of the cosmos and the cyclical, ordered renewal of nature were dependent upon this conjoined harmony.[34]

In recent years, the admirable intellectual efforts of several scholars have managed to integrate the results of archaeological, astronomical, epigraphic, and iconographical studies with the analysis of myths and the observation of religious practices of present-day Indians and farmers.[35] The result is a new image of the Divine Twins' voyage to the netherworld and a new interpretation of the birth of the corn god, two central themes in Mesoamerican cosmogony.

In the first place, it can be stated with certainty that the great mythological poem of the *Popol Vuh* refers, in its first part (narrating the efforts made by the gods to create the present era and new humanity), to a creation of the civilized world, which for the classical-era Maya was one governed by agriculture and represented by the domestication of the corn plant, its prodigious annual death and resurrection. The entire first part of the myth can be read as a metaphor of the seed, the ear of corn, and the conversion of the corn plant into the flesh of human beings and into the effigy of gods and rulers who controlled the cosmic forces.

The metaphoric play between the various phases of the plant's cultivation and the events occurring during the twins' voyage to the underworld appears in almost all the scenes described in the *Popol Vuh*. For example, the descent of the first pair of twins, Hun Hunahpú and Vucub Huhpú, to Xibalbá can be interpreted as an attempt to arrive at an agreement between the farmers on the earth's surface and the gods residing in the netherworld. The book the Maya called the dawn of life says that the masters of Xibalbá were bothered by the noise made by Hun Hunahpú and Vucub Hunahpú playing ball on the eastern court of the surface of the earth. This noise on the earth's surface can be interpreted as the disturbance caused by farmers cleaning, clearing, and preparing the soil to plant the corn during the months of February and March, before the first rains. The masters of Xibalbá were perturbed not only by this trespassing into their domain but also by the lack of an established agreement with the inhabitants of the earth's surface to control these matters.[36] This is why it is said in the *Popol Vuh* that the masters of Xibalbá got angry and ordered the twins to come down to the netherworld. As we know, the twins' first descent ends with Hun Hunahpú's death by decapitation on the ball court.

If, as has been seen before, Hun Hunahpú is the First Father, the corn god, then we can say that his decapitation corresponds to the cutting off of the corn during the harvest and to its subsequent planting inside the earth as seed. This event of agricultural life is transformed in the *Popol Vuh*. Hun Hunahpú's decapitated head is situated in the ball court of Xibalbá, the sacred place of transformations, hung upon a tree that has never flowered. Since Hun Hunahpú's skull is the first corn seed planted in the earth, it germinates miraculously and is transformed into a tree laden with fruit. Its germinating power is clearly expressed in the fertile encounter between Ixquic, a daughter of the masters of the netherworld, and Hun Hunahpú's skull. The *Popol Vuh* recounts that Ixquic was strangely attracted to this tree laden with fruits, among which was hidden Hun Hunahpú's skull. The skull drips saliva onto Ixquic's hand, thereby impregnating her. This is probably another symbolic representation of the encounter narrated on classical-period Mayan vases where Hun Nal Ye, the First Father, and the beautiful nude women of the netherworld meet. (See fig. 3.27b.)

This supernatural fertilization is equated with the phenomenon of the germination of the corn seed inside the earth. It also mythologically relates the event of Ixquic's pregnancy, a woman of the netherworld, and the birth of Hunahpú and Xbalanqué, the sons of Hun Hunahpú and Ixquic, who, like the corn plant, are born on the surface of the earth. In other words, underneath the language of myth, we witness the union of the reproductive forces contained in the corn seed and the germinal juices inside the earth. This conjunction produces the miracle of the corn plant's gestation.

Nevertheless, Hun Hunahpú does not get reborn. The masters of Xibalbá decide to retain him inside the earth until human beings, the farmers, pay tribute owed to the gods of the netherworld.[37]

Thus when the sons Hunahpú and Xbalanqué return at the next planting and disturb the surface of the earth by clearing it and working the land to introduce new seeds, once more the masters of Xibalbá are bothered and decide to call them into the netherworld. As we know, the Divine Twins use agility, intelligence, and cunning to vanquish the masters of Xibalbá at the ball game. They evade the successive traps, sacrifice the masters, and return victorious to the earth transformed into luminous stars. Their victory, as is said in the *Popol Vuh* in mythological language, meant the triumph of life over death, the retrieval of the bones of their fathers, the acquisition of the precious grains of corn from the hidden mountain of sustenance, and the prodigious rebirth of nature on the earthly surface.

The twins' descent to Xibalbá in the *Popol Vuh* and Quetzalcoatl's descent to the dominions of Mictlantecuhtli have the same purpose: to retrieve the seeds and bones of exanimate humanity in order to ensure periodic regeneration. The voyage to the netherworld is also both a retrieval and a pact. In vanquishing the Masters of Death through cunning strategies, the twins of the *Popol Vuh* and Quetzalcoatl denote the superior condition of the emissaries of the sky over the residents of the underworld. They are, however, obliged to reduce their pretensions of immortality and make a pact with the regents of the netherworld. According to this pact, the gluttonous earth will periodically return vegetation, dead beings will be reborn in their children, and the stars will illuminate the earth once again after its nocturnal transit through the underworld on the condition that a tribute of cosmic vitality be left inside the earth. Death, or the periodic sacrifice of life, was regularly consumed within the earth in such a way that life was reborn from the seed of the dead in a continuous and unalterable cycle.

This agreement between the celestial deities and those of the netherworld is present in all the creation myths of Mesoamerica's new humanity. In a deeper sense, the retrieval from the netherworld of the buried bones of ancient humanity by the divine emissaries recalls and actualizes a more ancient practice: the cult of the ancestors. When Hunahpú and Xbalanqué beat the masters of Xibalbá, the first thing they do is attempt to return their sacrificed parents to life. However, their efforts fail, and they then exclaim: "You will be invoked by name," "you will be adored first by noble sons, by civilized servants. Your names will not be lost."[38] This rite is the same as the one Ce Acatl Topiltzin Quetzalcoatl performs when he is informed of the death of his father. Tirelessly, he searches for his remains, and when he finds them, he honors them with ceremonies, celebrates his burial, and raises a temple to commemorate him.

The birth of the corn god, which in Mayan creation myths is the first act of the new cosmic era, sealed another fundamental pact between the gods and the inhabitants of the land. In this case, the resurrection of the corn god meant the appearance of food for human beings, whose flesh, according to the *Popol Vuh,* was made from corn dough. In exchange for the gift of giving life to new humanity and ensuring its reproduction through successive generations, the gods asked men and women to reciprocate by remembering and nourishing their protectors, particularly through the sacrifice of their own blood.

The irrefutable proof of the superior value of the netherworld in Mesoamerican thought is that it was considered the privileged space of the creation of the cosmos, the site where destructive chaos was eliminated and order was imposed. The resurrection of the corn god, in linking myths of creation with the origin of the cosmos, established the theogonic paradigms and primordial images according to which the Mayan peoples conceived of the foundation of all human and supernatural things. As we know, the initial tracing of the cosmos, its division into three vertical levels and four corners or spaces, the foundation of the cosmic tree in the center of this space, the birth of the gods, human beings, plants, and the goods of sustenance for life, the creation of time, the calendar, and writing are all primordial actions born with the beginning of the cosmos and from then on and for all time would mark the shape of human things and actions. "For the ancient Maya, Creation was at the heart of everything they represented in their art and architecture. When we take a second look at their temples, ball courts, statuary, murals and ceramic art in the light of our new understanding, we are overwhelmed by how these objects mirrored the Maya's unique vision of reality." This unified vision of life was so strictly connected to the primordial creation of the cosmos that it has been rediscovered and explained in an admirable book specifically concerned with the Mayan cosmos.[39]

From the Olmecs to the Maya, via the Izapa culture, creation myths and the first pantheons of the gods were based on fertility cults. From approximately 1000 B.C., the corn god is present in Olmec culture. This cult is connected, from then on, to four moments in the cultivation of the corn plant: its cutting or decapitation at harvest time, its burial as a seed in the netherworld, its voyage through the depths of this region (during which the seed is fertilized with the juices of the earth), and the appearance of the corn plant on the earth's surface in spring. Theology and agricultural myths combine these four periods of the corn plant's development and transform them into the key episodes in the lives of Hun Nal Ye, Hun Hunahpú, and Quetzalcoatl.

Probably ever since the Olmecs, and definitely since the Mayan era, fertility cults were associated with the resurrection of the corn god and with the festival that begins the agricultural year, which celebrated these events. In this festival, the majority of the population gathered together. The supreme governor, invested with his powers of great shaman, captain of the armies, and head of the kingdom, was the principal who officiated the rites that revived the moment of the world's creation and invoked the protection of cosmic forces regulating existence on earth. The sacrifice the governor made of his own blood ratified the primordial pact between the gods and human beings, according to which the latter had to nourish the former with their most precious substance.

The Mayan kings of the classical period would conduct great festivals marking the annual change of seasons. One of the greatest was this celebration of the beginning of the agricultural year in March and April, when the exalted moment of the creation of the cosmos and the beginning of counting time was relived. Each year, the spring equinox was celebrated as the beginning of the agricultural year at the arrival of the first rains. Each fall, at the equinox, the harvest festival celebrated the beginning of the dry season. In these festivals, the supreme governor would stand before his people to ratify his power over the supernatural forces controlling seasonal change and regulating the renewal of plants and food. The legitimacy of the Mayan king was founded on his capacity to manage these forces, invoke the propitiatory powers of the ancestors, and keep the kingdom safe from the evil tricks of its enemies. In other words, the main activities of this sovereign were linked to his control of supernatural forces, especially those of the netherworld, the dark place upon which the renewal of human beings, plants, and stars depended.

Recent archaeological explorations at sites in La Venta and Chalcatzingo revealed plazas and monuments depicting cults dedicated to the netherworld which were associated with fertility. Representations of caves inside the netherworld, large mosaics in the form of buried masks in the ceremonial plazas, and pieces of jade containing a character whose split open head sprouts corn plants all are evidence of a belief in the reproductive powers of the underworld.[40] One of the most remarkable traits of the peoples who flourished in Mesoamerica is the continuity and vitality of this belief.

Fig. 3.32. The birth of the corn god represented in a column of the Lower Temple of the Jaguars in Chichen Itza. Drawing based on Taube, "The Iconography," figs. 1b and 19a.

In Teotihuacan, from the foundation of this majestic city, the cult of fertility and caves was dominant. The existence of a cave dedicated to these cults seems to be the origin of the construction of the gigantic Sun Pyramid. Some suggest that the cave found under this pyramid can be related to an ancient eschatological myth whereby the first humans were born from caves.[41] Others call the most prominent deity of Teotihuacan the "Goddess of the Cave" because her body seems to sprout from a base in the form of a cave, and her cult is associated with water, fertility, and agricultural abundance.[42] The image of a mountain existing inside the earth whose center contained nutritious seeds, and especially corn, is one of the most frequently repeated iconographical motifs in Mesoamerican representations. It is the central image on Mayan funereal vases, where the corn god is seen rising from the depths of the earth, carrying corn seeds retrieved from the inside of the first mountain or cave of sustenance. Taube has shown that this is an image that persists through the end of the classical period and into the postclassical period, since it is known that a similar image of the corn god exists at Chichen Itza (fig. 3.32) and a sculpture in this style at El Tajín shows Quetzalcoatl carrying the corn plant he retrieved from the netherworld (fig. 3.33).[43]

As we have seen, the conception of a cave inside the earth where the essential sustenance is situated remains the most constant image in the fertility myths and cults as well as the central theme of the myth of the corn

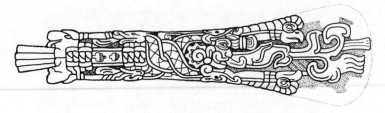

Fig. 3.33. Palm in the style of El Tajín, representing Quetzalcoatl transporting a corn plant. To visualize it better, the figure has been placed horizontally. Drawing based on Taube, 1986, 59, fig. 6.

god's resurrection for the classical Maya, the Toltecs, the Mixtecs, the Mexicas, and the peoples of the southwestern United States of America.[44]

In the Mesoamerican conceptions of the origin of plant and human life, essential seeds reside inside the earth; their retrieval and transformation into human food implies an agreement with the gods of both the netherworld and the celestial region. The most popular version of this idea was spread through the myth of the Divine Twins, which Michael Coe compares to the *Ramayana* or the *Mahabharata* in Hindu literature or the *Odyssey* in Western literature. The Divine Twins popularized throughout all of Mesoamerica the gesture of retrieving and resurrecting the corn seed from the depths of the netherworld.[45] According to this theological and mythical conception, human beings were made out of the most precious substance in the vegetal kingdom: they were flesh-and-blood, heart-and-soul corn. Thus, in these myths, the advent of new humanity is preceded by the resurrection of the corn plant and the corn god.

Another example of the consistency in the founding acts of the first creation throughout time is the image of the first opening up of the earth, the passageway allowing for the communication between beings in the netherworld and those in the terrestrial region.

The image of the opening in the earth in the form of a "V" or a "U" is seen on Olmec and Mayan monuments as equated with a passage through which beings and forces transit from one cosmic region to another. For centuries afterwards, this meaning remained the same. In a study on the V-shaped fissure in the Mixtec codices, Peter T. Furst has shown that, like the Olmecs, the Mixtecs used this symbol to indicate a cosmic passage between the netherworld, earth, and celestial region.[46]

The most spectacular images of the passage from one region to another are those of the Mixtec god Nine Wind and the king of Quiriguá. In one image, Nine Wind descends from the nocturnal sky to earth. (See fig. 1.17.) In the other, the king of Quiriguá wears a jaguar mask and performs the ritual dance of his self-sacrifice before throwing himself into the middle of the earth through a V-shaped fissure (fig. 3.34).[47] If this last interpretation is correct, then the symbolism of this monument is one more version of the famous stone that covers Pakal's sarcophagus in Palenque (fig. 3.35). There, too, according to traditional interpretations, the final moment in which Pakal last contemplates the light of the sun is depicted as he begins his descent into the depths of the monster of the earth, who receives him with open jaws.

Nevertheless, the facts presented here allow for a different interpretation of this image. If we review the iconographical sequence showing Hun Nal Ye moments before his resurrection, we see that in these scenes he is first

Fig. 3.34. The deceased king of Quiriguá (Guatemala) performs the ritual dance of his sacrifice and buries himself in the ground in Monument 24 from Quiriguá. Drawing based on Baudez, 1988, 144.

Fig. 3.35. King Pakal on the cover of the sarcophagus of
the Temple of the Inscriptions at Palenque. Drawing
based on Robertson, 1983, 99.

dressed in his splendid jade costume and then later begins the dance preceding his resurrection. His appearance on the earth is a jubilant act celebrating
the rebirth of the god and the corn seed. It is clear that, according to these
images, Hun Nal Ye is not a god of death but rather the god of resurrection.
Likewise, if we observe that, in the magnificent relief covering Pakal's sar-

cophagus, he is wearing the same net dress as the corn god and that he, like the corn god, just before his appearance on earth, performs the ritual dance of his resurrection, we can interpret this image on the monument as one commemorating Pakal's resurrection. The resurrection is the exalted moment in which the dead king is reborn in the afterworld transformed into a god. The transformation of the dead king into a god or divine ancestor was, from beginning to end, the final objective of the funerary ritual surrounding the burial of Mayan kings.[48]

As we have seen, the death and resurrection of the corn god are closely connected to dynastic succession. The altar of the Foliated Cross of Palenque shows that the cycle of death and resurrection of corn had been linked to the continuity of the royal lineage and the maintenance of cosmic balance, both functions and the main responsibility of the supreme governor. In other words, the great earthly and cosmic disturbance implied by the disappearance of vegetation, the loss of an individual for the society, or the death of the king for the stability and continuity of the kingdom were the great dangers that the ceremonies surrounding the great mystery of the death and resurrection of the corn god sought to avert.

As can be seen, one of the objectives of the creation myths was to organize the cosmos according to regulating principles, to give it firm support for the created order, and to ensure the continuity of the cosmic and human cycle. In this first phase of creation, when the regions of the cosmos and its attributes are defined, the relationship between the netherworld and the earth's surface is what myth and theology most painstakingly attempt to regulate. The myths of creation and theological discourses repeat insistently that, before becoming the region of death, the netherworld is actually the realm where the mysterious process of the transformation of matter occurs and the sacred zone that produces the forces ensuring the continuity of life. Therefore, in all the creation myths, the netherworld, an obscure matrix inhabited by the productive forces of vegetation, stars, and living beings, is the place where new creation is born.[49]

The Appearance of the Earth and the Creation of the Sun

At the conclusion of the first creation and once the regulatory principles of the celestial harmony were established, the gods labor to order the earth. They have had it emerge from the primordial waters and endow it with creative and reproductive powers. The surface of the earth is filled with valleys, mountains, rivers, lagoons, and canals where plants and animals of different species multiply. Once the gods have made this varied and secure scene emerge, they begin the creation of human beings. The majority of the sources signal that it is only after various attempts that this is accomplished. The ordering of the cosmos culminates with the last creation, human beings made of corn and the brilliant appearance of the sun.

According to the *Popol Vuh,* the creator gods said: "The time has come for the dawn, the end of the work and the appearance of those who have to sustain and feed us." Then the gods got together, "and they conferred in the darkness of the night . . . and they found and discovered what had to be put into the flesh of man": corn. Four animals, the mountain cat, the coyote, the parakeet (magpie or parrot), and the stag (or deer), revealed where the yellow and white corn spikes could be found. And then the creator gods ground up the yellow and white corn and made a dough from which "they created the muscles and vigor of man": "the first man was *Balam Quitzé,* the second *Balam Acab,* the third *Mahucutah* and the fourth *Iqui Balam.*" These were "the progenitors" of "the small tribes . . . and the large tribes . . . , the origin of us, the Quiché people."[50]

Nevertheless, even when the earth had appeared and was inhabited, the cosmos remained overwhelmed by darkness and lacked any movement. Then the gods agreed to create the sun, the most important event since the first creation, according to the cosmogonies. In these accounts, the appearance of the sun is the culminating action of a series of primordial creations, the moment in which the face of the earth is lit with the golden light of the star and its surface is heated and comes to life. According to these texts, only then does the created world acquire life and have all its parts begin to move rhythmically around the sun. The stars follow the sun, and this movement produces the change from day to night and the seasons. All the parts of the immense cosmos take on a movement regulated by the trajectory of the sun. Thus, the sun is the regulator of all the forms and phases of time.[51]

The birth of the sun is the explosive event in the series of primordial creations involving the creator gods. The appearance of the sun brings with it the union between space and time because in its daily path it touches the three levels of vertical space (the netherworld, the earth, and the sky). Its annual rotation travels the four corners of the cosmos, in such a way that its transit through cosmic spaces is a spatial and temporal sweep that stipulates the balances and fundamental relationships of the created universe (fig. 3.36).

A.

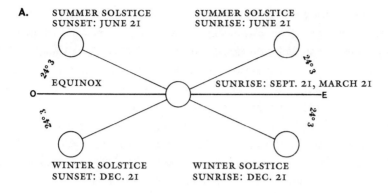

SUMMER SOLSTICE
SUNSET: JUNE 21

SUMMER SOLSTICE
SUNRISE: JUNE 21

24°3

24°3

EQUINOX

SUNRISE: SEPT. 21, MARCH 21

O —————————————— E

24°3

24°3

WINTER SOLSTICE
SUNSET: DEC. 21

WINTER SOLSTICE
SUNRISE: DEC. 21

B.

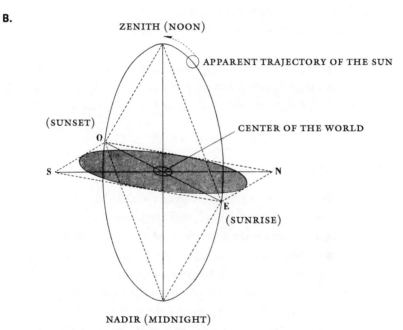

ZENITH (NOON)

APPARENT TRAJECTORY OF THE SUN

(SUNSET)

CENTER OF THE WORLD

O

S

N

E

(SUNRISE)

NADIR (MIDNIGHT)

Fig. 3.36. The four "corners of the sky" in the solstices and the central point in the sun's movement through the zenith. Drawing **(a)** based on Villa Rojas, 1986, 135, fig. 2, and **(b)** on Markman and Markman, 1989, 121.

Likewise, the accounts of the last creation declare that, from the first appearance of the sun, the relationships between the cosmic and human order are verified by special emissaries: Hun Nal Ye, Ehécatl, or Quetzalcoatl. Ehécatl, in the Mixtec tradition, and Quetzalcoatl, in both the Toltec and Nahuatl traditions, appear in the cosmogonies as the cultural heroes who fulfill the role of transmitting the basic necessities to humanity. These are supernatural beings who, as shown in the codices and pictorial and sculptural representations, travel from the nocturnal sky or the netherworld to the earth in order to communicate the mysteries of life to human beings. In the Mayan tradition, Hun Nal Ye is clearly a tellurian deity who carries food and the goods of civilization from the netherworld to the earth's surface. Thus, according to Mayan, Mixtec, Toltec, and Mexica mythology, it is from the netherworld, through the intermediary of divine emissaries, that goods and knowledge arrive on the earthly world for the development of life. Hence the pact between the gods and new humanity is defined: creation is an act of the gods, and the mission of humans on earth is to conserve the basic principles of this divine creation and honor the founding gods through sacrifice.

The Chronicle of the Lineages, Dynasties, and Kingdoms

Once this second act in the process of the ordering of the world occurs, the mythical texts change themes and characters. The important theme now in the creation stories is the appearance of distinct ethnic groups, the definition of their origins, languages, and specific traditions, and the beginning of their migrations, under the tutelage of guiding leaders who keep close contact with the gods while they lead their people to the promised land. Some texts narrate the disappearance of these leaders endowed with supernatural powers. When they die, they leave their descendants their remains in the form of sacred votives and are then substituted by leaders with entirely human characteristics who create dynasties, undertake wars and conquests, arrive at the lands announced by these ancestors, and establish powerful kingdoms.

In some creation stories, this part is transformed into a narrative of the dynasties that governed these peoples, for example, the Mayan text written on the temples of Palenque or the Vienna Codex. However, for the most part, as observed in Quiché, Cakchiquele, and Nahuatl texts, the account is transformed into a chronological narration of events, in which the key deeds of the ethnic group are enumerated alongside the succession of rulers. In any case, what is underscored in these texts is the continuity between the origins of the creation and the earthly history of the groups and kingdoms that emerged from this fundamental genesis. Thus, the theme most emphasized in the creation stories is the link between sacred origin and earthly descendence. (See table 2.)

In these texts, there is a striking resemblance of form and content. Although these were produced by groups as different as the Palenque Maya, the Oaxaca Mixtecs, the Guatemala Quichés, and the Toltec and Nahuatl peoples of central Mexico, they all project the basic unity in the mythical thought of diverse Mayan peoples. Long ago, these peoples invented a canon to explain their origins and conserve and transmit their memory. This model integrated the original foundation of the cosmos with the birth of the sun, which breathed life and order to the different parts of the created world, and, finally, with the origin and development of the ethnic groups that founded memorable cities and nations.[52]

Table 2. Comparative Chart of Indigenous Texts Relating the Origin of the Cosmos and the Founding of Its First Kingdoms and Dynasties

The Palenque Myth of the Origin of the Cosmos and the Palenque Kings	The Vienna Codex (Pre-Hispanic)	The History of the Mexicans (A.D. 1531)
On December 7 of the year 3121 B.C., when chaos reigned and the eight Lords of the Night governed, the First Mother was born. Likewise, on June 16 of the year 3122 B.C. the First Father was born.	Meeting between 9 Wind and the creator gods, who endow him with emblems and divine attributes and instruct him as to his mission on earth.	In the heavens of the thirteenth firmament, the creator gods Tonacatecutli and Tonacihuatl produced four gods, who began the creation of the cosmos, created fire, a half sun, a man and a woman, and the underworld and water gods. Later, the four gods agreed to bring forth the earth, and seeing that the sun illuminated little, they decided to create one that would light up the whole earth.
	Descent of 9 Wind to earth, where he separates the sky and the waters from the surface of the earth.	
	Birth of the Mixtec gods and the Mixtec lineage from the Apoala tree.	
	Discovery of the Mixtec land and useful plants.	
		Tezcatlipoca, Quetzalcoatl, Tlatocatecutli, and Chalchiuhtlicue tried four times to create a new sun and a new humanity, and four times these projects were destroyed by cosmic catastrophes.
Eight years after this event, thirteen *baktunes* had passed, and the new creation was begun, after which the passing of the years and days began to be counted. As soon as the new creation was begun, the First Father arranged the order of the universe and imposed regularity upon the passing of time.	Birth of the sun and the beginning of the flow of time. Establishment of the ceremonies and rites of propitiation for the preservation of the earthly and cosmic order.	The destruction of the last sun caused the sky and the land to stick together, so the four gods decided to separate them and found a habitable world. Tezcatlipoca and Quetzalcoatl raised the sky and turned themselves into trees to support it.
		Later they created fire and the *macehuales* and decided

The Legend of the Suns (A.D. 1558)	The *Popol Vuh* (A.D. 1554–58)

Through the suns 4 Tiger, 4 Wind, 4 Rain, and 4 Water, the sun presided over four catastrophic attempts to create the cosmos and humankind.

Upon the disappearance of the last sun, Titlacahuan advised a man and a woman to carve an opening in an *ahuehuete* tree and to take shelter there in order to survive the flood. After this, they built a fire and roasted a fish to assuage their hunger; but Titlacahuan punished them because they filled the sky with smoke and caused it to dry up.

Quetzalcoatl descended into the underworld to search for the bones of the ancient humans. The gods of the underworld refused to give him the bones, and they schemed to frustrate his effort. Finally they agreed to give him the bones on the condition that he would not keep them forever. Quetzalcoatl managed to take them to Tamoanchan, where the gods ground them up and Quetzalcoatl spilled the blood of his male organ over the ground bones, out of which were born the "vassals of the gods."

Then Quetzalcoatl discovered that the corn was being stored in the Tonacatepetl. He stole a few grains and took them to Tamoanchan, where the gods chewed them and then put them into the mouths of human beings.

Once these events had taken place, the gods agreed to create the sun. Nanahuatl put himself into the divine oven and was transformed into the sun. Napatecutli was turned into the moon. However, after it was born, the sun remained in the sky for four days without moving. Seeing this, the gods, reunited in Teotihuacan, sacrificed themselves, and with their blood they gave movement to the sun.

The gods of creation were in the primordial waters when chaos still ruled and all was darkness and silence. They arranged for the appearance of the earth, created the plants and animals, and attempted three times, unsuccessfully, to create human beings.

Before recounting the gods' fourth attempt, the text relates the adventures of the Divine Twins in the underworld. Upon defeating the Lords of Xibalbá, the Divine Twins created the favorable conditions for the earth and the sky to receive human beings.

Having defeated the Lords of Xibalbá, the creator gods attempted a fourth and successful creation of human beings, which were made out of corn. This occurred while darkness still reigned. Thus were born the first four humans, Balam-Quitze, Balam-Acab, Mahucutah, and Iqui-Balam, who, upon receiving their respective female mates, founded the first Quiché lineage.

Each clan decided to have its own patron gods. To do so, they agreed to go to Tollan, in the east, where each clan received its respective Tohil god (the god of guidance), created fire, and, under the advice of this god, decided to leave Tollan and look for a permanent site in which to settle.

Their pilgrimage culminated when the Morning Star signaled the impending appearance of the sun. In awe, they witnessed the first sunrise.

The first leaders of the four clans died and

Table 2 (continued)

The Palenque Myth of the Origin of the Cosmos and the Palenque Kings	The Vienna Codex (Pre-Hispanic)	The History of the Mexicans (A.D. 1531)
Seven hundred fifty-four years after the creation of the new era the sons of the First Mother and the First Father were born. God I, a god associated with Venus, was born October 21 of the year 2360. On November 8 of the year 2360 God II, who had a snake leg and was the god of the ancestors and of blood sacrifice, was born. God III, or the Jaguar God, was born October 25 of the year 2360 and is also known as Aha-Kin or Lord Sun.		to create a sun that would shine and give warmth to the earth. The son of Quetzalcoatl, Nanahuatxin, turned himself into the sun, by means of sacrifice, and the moon began to follow him. Later they created a new generation of *macehuales,* and war, to satiate the sun with the blood of the defeated.
The Palenque text has the governing dynasty of Palenque descend directly from this divine pair. It declares that U-Kix-Cham, born on March 11 of the year 993 B.C., was crowned king on March 28, 967 B.C. From this legendary king, the text makes a leap in time to meet up with the founder of the Chan-Bahlum dynasty, Chan-Bahlum I, from whom Chan-Bahlum, author of the Palenque text, took his name.	Chronological history of the Mixtec lineage, which begins in the year A.D. 720 and ends ·in A.D. 1305. In the Vienna Codex, this history appears in reverse.	Following this, the text relates the origin of Ce Acatl Topiltzin Quetzalcoatl and the migration of the Mexicans, from Aztlan to the founding of Tenochtitlán.
Source: Schele and Freidel, *A Forest of Kings.*	*Sources:* J. L. Furst, *Codex Vindobonensis;* Caso, *Reyes y reinos de la Mixteca;* Kingsborough, *Antigüedades de México,* study and interpretation by José Corona Núñez.	*Source:* Garibay, *Teogonía e historia.*

Note: Translated by Laura Benali. The above table compares the five texts on the following bases:
1. The first cosmogenic creations (first section across)
2. The creation of the sun and the beginning of time and life on earth (middle section across)

The Legend of the Suns (A.D. 1558)	The *Popol Vuh* (A.D. 1554–58)
	left to their descendants bundles containing their remains, which their descendants agreed to honor.
Following this, the text relates the myth of the four hundred Mixcohuas, the Ce Acatl's birth and childhood, and the destruction of the kingdom of Tula. The last, very brief section relates the principal occurrences during the governance of the Mexican kings, from Acamapichtli to Axayacatl.	Their heirs decided to return to the east, to Tullan, to receive the emblems of power, which Nácxit-Quetzalcoatl granted to them. They continued their pilgrimage, founded villages, and became a powerful kingdom. The text describes the successive feats of the generations of leaders that protected them and made them great.
Source: Códice Chimalpopoca (Leyenda de los Soles).	*Source: Popol Vuh,* trans. Recinos; Tedlock, *Popol Vuh.*

3. A historical account of the governing dynasties and main events for the ethnic group (bottom section across)

FOUR

Toward a New

Interpretation

of the Myth of

Quetzalcoatl

As the reader has observed, in the last decade new images of the Quetzalcoatl myth have appeared owing to the deciphering of the Mayan glyphs, new archaeological discoveries, contributions from epigraphy and iconography, and studies on astronomy, myths, gods, cults, and religious symbols. Each one of these perspectives has forged new versions of the multiple episodes that compose the saga of this variable figure. Stimulated by these discoveries, I could not resist the compulsion to develop my own interpretation of Quetzalcoatl. My approach is historical in that my focus begins with the birth of the myth in the distant ages of the creation of the cosmos and ends with its exuberant proliferation in the epoch of Mexica splendor. As can be appreciated, this reconstruction of the most ancient and changeable myth of Mesoamerica is based on a new reading of the language of myth in light of the abundant iconology describing the saga of Quetzalcoatl. It is also supported by new interpretations that have modified and enriched the most distant past of Mexico's history.

The Origin of the Cosmos and the First
Tasks of (Hun Nal Ye) Quetzalcoatl

The *Popol Vuh* narrates that when the gods undertook the first creation, there was no light or time: "Everything was in suspense, everything calm and silent; everything immobile, quiet, and the vastness of the sky was empty space. . . . Neither man nor animal yet existed . . . no stones, caves, ravines, grass or woods: only the sky existed. The face of the earth could not be seen. There was only the calm sea and the sky in all its vastness."[1]

In this first image of the Mayan cosmos, only the primordial waters were visible and the vacant space of the sky. Before this desolate world, the gods agreed to form some creatures to populate the earth who would worship and feed them in return. They first created some animals, who multiplied on the surface of the earth. However, when the gods asked them to pronounce the names of their creators and invoke them, the animals spoke only in incomprehensible voices.

Upon their second attempt, the gods ordered the creation of other beings and that the animals would live in the ravines and woods and their flesh would serve as food. They said: "We now attempt to make obedient beings who will sustain and feed us." They then formed some beings out of mud, but these were delicate creatures who lacked understanding and did not multiply. Once these first human beings came into contact with water, they could not survive, and this second creation was eradicated.

When the gods tried a third time to create human beings, they consulted with Ixpiyacoc and Ixmucané, the grandfather and grandmother who were expert in the divining arts. Following their advice, the gods formed a man and a woman out of wood, and this pair multiplied. However, when the gods perceived that their creations had no soul and could not remember their creators, they caused a flood that destroyed the wooden people.

According to the *Popol Vuh*, when this flood occurred, forces emerged which disrupted the cosmos and prevented it from taking shape. The flood episode is the most dramatic of these destructive events and is frequently cited in the Mayan narratives referring to the creation.[2] Various texts present this cataclysm as a cosmic battle between the heavens and the earth (fig. 4.1). These mention that at the end of the deluge the only thing left in the immensity of the water was a large caimanlike animal. The Nahuatl narratives offer similar imagery. In both the Mayan and Nahuatl cosmogonies, the great caiman or tortoise symbolizes the earth floating in the primordial waters,[3] one of the most frequent images found in Mesoamerican creation myths (fig. 4.2).

After the first frustrated attempts to create the world, the gods perceived their impotence in controlling these loose forces and decided on the inter-

Fig. 4.1. The flood scene in the Dresden Codex. In the upper section, a goddess is seen pouring water from a pitcher. Another current of water also flows from an animal's mouth. Below, there is a black Chac with warrior decorations. Drawing based on Thompson, 1988, fig. 74.

vention of mediators who make contact with the destructive powers of the heaven and netherworld. In Mayan mythology, these intermediaries are the Divine Twins. The narration of their adventures takes up a good part of the *Popol Vuh*. Their deeds predate the definitive creation of the world and are therefore actions that prepare the present era. It is said in the *Popol Vuh* that when darkness reigned and there was no sun, Ixpiyacoc and Ixmucané engendered Hun Hunahpú and Vucub Hunahpú. Hun Hunahpú, which translated literally means One Blowpipe or Culverin, married first and had two sons, Hunbatz and Hunchouén, who were great sages and diviners.

"They were flautists, singers, blowpipers, painters, sculptors, jewelers and silversmiths." An image of this pair can be seen on a Mayan vase from the classical period, where they are presented, poised to begin their artistic work, with conch shells containing dyes for painting (fig. 4.3).

Unlike their brothers, Hun Hunahpú and Vucub Hunahpú were occupied with hunting with blowpipes and playing ball all day on a court with an earth-covered surface. One time, when Hun Hunahpú and Vucub Hunahpú were playing ball, they were overheard by the Lords of Xibalbá, who lived in the netherworld. This is when they said: "What are they doing on the earth? Who is making so much noise and making it tremble? Let them come and play ball here, where we will beat them!" The Lords of Xibalbá arranged this meeting, although their role was to produce illnesses that provoked pain, malaise, and death.

The twins accepted the invitation. They put the oilskin ball and their playing gear in a hole in the roof of their house and followed the messengers who led them on the path inside the earth to Xibalbá. "Thus they were

Fig. 4.2. The great caiman resting in the primordial waters. Drawing based on Maudslay, 1974, vol. 1, fig. 95c.

Fig. 4.3. Probably a representation of Hunbatz and Hunchouén as painters and artists. The character on the right has the face of a monkey, the animal into which both brothers were transformed, according to the *Popol Vuh*. Drawing based on Kerr, 1989, 377.

descending the path to Xibalbá, going down very steep stairs." They crossed deep ravines and "crossed the river that runs between thorny gourd-trees." "Then they arrived at the banks of a river of blood and crossed it without drinking its waters; they arrived at another river of plain water and they were not beaten. They then went ahead until they arrived at the intersection of four paths." One of the paths was red, one black, one white, and the other yellow. The black path spoke to them in this way: "I am the one you must take . . . and there they were beaten."

From this point on in the text, there is a repetition of how the twins were already vanquished by the Lords of Xibalbá, because they were unwittingly falling into one trap after the other. When they arrive at the lords' reception room, they are at once deceived, since they greet some disguised puppets as the Lords of Xibalbá, who burst into laughter. They are invited to sit down on a bench, and the bench turns out to be a fiery stone that burns their buttocks, and, once again, the Lords of Xibalbá find this hilarious. The lords put the twins in a dark house to spend the night, with a torch pine and cigar for light, but they insist that these not be consumed and that they be returned whole at dawn. The twins do not pass this test, and the Lords of Xibalbá decide to sacrifice them: "Before burying them, Hun Hunahpú's head was cut off," and they ordered that it be hung from a tree near the ball court. "And having gone to hang the head on the tree, all of a sudden this tree that had never bloomed was covered with fruits" (fig. 4.4).

The news about this marvelous tree reached the ears of a damsel of Xibalbá called Ixquic. " 'Why not go and see this tree of which they speak?'

exclaimed the young girl. And she started off right away and soon arrived at the foot of the tree. 'Oh!' she exclaimed, 'what fruits are these that this tree produces? . . . Would I die or lose myself if I cut one of them off?' said the damsel."

Hearing this, Hun Hunahpú's skull, which was hidden among the gourds in the tree, said: "'What is it that you want? These round objects that cover the tree's branches are nothing more than skulls. . . . Do you truly want them?' When the youthful maiden responded affirmatively, at this moment, the skull spit out a stream of saliva which fell directly in the palm of her hand. Then the skull said: 'In my saliva and my spittle, I have given you my descendants. . . . Know then, that on the surface of the earth, you will not die. Trust in my word.'"

This miraculous fertilization inside the netherworld is the origin of the

Fig. 4.4. This image is similar to the scene in the *Popol Vuh* in which the head of Hun Hunahpú is transformed into a tree brimming with squash. Drawing based on Taube, 1985, 176, fig. 4c.

second pair of twins, the sons of Hun Hunahpú and Ixquic. According to the myth, Ixquic managed to escape the region of Xibalbá and give birth to Hunahpú and Xbalanqué on the surface of the earth. This ascension up to the earth concludes the first series of episodes situated in Xibalbá.

Hunahpú and Xbalanqué are born on the surface of the earth, where they encounter the envy of the first sons of their fathers, Humbatz and Hunchouén. Cleverly, they get rid of their elder brothers, who are transformed into monkeys. Then they attempt to gain the confidence of their mother and grandmother. The most ancient images that the texts present of this pair depict them as hunters or ball players and detail their identifiable personal traits (fig. 4.5). After a series of adventures, the twins find out that their fathers, before leaving on the doomed trip to Xibalbá, buried their playing gear in the roof of their house and that their grandfather hid this fact from them to protect them from suffering the same fate as their fathers did.

The youths find the hoop, gloves, and ball and go back to play on the ball court. A short while later, the Lords of Xibalbá speak out: "Who is coming back to play on our heads and bother us with this racket? Is it possible that Hun Hunahpú and Vucub Hunahpú, who wanted to outdo us, never died? Go and call them right away!"

As the readers of the *Popol Vuh* know, the twins accepted this challenge and decided to travel to Xibalbá. However, before this second trip, while obscurity and chaos still reigned, they accomplished other exceptional deeds: they confronted Vucub Caquiz and his sons, Zipacná and Cabracán.

The *Popol Vuh* states that when the flood occurred and destroyed the humans made of mud, when there was still no sun or moon over the earth, some ostentatious beings appeared whose sole ambition was to outdo themselves and dominate. One of these was named Vucub Caquiz, who proclaimed: "I am the sun, I am the light, the moon. . . . Great is my splendor." His appearance was that of a great bird with brilliant emerald eyes, bright teeth, and a silver-colored nose. The other show-offs were his sons: Zipacná, who was said to have made the earth, and Cabracán, who had the powers to make the earth tremble.

The creator gods did not appreciate these self-worshiping beings and asked the twins to do away with them. Hunahpú and Xbalanqué accepted this challenge. First, they confronted the great bird, Vucub Caquiz (who in the vases and texts of the classical period is called Itzam Yeh). They knew that every day he would alight on a nance tree to eat its fruits. They hid in

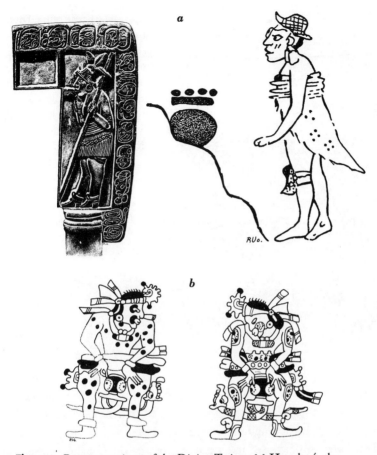

Fig. 4.5. Representations of the Divine Twins. **(a)** Hunahpú, the older brother of the Divine Twins, dressed in a hunter's costume (*left*) and as a ball player (*right*). Drawing based on Coe, 1989, figs. 9 and 15. **(b)** Representation of the Divine Twins on the Mayan vases of the classical period. On the left, Hunahpú, whose name on the vases is One Ahau, can be recognized by the black painting on his body. On the right, Xbalanqué, the Yax Balam of the classical period, is distinguished by the pieces of jaguar skin attached to his body. Drawing based on Hellmuth, *Monster und Menschen,* figs. 426 and 427.

Fig. 4.6. The battle of the Divine Twins with Vucub Caquiz on a stele in Izapa from the end of the formative period or beginning of the present era. In this scene, Vucub Caquiz descends to the nance tree, where the twins await his arrival. Drawing based on Smith, 1984, fig. 55a.

the branches of the tree, and when Vucub Caquiz arrived, Hunahpú shot him with his blowpipe, which hit him in the jawbone and knocked him down from the tree. Hunahpú then attempted to overtake him, but Vucub Caquiz tore off his arm and managed to escape.

These scenes, illustrated in a book written by the Quichés at the beginning of the sixteenth century, are the same as those recently discovered by archaeologists engraved in two stelae in Izapa from the formative or pre-classical period. In the first (fig. 4.6), Vucub Caquiz is seen descending from the nance tree, guarded by the twins on each side. In Stele 25 (fig. 4.7), other investigators recognize Vucub Caquiz perched next to Hunahpú, who is missing his left arm. The importance of the confrontation between Vucub Caquiz and the twins is signaled by the numerous images that represent this episode in the Mayan vases and funerary plates of the classical period (fig. 4.8, plate 6).[4]

After the battle at the nance tree, the twins were accompanied by an old man disguised as a medicine man and thus were able to enter Vucub Caquiz's house, kill him, and recover Hunahpú's arm. Then they gloried in their ingenuity and did away with Zipacná and Cabracán.

Once this memorable deed was accomplished, the twins accepted the challenge of the Lords of Xibalbá and initiated their descent into the netherworld. They eluded rivers and ravines and the traps that had snared their fathers. They survived the struggle of spending the night in the Dark House. Mayan funerary vases show various scenes of this voyage and the confrontation between the twins and the Lords of Xibalbá (fig. 4.9, plate 7a). In his first studies on the twins' adventures in Xibalbá, Michael Coe recognized scenes in which they were presented with regents of the netherworld and

Fig. 4.7. Izapa's Stele 25 showing another episode in the battle between Vucub Caquiz and the Divine Twins. Here, Hunahpú contemplates the great bird that has pulled off his arm. Drawing based on Smith, 1984, fig. 56c.

talking with Itzamná, one of the main gods (fig. 4.10), and others in which Hunahpú perforates his penis to let his blood flow (fig. 4.11).

Surprised by the twins' abilities, the Lords of Xibalbá challenged them to a ball game (plate 7b). At the beginning of the game, they grabbed the flint knife to sacrifice the twins, who claimed to have come to play, not to be sacrificed. After resuming the game, the twins managed to win the match. Shamed, the Lords of Xibalbá attempted other tricks to beat the twins during the night, but the twins once again managed to humiliate them and avoided the dangers of the House of the Razor-Knives.

Desperate, the Lords of Xibalbá subjected the twins to all kinds of trials: the Cold House, the Tiger House, the Fire House, but in each case, they came out unscathed. "What race are these? Where do they come from?" the Lords of Xibalbá wondered. They then decided to put them in the Bat House to see if they would die there. But the twins slept inside their blow-pipes and thus escaped this danger. Nevertheless, in the morning, Xbalan-qué asked Hunahpú if the dawn had already broken and asked him to look outside. When Hunahpú stuck his head out, it was immediately cut off by the bat Camazotz, and his body remained decapitated (fig. 4.12, plate 8).

Joyfully, the Lords of Xibalbá went to hang Hunahpú's head at the ball court. But Xbalanqué, with the help of "many sages who came then from the sky," recomposed the decapitated body of Hunahpú with a tortoise shell. Thus, at dawn, the twins returned to the patio of the ball court to confront the Lords of Xibalbá. When the ball was in play, it shot out of the court, and then a rabbit adopted its form, and through it, the Lords of Xibalbá went

Fig. 4.8. Representation of the battle between Vucub Caquiz and the Divine Twins on a Mayan funerary vase. Here Hunahpú is seen shooting through his blowpipe at Vucub Caquiz, who is stuck in a tree. Hunahpú is wearing a hunter's costume and hat. Drawing based on Kerr, 1989, 169.

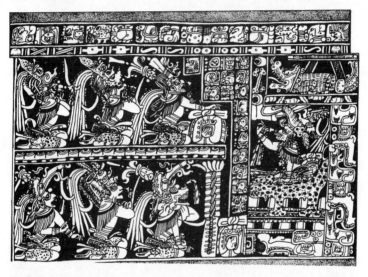

Fig. 4.9. (a) Scene of the meeting between the Divine Twins and the Lords of the Netherworld. Polychrome vase from the north of Petén representing the god Itzamná, lord of the netherworld, seated on his throne (*left*), and the twins Xbalanqué and Hunahpú. Drawing based on Robicsek and Hales, 1981, fig. 41a. **(b)** Mayan funerary vase called the Seven Gods. On the far right, seated on a jaguar throne, the main god of Xibalbá, the so-called God L, presides over a rite preceding the creation of the cosmos. Drawing based on Coe, 1973, 109.

away. Xbalanqué took advantage of this moment to retrieve Hunahpú's real head and restore it to his body. When the Lords of Xibalbá returned, the two brothers confronted them and returned to the game.

Convinced that the Lords of Xibalbá were intent upon sacrificing them, they consulted two diviners, Xulú and Pacam, to whom they communicated a plan to trap the lords. So when the lords sent before them a great hearth,

Fig. 4.10. (a) In a scene depicting their travels through the netherworld, the twins meet one of the main lords of this region, who points to a plate with a crocodile. Drawing based on Coe, 1989, fig. 19. (b) Vase with one of the twins conversing with a character from Xibalbá. Drawing based on Coe, 1982, 51.

Fig. 4.11. Blood spouts from Hunahpú's penis on a vase from Huehuetenango. This is another inexplicable episode from the saga of the twins in the netherworld. Drawing based on Coe, 1989, fig. 17.

they appeared to accept their fate and jumped into the fire. Seeing this, the lords "were filled with happiness" and called Xulú and Pacam, the diviners, to ask what should be done with their bones. The diviners said that first the bones had to be ground up and then sprinkled into the river, which was exactly what they had to say according to the twins' plan to trick the Lords of Xibalbá. Thus it was done, and the dust from the bones rested on the bottom of the water, and from this dust the twins were reborn transformed into "beautiful boys."

The twins had, among other talents, the ability to transform their appearance. They appeared as two poor, elderly people before the inhabitants of Xibalbá and began to perform dances and marvels. "They burned the houses as if they were really burning and then turned them back to the way they were before." But the feat that the netherworld beings of Xibalbá most admired was when they "would kill each other" and then, a second later, come back to life. The news of this astounding feat reached the Lords of Xibalbá, who sent for the twins to perform before them. The twins performed their dances, killed and resuscitated a dog, and burned down and restored the house of the main Lord of Xibalbá.

Xbalanqué sacrificed Hunahpú, cut him to pieces, and then returned

Fig. 4.12. A Mayan plate representing the bat Camazotz, famous for his act of decapitation. On the borders of the plate, the figure of two characters can be seen, which some interpret as being representations of the Divine Twins. Drawing based on Reents-Budet, 1994, fig. 6.51.

him to life. The Lords of Xibalbá were astonished. Enthusiastically, they requested that the twins perform the same feat with them. So the twins sacrificed the two main Lords of Xibalbá, Hun Camé and Vucub Camé, but did not restore them to life. Then they revealed their true identity to the inhabitants of Xibalbá and proclaimed themselves the "avengers of the pain and suffering" of their fathers, dead because of the Lords of Xibalbá. They humbled the inhabitants of Xibalbá, who were prohibited from playing ball and taking full possession of any and all human beings. The twins declared that "the sons of distinguished men will not belong to you and will move away from your presence. The sinners, the evil ones, the sad and misbegotten who give in to vice," will be the only ones to reside in the region of Xibalbá.

Nevertheless, the twins were not able to restore their father and uncle to life. Instead, Hunahpú and Xbalanqué promised them immortality through permanent remembrance of them and the continuity of their lineage. They said: "You will be invoked by name. . . . You will be adored, first by the illustrious sons and by civilized vassals. Your names will not be forgotten." Thus, it was established that through them the lineage would continue as would the memory of their ancestors.

These two parts of the *Popol Vuh,* the one relating the frustrated attempts at creating the cosmos and the one narrating the adventures of the two pairs of Divine Twins, lead into a third part, in which the creation of human beings, the appearance of the sun, and the ordering of the cosmos are recounted.

The Divine Twins' deeds can be interpreted as a preparation for the final creation. Their memorable victories over vainglorious beings who pretended to be the sun and the moon, and over the Lords of Death who governed Xibalbá, are acts that prepare for the creation and ordering of the cosmos. The destruction of the false sun and the false moon eradicates the conflict among the celestial powers and victory over the Lords of Xibalbá in the uncontrolled destructive forces of the netherworld. The destruction of the regents of the netherworld meant that the inside of the earth was no longer to be the insatiable mouth through which living beings, stars, and seeds disappeared. The Divine Twins force the Lords of Xibalbá to allow the regeneration of life, the conservation of genealogical memory, and the continuity of lineages through the succession of fathers by sons. In this way,

Fig. 4.13. The four cosmic trees with their deities and symbols, according to the Mesoamerican interpretation of the four-part division of space. Drawing based on the Fejérváry-Mayer Codex, plate 1, Kingsborough, 1967.

instead of being only a region of death and destruction, the netherworld is converted into a zone of gestation, transformation, and regeneration.

Once these pacts with the powers of heaven and the netherworld are established, the creator gods begin the task of organizing the cosmos and putting it into motion. First, they lift up the celestial vault, which had fallen during the last flood, by placing trees to support the sky in the four corners of the cosmos (fig. 4.13). They also have the earth emerge from the primordial waters. These acts that constitute the cosmos are depicted as key scenes in all the narrations of creation in Mesoamerica.

After the ordering of the universe, events follow which transform the netherworld into the most important region of the cosmos. On one side of the ball court, the original place of sacrifice and the center of the netherworld, the First True Mountain (Yax Hal Witz) rises up, with its humid cave interior containing the nutritious seeds and fertilizing juices (fig. 4.14). With the cords and measures used to establish the four corners of the universe, the center of the cosmos was fixed. It was at this foundation site on the surface of the earth that a tree was erected whose trunk was planted in the netherworld and whose top branches touched the celestial region (fig. 4.15).

From this model cosmogony, all the Mesoamerican cities erected their main plazas using architecture dominated by a sacred mountain of sustenance, a ball court, and a cosmic tree that adjoined the town and the five magnetic points of the cosmos. In the most ancient ceremonial traces of Mesoamerica, the drawing in La Venta, the Olmecs built an artificial mountain (fig. 4.16) in the center of a large submerged plaza that simulated the reservoir containing the primordial waters. They deposited elaborate offerings inside the earth and erected stelae to represent their rulers. The most synthetic expression of this cosmogram can be seen in a small piece in the Dallas Museum, where the Olmecs' genius is represented in the image of the First True Mountain rising up from the underworld and above it a cosmic corn tree, flanked by the four corners of the universe (fig. 4.17).[5]

In Teotihuacan, if we associate the image of the Goddess of the Cave, who prodigiously brought forth water and made the plants germinate, with the painting called Tláloc's Paradise in the lower section (fig. 4.18), we have before us another version of this cosmic geography. Above, the goddess emerges in grandiose fashion from the humid cave of the netherworld and rises up like a cosmic tree to the celestial region. Her fertilizing power makes the plants sprout on the earth's surface. Below, the First Mountain that sprang up on the day of the creation (painted with points that seem like seeds) can be seen as two currents of water flowing from within it, making plants and flowering trees appear. The diminutive humanity that populates this agricultural paradise plays ball and celebrates the abundance of goods emanating from the mountain of sustenance.[6]

When the texts engraved on a stele in Quiriguá and on the temples of Palenque were deciphered, the interpretation of these symbols was enriched with episodes from the marvelous history of the creation of the Mayan cosmos. In Mayan cosmology, the ancient date of 3114 B.C.E. is recorded as the end of a period of thirteen cycles, or *baktunes,* and the date when the First Father, called Hun Nal Ye, One Corn, was born. Hun Nal Ye created a house in a place called Risen Sky and divided it into eight parts, following

Fig. 4.14. Painting of Yax Hal Witz, the First True Mountain, which rose on the day of the creation of the cosmos, on a Mayan vase from the classical period. Drawing based on Reents-Budet, 1994, fig. 5.40.

Fig. 4.15. Representation of the cosmic tree in the center of the altar of the Foliated Cross of Palenque. A face of the monster of the earth symbolizing the netherworld can be seen on the lower section. In the middle section, corresponding to the earth's surface, corn plant leaves and husks with human faces are evident. In the upper section, there is the symbol of the celestial bird. Drawing based on Schele and Miller, 1986, 115.

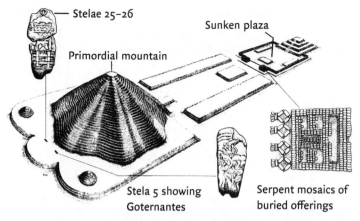

Fig. 4.16. La Venta Complex. Reconstruction of the sacred center of La Venta, with the representation of the primordial mountain, the sunken plaza, the buried offerings, and its stelae or stone trees with the effigies of their rulers. Drawing based on Freidel, Schele, and Parker, 1993, fig. 3.4.

the four cardinal points and the four intercardinal corners of the earth. In the same place, he dedicated the three stones marking the center of the cosmos and erected the cosmic tree called Wakah Chan, the name of the tree in the center of the altar at the Temple of the Cross in Palenque (fig. 4.19).[7]

After these exceptional deeds, Hun Nal Ye is the protagonist of the main act of the cosmogony when he is resurrected in the netherworld in the form of an extraordinarily beautiful youth. This youth carries the precious corn seeds recovered from Xibalbá. The story of the resurrection of the corn god is known not from the deciphering of the Mayan glyphs but rather from a series of painted scenes on funerary vases from the classical period.

The funerary objects record in images three significant events in the Mayan creation myth: the battle between the Divine Twins against Vucub Caquiz, the voyage of Hun Nal Ye to the region of Xibalbá, and his glorious resurgence from the depths of the underworld. The scenes that illustrate the conflict between Vucub Caquiz and the Divine Twins are a visual representation of the same episodes related in the *Popol Vuh,* nine or ten centuries later. However, the sequence of images that narrate Hun Nal Ye's voyage in the netherworld depicts episodes of this saga which are not included in the sacred book of the Quichés.

Fig. 4.17. Primordial Olmec cosmogram. In this
small plaque, Olmec genius synthesized a vision of the
cosmos propounded throughout the Mesoamerican
world. On the borders, the four directions and four
corners of the cosmos are depicted. In the lower
section of the figure, the First Mountain is crowned
with a cosmic tree (a corn plant), with four grains of
the same plant, one on each side. The four grains
symbolize the four directions or corners of the cosmos;
the corn plant makes the fifth, the center from which
the vertical cosmic tree sprouts. Drawing based on
Schele, 1994, fig. 11a.

Even when these images seem unconnected, ordering the events as follows would be possible. The first scene would correspond to Hun Nal Ye's
fall into the aquatic, dark medium of Xibalbá. In penetrating into this region, the corn god confronts characters who threaten him with hatchets
and other instruments of decapitation (fig. 4.20). He then continues his
adventure, probably a sexual encounter, with some naked young women
(fig. 4.21). Then comes the episode of his canoe trip in the cold waters of the
netherworld, accompanied by two rowing gods. Other scenes indicate that
the canoe ends up capsizing in the depths of the underworld. As we know

from our reading of the *Popol Vuh,* Hun Nal Ye descends to the netherworld in search of the hidden mountain of sustenance, the place where yellow and white corn was kept.

Another vase depicts three episodes of Hun Nal Ye's voyage to the netherworld. In the lower section, the god appears in the position of a new-born baby, as if he had just been born from the jaws of a serpent. In the upper section, where he is represented with a youthful appearance, the rowing gods steer him in the canoe, and he carries a bag on his chest with grains of corn (fig. 4.22). In other words, in these images, Hun Nal Ye returns

Fig. 4.18. Representation of the cosmic tree, the cave of the netherworld, and the First Mountain, in the Tepantitla mural, Teotihuacan. Drawing based on the reproduction of this painting in the Museo Nacional de Antropología and on Schele, 1994, fig. 18.

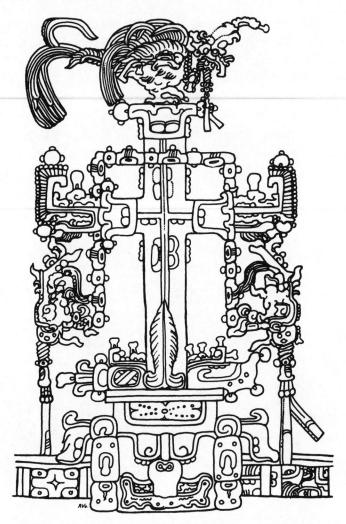

Fig. 4.19. The cosmic tree called Wakah Chan on the altar of the Cross of Palenque. This tree repeats the three cosmic levels that appear in figs. 4.15, 4.17, and 4.18. Drawing based on Freidel, Schele, and Parker, 1993, fig. 2.8b.

Fig. 4.20. The corn god confronts menacing characters in the netherworld. Drawing based on Kerr, 1989, 269.

a

b

Fig. 4.21. (a) The corn god departs the netherworld with nude youths. Drawing based on Robicsek and Hales, 1981, 67. (b) Polychrome Mayan vase with the corn god already dressed, conversing with two nude women in an aquatic medium. Drawing based on Coe, 1973, 25.

from the place where the sustenance had been hidden and carries back the precious cornstalks. In the last scene on the left, two women help him to put on his jade cylinder and sphere dress.

The participation of women in the preparation of the rebirth of Hun Nal Ye is particularly accentuated in the funerary vases of the classical period. In a drawing, two naked women help him with his jade cylinder and sphere

Fig. 4.22. Mayan funerary vase showing three episodes of Hun Nal Ye's voyage to the netherworld. In the lower section, the corn god appears to be lying down, as if he were just born. In the upper right section, he is seen in the middle of the rowing gods, carrying a bag with the grains of corn recovered from the mountain of sustenance. On the left side, two nude women help him to dress. Drawing based on Freidel, Schele, and Parker, 1993, fig. 2.27.

dress. My interpretation is that the women are a symbolic representation of the juices of the earth, and their encounter with Hun Nal Ye is equivalent to the sexual act incubating life in the underworld. In line with this interpretation is the scene in which the women help Hun Nal Ye get dressed, which would correspond to the biological process through which the juices of the earth endow the corn plant with its stalk and precious leaves.

The funerary vases include other episodes from Hun Nal Ye's voyage which are not recorded in the *Popol Vuh*. Even when various images cannot be deciphered, the most probable interpretation is that they refer to the twins' search for the First Father in the region of the netherworld. Thus, one of the most mysterious scenes is the one showing the Divine Twins meeting some stags. Some authors have called attention to these strange images but have not explained them.[8] Another mysterious scene is the twins' visit to a palace and their prostration before three elegantly adorned women (fig. 4.23).

What is certain is that these scenes, and those that refer to dressing Hun Nal Ye, culminate in a dance that appears to be the celebration of his triumph over the Lords of Xibalbá and precedes his resurrection. Among the many pieces showing this dance, there are a few that stand out: one (fig. 4.24) in terms of how dynamically it is painted (see also figs. 3.25 and

Fig. 4.23. The Divine Twins are prostrated before three elegant women seated on a throne. On the left, a character with a hatchet hits the palace walls and makes a hole in the roof through which rays of sunlight shine. Photograph taken by Kerr, 1990, 285.

Fig. 4.24. Hun Nal Ye celebrates his resurrection with a dance. In this extraordinary painting, the profusely decorated corn god is assisted by some dwarves. Drawing based on Coe, 1978, 14.

Fig. 4.25. Painting on a Mayan vase from the classical period showing some youths dressed like the corn god performing a dance along with old characters (the Lords of Xibalbá) who are covered with ornaments and decorative costumes. Drawing based on Coe, 1989, 98.

Fig. 4.26. Hun Nal Ye (*left*) emerges from inside the earth with a bag containing precious seeds of corn. Drawing based on Robicsek and Hales, 1981, fig. 59.

3.29), and the extraordinary vase (fig. 4.25) that shows the twins celebrating their victory over the Lords of Xibalbá.

Finally, there are the scenes describing the climax of this succession of dramatic events: the sprouting of the corn god from the depths of the earth. One vessel shows the rowing gods accompanying Hun Nal Ye to his glorious rebirth (fig. 4.26). The corn god (on the left) sprouts from a tortoise shell (caparison), with a bag containing the precious corn seeds. In another finely illustrated plate, Hun Nal Ye comes out of the split in a tortoise shell (carapace) and is received by Xbalanqué and Hunahpú (fig. 4.27). Another vase represents the same jubilant scene, with the twins, one on either side, helping the First Father to exit the netherworld (fig. 4.28).

Comparing the prodigious adventures of the twins narrated in the *Popol Vuh* with the studies in which the texts and symbolism of the Mayan monuments are deciphered,[9] one has the impression of having encountered a large slice of human history and having touched something deep within this history. We soon perceive that for more than fifteen centuries, from Palenque to Copán, the Maya were recounting the same history of the origins of the cosmos and the bases of civilized life.

As the most ancient engraved images of the Divine Twins from the Izapa stelae suggest, it is possible that this myth began to be recounted from preclassical times, many years before the present era. Most probably, the myth

Fig. 4.27. Hun Nal Ye is reborn inside the earth, represented in this scene by a tortoise shell. Xbalanqué (*right*), pouring a pitcher of water on the gash in the earth, and Hunahpú (*left*) receive him. Drawing based on Robicsek and Hales, 1981, vase 117.

Fig. 4.28. The resurrection of Hun Nal Ye painted on another Mayan vase. Xbalanqué, on the right, and Hunahpú, on the left, help him to get out of the inside of the earth. Drawing based on Robicsek and Hales, 1981, 155.

was born with the beginnings of civilization, when the Mesoamericans discovered the secret of cultivating plants and founded their life on agriculture. Classical Maya engraved their cosmogony on various monuments in Quiriguá, Bonampak, Copán, and Palenque, indicating that originally this was an agricultural myth, in which the narration focused on the corn plant's sprouting from the depths of the earth. Through the texts, paintings, and stelae from this period, we know that the Mayan leaders transformed the appearance of the corn plant into a divine gestation. They built their conceptions of the cosmos, human beings, and civilized life around the god who created the most precious food. The fact that Mayan cosmogony refers to the present creation of the cosmos as an agricultural awakening, and has new humanity sprout from corn dough, reveals that, for the most ancient peoples, civilization was born with the origins of agriculture and the cultivation of corn.

Another feature that distinguishes this cosmogony is the connection of the planting cycle and the harvesting of the corn plant with the succession of the dynasties recorded in Palenque. In the altar at the Temple of the Cross in Palenque, Pakal is depicted as being succeeded by his son Kan Balam. Below the Pakal figure, an effigy of the corn god is resting in the netherworld, while Kan Balam appears to sprout from a corn leaf and is wearing the costume the corn god wears at his resurrection. In other words, whereas Pakal descends to the underworld, like Hun Hunahpú, Kan Balam ascends to this region, transformed into Hun Nal Ye, the youthful corn god. (See fig. 3.26.)

Further proof of the classical Maya's identification of the myth of the death and resurrection of the corn god with the dynastic cycle of the death and resurrection of kings is evident in the magnificent relief on the stone covering Pakal's sarcophagus. In this famous monument, Pakal appears dressed in the corn god's green jade suit. He has been transformed into Hun Nal Ye and as such is reborn from the depths of the netherworld, transformed into the god and ancestral leader of the kingdom of Palenque. Thus, at the same time that on the surface of the earth the new governor takes the place of the defunct king, in the underworld, the dead king abandons this region and is transformed into an immortal god.[10]

Furthermore, alongside the development of the religious view of the world through which the attributes of the corn god and the origin of the cosmos were described, the myth of the Divine Twins was energetically developed. This myth is a popular version of conceptions relating to the creation of the cosmos and the origin of the gods that are known to us through the Mayan texts and codices. Today we see that Hun Nal Ye, the Mayan corn god from the classical period, is Hun Hunahpú, the older brother of the first pair of twins in the *Popol Vuh* who accepted the challenge from the Lords of Xibalbá to descend into the netherworld. The vessels and funerary objects dating from the classical period confirm this identification and, along with the *Popol Vuh,* that Hunahpú and Xbalanqué, the Divine Twins, are the sons of Hun Nal Ye, the agents whose cunning strategies outfox the Lords of Xibalbá and return their father to earth. Just like the corn plant, Hun Nal Ye ascends to the surface of the earth carrying the precious grains of corn, which he provides to form the flesh of human beings and food for future generations.

This popular version of one of the most ancient cosmogonies of Meso-america has had the longest life. As with all myths, it was passed down from generation to generation through an oral tradition. We also know that there was a dramatized version of the epic of the Divine Twins whose origins are surely contemporaneous with those of the myth. On June 24, 1543, the Franciscan friars of the province of Verapaz in Guatemala saw a theatrical representation of this ancient drama during a festival celebrating the anniversary of the foundation of the town of San Juan Chamilco. On this day, probably ignorant of the origins of the story and its significance, the friars saw the Divine Twins come to life to battle the fearsome Lords of Xibalbá. The scenery was magnificent and included the sound of snail trumpets, drums, and cymbals as well as other ancient instruments during the frenetic dance when the lords are finally destroyed.[11]

We also know that toward the beginning of the sixteenth century there was a version of this story painted on the ancient Mayan books, since the Quiché editors of the *Popol Vuh* seem to refer to paintings or ancient codices.[12] Father Ximénez writes in his *Historia de la provincia de San Vincente de Chiapas y Guatemala* (History of the province of San Vincente de Chiapas in Guatemala) that the stories of the *Popol Vuh* which he collected in the town of Chichicastenango "were the doctrine that the Indians first swallowed with their mothers' milk and everyone knew them by heart." He adds that in this town it was reported that "those books had a lot to do with each other."[13]

The Transformations of the Plumed Serpent

Perhaps the best-known image of Quetzalcoatl is the snake with feathers, or the Plumed Serpent. In the Mesoamerican tradition, the serpent is associated with the reproductive powers of the earth and fertility. This is the very image of resurrection: each year it changes its skin and is regenerated. Besides, we know that in "indigenous mythology, serpents and rainfall are closely related. These reptiles are considered to be the image of the thunderbolt and this is why people from Tláloc, messengers who spread the rains . . . and lightning and thunder, carry serpents in their hands."[14] Inga Clendinnen observes that the imposing Mexica sculptures of the serpent accentuate its great fangs and coiled body, which spirals around like a sea snail. In most of the sculpture and painting, the rough skin and scales of the serpent are transformed into a crown of feathers or simulate vegetal exuberance, corn husks sprouting from its body. These are representations that masterfully unite the very fine treatment of stone with the supernatural representation of the deity.[15]

The bird, in turn, is an image associated with the sky and the divine forces that inhabit this region. Yet, from the color and size of the feathers covering the serpent's body, it is clear that the plumage is from one bird in particular: the green plumed *quetzal*, the most beautiful bird of the tropical jungle. The quetzal's brilliant and brightly colored feathers were a synonym for magnificence, splendor, and wealth for Mesoamerican peoples. "The feather filaments are light, long, and glossy, so that the smallest movement sets them shimmering. And the color, a gilded emerald haunted by a deep singing violet blue, is extraordinary: one of those visual experiences quite impossible to bear in mind, so that each seeing is its own small miracle." [16]

The iridescent plumes of the quetzal were the main decoration on the rulers' costume. Alone or accompanied by other adornments, the green feathers of the quetzal were identified as something precious. When these feathers crowned the official garb and royal insignias, they expressed the splendor that surrounded high office.

Uniting into one single entity the attributes of the serpent and the bird, metaphorically combining both the germinating powers of the earth and the creative powers of the sky, the Plumed Serpent became synonymous with the Precious Twin.

From the most ancient times until the Aztec era, it seems that the meaning of the Plumed Serpent was associated with vegetal renewal. The green plumes of the quetzal which covered the serpent's body were a symbolic representation of the time of year when the dry season was substituted by the greening of vegetation. The earth, represented by the rough skin of the serpent or caiman, would be covered by the green leaves of the corn plant. In the Mesoamerican imagination, this marvelous agricultural phenomenon took the form of a plumed serpent. The green shoots of the corn plant, which always sprouted a few days after the first rains, would form a carpet of green feathers over the fields, the fullest image of the flourishing of life for these peoples.

The green of the first sprouts of the corn plant was transformed into the symbolic color of vegetal renewal, the color most appreciated by Mesoamerican peoples. The symbolic value of this color is also connected to jade. Jade is the most precious and valued of stones as well as a symbol of vital energy and the adornment that distinguished the sovereign and members of the noble lineages. Ever since the Olmecs, there was a custom of hanging a *chalchihuitl,* or round, green stone, in the mouth of the dead, as a talisman to ensure later rebirth. This same stone with brilliant green tones was selected to adorn the frontal band worn by the rulers and to signal the connection between these personages, the corn, and the vital energy animating the cosmic and human order.

In the so-called Plumed Serpent Temple in Teotihuacan, constructed in the middle of the second century A.D., this entity is represented with symbols that we will later recognize in monuments at sites and within cultures as different as Xochicalco, Cacaxtla, El Tajín, Tula, Chichen Itza, Cholula and, Mexico-Tenochtitlan. In the altars of this edifice, the undulating body of a rattlesnake is seen covered with precious, quetzal plumes. At the bottom of the serpent body, a sculpted serpent head sprouts from a circle of petals or plumes. Beside this sculpture there is another strange figure, in the form of a mask, which has been given various interpretations. (See fig. 1.2.)

Several scholars, each with a different emphasis and focus, suggest that these representations allude to the cycle of rainy and dry seasons, attributing the sculptural ensemble to a symbolism related to the celebration of vegetal renewal.[17] Even when the interpretation of these figures continues to be debated, there is a consensus regarding the Plumed Serpent as a symbol of vegetal renewal. The Plumed Serpent represented in the altars and talus of this monument is surrounded by conch shells, snails, and *chalchihuites,* objects indicating the reproductive quality of the waters, and more precisely, the combination of the fertilizing powers of the earth and the sky.

Pedro Armillas, seeking an explanation for the feathers covering the serpentine bodies in this monument, recalls a Nahuatl song dedicated to Xipe Totec, the Mexica god of springtime and vegetal renewal, which shows the identification of quetzal feathers with vegetation. In this song, Xipe Totec is asked to make the rain fall "so that the dry earth will change its cloak of fire, *xicoanahualli,* for that of the quetzal serpent, *quetzalcoanahualli;* who rains down its water of precious stones so that the *xiuhacóatl,* the fire snake, the dryness, turns into Quetzalcóatl, the earth covered with vegetation."[18] There are also Mexica sculptures with mature cornstalks growing out of serpents' scales.[19]

Another Nahuatl text also demonstrates that this is the meaning of the green quetzal feathers on the serpent's body. This text relates the story of a bet between the legendary Huémac, king of Tula, and the people of Tláloc (the Tlaloques), providers of the rain.

Huémac confronts the Tlaloques on the ball court, proposing that if they win the match, they will receive their *chalchihuites* (round jade stones) and precious *quetzalli* (quetzal bird feathers), alluding to the material value of each of these objects. The Tlaloques agree and add that Huémac will receive the same if they lose, alluding to the symbolic value of these objects. Huémac wins the game, and the Tlaloques, instead of giving him these desirable green stones and brilliant, rich plumes, offer him *elotes* (green corn on the cob) and precious leaves of green corn in which the *elote* grows. Angry, Huémac throws away the *elotes,* saying: "Is this all I win? No *chalchihuites?* No *quetzalli* plumes? Get rid of these things!" The story recounts how the Tlaloques represented ancient wisdom before the newcomer Huémac. They decide to deliver the precious stones and rich plumes that Huémac demanded, but in vengeance they bury the true riches they had promised. As a consequence of this decision, for four years there are droughts and frosts that overwhelm the Toltec farmlands, and "they lost the fruits of the earth."[20]

The tellurian symbolism of the Plumed Serpent is clearly an allusion to the sprouting of the first leaves of corn, modified much later, along with the ancient symbolism of the corn god. Most of the transformations in the figure and meaning of the corn god occurred during the height of the Toltec period, as its influence spread throughout different areas in Mesoamerica. Most of the symbols and names that at this time referred to Quetzalcoatl, Kukulcán, Gucumatz, or Náxcit are represented by the Plumed Serpent. Yet this emblem, instead of referring to vegetal renewal or the ancient corn god, now seems to be connected to political or military office. In the chronicles written by the Cakchiqueles and Quichés, the names Kukulcán, Gucumatz, Nácxit, Plumed Serpent, or Quetzalcoatl refer to a captain who had supernatural powers, conquered and waged war, founded cities that were transformed into the heads of kingdoms, and built grandiose temples that bear his name. The origin of this character, his emblem, and attributes converge at Tollan, the wonderful city where, according to Toltec songs spread by the Aztecs, the symbolism of imperial grandeur, the force of military power, the prestige of a sacred site, the abundance of material goods, and the splendor of civilization were all joined in one place.

From Ancient Corn God to the Figure of Topiltzin Quetzalcoatl of Tula

The passage from the ancient kingdoms to the so-called postclassical period has not been the subject of many studies and is one of the most confusing periods of Mesoamerican history. Perhaps historians have resisted studying this period because of its tragic history, replete with destruction. Suddenly, at the end of the seventh century, the powerful states that the Teotihuacanos and Zapotecos had constructed were destroyed by violent revolts. Later, between the eighth and ninth centuries, each one of the small Mayan kingdoms succumbed to the same destiny or was abandoned and then absorbed by the jungle brush. Although the fall of these ancient political organizations has no clear explanation, it created a power vacuum and opened the door to successive invasions and migrations. Buffeted by turbulence and instability, this period witnessed the blurring of all borders (geographical, political, ethnic, religious, and cultural) and the rise of new political and social organizations. Infrequently studied, this period is also difficult to understand because of the changes taking place at this time. On the one hand, it continues previous traditions, and on the other, new religious and political conceptions are formed.

At the end of the ninth century, the groups of Zapotecos, Maya, and Teotihuacanos who had survived this unrelenting destruction must have felt they were witnessing the worst catastrophe in all of human experience. In a few short years, political constructions that had required centuries to be built were dismantled. Royalty and the divine figure of the sovereign, the two institutions that had forged the splendor of the ancient kingdoms, were razed to the ground. The royal palace and the monuments of the ceremonial center fell to pieces or disappeared in devastating fires. Profanations and lootings occurred at the tombs constructed as the eternal resting places for deified ancestors. Images of the revered gods were destroyed. Assassinations and persecutions of the leading groups transformed flourishing cities into precarious agglomerations, exposed to assault from foreigners or bloody internal rivalries. Violence and insecurity characterized this long period of destruction followed by famines and epidemics that increased the panic and led the population to migrate in a desperate fashion.

In this setting, armed contingents began to appear more and more to protect the massive migrations from north to south and from south to north. It became frequent to see armed bands going from one place to another in search of booty. There are no texts to tell the tragic events of these years that darkened Mesoamerican history. The only witnesses we have are the remains of burned cities, destroyed temples, profaned tombs, populations consumed by hunger and illness, desolate lands, and walled cities built up at inaccessible heights. Perhaps the most representative vestiges of the period are the war symbols.

Between the seventh and ninth centuries, almost all the ancient cities were abandoned after having been burned down and sacked. The new cities founded between the ninth and twelfth centuries multiply the emblems of war, conquest, and blood sacrifice. During this period of instability and constant migrations, a transformation occurs in the kingdom of Toniná, ensconced in the mountainous backbone of Chiapas, which turns into a military power and the protagonist of great deeds. Its annals record with pride the captivity of the powerful lord of Palenque, K'an Hop'-Chitam, on August 26 in A.D. 711, the subjugation of the lord of Bonampak, and the razing of Palenque in the year 730.[21] The most important monuments of this kingdom, built in the form of an impregnable bastion, are the stelae showing its rulers transformed into victorious chiefs or the terrifying stuccos exalting ritual decapitation (fig. 4.29).

During the period between A.D. 600 and 900, the kingdom of Xochicalco was also flourishing in the western part of the Morelos Valley, high up on a steep site selected to ward off enemy attack. The primary symbolism associated with this great fortress is defensive, military, and sacrificial. Whoever has studied the site cannot help but observe the variety of influences that converge here, ranging from regions as different as the Mayan region to Teotihuacan, Oaxaca, Guerrero, and El Tajín. Nevertheless, none of these sources seems to predominate in the architecture, religious symbols, or art of Xochicalco. Xochicalco is most noted for its eclecticism, its use of ancient canons intermingled with new emblems and new symbolism.[22] Thus, there are indications that two pyramid-shaped monuments cohabited in its main plaza.[23] It is possible that one of these was dedicated to the ancestral deity (the Plumed Serpent) and the other to the state god in power, just as later in Tenochtitlan the twin sanctuaries of the Main Temple (the Templo Mayor, or Great Temple) were dedicated separately, one to Tláloc, the ancient god of fertility, and the other to Huitzilopochtli, the state god of the Mexica people.

Ever since the celebrated description given by José Antonio Alzate at the end of the eighteenth century, the main monument of Xochicalco has attracted the attention of those curious about and interested in Mexican antiquity (fig. 4.30). For many, this was the most realistic representation encountered of the emblem of the legendary Quetzalcoatl. Two centuries later, the image of Quetzalcoatl returned to haunt reflections upon this ancient fortress city. In 1962, César A. Sáenz discovered three stelae with engraved sculptures on all sides, intentionally buried in the floor of a temple (figs. 4.31 and 4.32). After studying these monuments, he concluded that two of the

Fig. 4.29. Decapitation scene in the extraordinary stucco mural discovered in a building in Toniná. Drawing based on Yadeun, 1992, frontispiece.

stelae (number 1 and number 3) were representations of Tlahuizcalpante-cuhtli, the Morning Star, one of the principal personas of Quetzalcoatl, and Stele 2 represented Tláloc.[24]

Ten years later, Esther Pasztory analyzed the glyphs, images, and symbols on these monuments and opted for a different interpretation. She corrobo-

Fig. 4.35. The Plumed Serpent on the mural of the Lower
Temple of the Jaguars in Chichen Itza. As in the classical
period, the central character in the painting performs a rite of
bloodletting (in this case, the blood of a sacrificed ball player),
in order to invoke a protecting deity. The Plumed Serpent
seems to sprout from the sacrificial vessel seen at the figure's
feet. Drawing based on Coggins and Shane, 1989, 42.

in the Palenque version, the pair of creator gods organize the different parts
of the cosmos and participate in the foundation of a new era, starting off
with the beginning of time and human life. However, the part corresponding to the human foundations and the beginnings of the kingdom is dominated by the birth of the protector gods of Palenque, the divine origins

Fig. 4.36. Plumed rattlesnakes decorate these facial ornaments found in the Cave-Reservoir of Sacrifices in Chichen Itza. According to Coggins and Shane, these ornaments cover the face of the character in figure 4.35. Drawing based on Coggins and Shane, 1989, 57.

of the Palenque dynasty, and the sacred and indestructible character of the continuity of the royal office. The sovereign is the incarnation of the First Father: like the god, he regulates the harmony of the cosmos, directs human destiny, and communicates with the ancestors and supernatural forces.

As has been observed, the creation text from Palenque is focused on the fertilizing forces of the earth and on the corn god, who appears as the First Father. This figure is the founder of a new cosmic era and the motor of the cycle of death and resurrection in nature, whereas the Toltec and Mexica cosmogonies are basically solar.

As opposed to the key central function of the sovereign in classical Mayan kingdoms, in Tula, Chichen Itza, and the Quiché and Cakchiquele kingdoms, the omnipresent figure of the king is substituted by Topiltzin Quetzalcoatl. Topiltzin Quetzalcoatl is commander in chief, the head of the kingdom, supreme priest, and civilizing hero all at once. In this new image of power, the myth of Quetzalcoatl clearly shows how the function of the warrior chiefs moved up a notch in the political hierarchy into a position closer to the highest-ranking powers in the kingdom.

Likewise, the myth indicates the presence of a form of political organization which differs from the Mayan city-state. The marvelous mythical

Fig. 4.37. **(a)** The emblem of the Plumed Serpent with symbols of Venus around it, accompanying a warrior, in Disk E from Chichen Itza. Drawing based on Barba and Piña Chan, 1989, 185. **(b)** Relief on a bench in the Warriors' Temple at Chichen Itza. Some warriors are decorated with the emblem of the Plumed Serpent and seem to be walking toward a central cult object, a *zacatapayolli* with three instruments for the blood sacrifice in a bowl of herbs. (Klein, "The Ideology of Autosacrifice," 298–303). Drawing based on Klein, 1987, fig. 4.

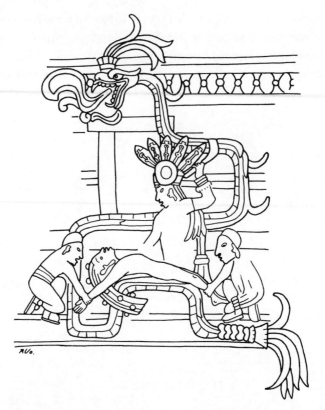

Fig. 4.38. Performance of a sacrifice in Chichen Itza under the emblem of the Plumed Serpent. Drawing based on Morris, 1931.

city of Tollan is a multiethnic polis, a metropolis dominating various regions and ethnic groups whose leaders are obliged to receive investiture, render homage, and pay tribute in this capital. In mythical language, these accounts reveal the advent of a form of expansive power which imposed a new way of governing through migrations and conquests. It appears that in the central and southern parts of Mesoamerica, there was a sort of confederation of various cities ruled by a collective power (*Mul tepal*). This new political organization was supported by military groups and sustained by tribute paid by those who had been conquered.[29] The myth does not explain nor does it describe this structure of power, but it does exalt its symbols. Tollan, the ideal metropolis, is the symbol that now synthesizes the prestige previously concentrated in the figure of the sovereign. It is the center of political power, the cradle of civilization, the seat of agricultural abundance, the residence of the gods, and the cosmic center maintaining the balance and harmony of the universe.[30] Rather than the figure of the sovereign, it is the city of Tollan that is the emblem of the kingdom and the symbol of universal and legitimate power.

In the same way as in the myth, the powers previously concentrated in the figure of the governor became the emblem of the metropolis reigning over various ethnic nations; the history of the human groups referred more to the ethnic groups and the state representing them, rather than to the sovereign leader. In contrast to the dynastic tales engraved by Kan Balam in Palenque, or the foundation myth in the Vienna Codex, in which the history of the kingdom is ciphered into the history of the dynasties, in the historical annals of the Quichés, Cakchiqueles, and Nahuatl peoples, in addition to their cosmologies, the narration is concentrated on the migrations and events involving the ethnic group. Rather than a dynastic history, collective memory or the ethnic nation is narrated along with the history of its rulers.

Fig. 4.39. The Plumed Serpent surrounds the figure of an eagle-man on a mural at Cacaxtla. Drawing based on *Cacaxtla,* 113.

The narration of the deeds of the sovereign, which previously reflected the history of the kingdom and its people, has been transformed through new social and political realities into the narrative of the origins and deeds of an ethnic nation.

The analysis of the changes occurring in the content of these myths reveals something even more compelling. The myth of the origins of the sedentary peoples, who in the case of the Maya or Mixtecs situated their origins within the borders of their own land, has now been displaced to a remote and foreign land. The Itzáes, Quichés, and Cakchiqueles all proclaim that their ancestors came from a distant place called Tollan, which was located in another region altogether. Likewise, the account of the migration from Tollan legitimates an invasion of foreign peoples into lands previously inhabited by native groups. In other words, the accounts of migrations, conquests, and settlements of these itinerant peoples radically transposes the origins of the native populations and imposes upon them another ascendancy and a new identity. From these invasions on, the Itzáes, Quichés, Cakchiqueles, and Mexicas claim a distinct origin, foreign to the location in which they have settled, and speak of themselves as descendants of Toltecs.

Besides this transposition of original roots, the invasion outside is concentrated on erasing the ancient past and exalting the domination of the invaders over the native populations. In the myths of origin which appear in these texts, the new arrivals are exalted over the previous inhabitants, the younger brother over the older brothers, the warriors over the farmers, and the fanatic veterans of a state god over the inhabitants who revere multiple deities. In the majority of these origin myths, the legitimacy of the invaders relies on the superiority of their weapons, marriage with native women, and the appropriation of ancient and prestigious knowledge by the newcomers.

The myth has given way to historical realities, and in turn historical reality has been transformed, as Marshall Sahlins states, into a metaphor of mythical foundations.[31] The myth of Ce Acatl Topiltzin Quetzalcoatl's marvelous Tollan, origin of power, arts, and sciences, cradle of gods, and the absolute center of the cosmos, became the guiding light for the migrations that led Itzáes, Quichés, Cakchiqueles, and Mexicas to found powerful kingdoms dominating the central and southern regions of Mesoamerica from the eleventh century to the Spanish invasion. Quetzalcoatl was transformed into the most variable, charismatic, and ubiquitous presence in the land, a character who from then on acquired the attributes of limitless metamorphosis, resurrection, and multiplication.

The Mexicas' Quetzalcoatl

As we have seen, each political or cultural change elicits profound transformations in the personality, symbols, and significance of Quetzalcoatl. One of its least studied contrivances is the one that enabled the Aztecs to appropriate this charismatic figure and assimilate it into their own political and religious conceptions.

The surest method of recording the changes human actions have wrought on history is to analyze their evolution by following the course of events from past to present. Until recently, this perspective could not have been applied to the most ancient past of Mexico because of the lack of creditable archaeological and historical data. It is also true that since the Spanish Conquest we have become accustomed to seeing this past through the image of it the Mexicas have given us. What we knew of Mexican history was the Mexicas' impact on ancient times, and this formed the dominant, longstanding image of Mesoamerica's past.

This perspective has begun to be modified. In its place, a very ancient history is emerging, deeper and denser, which speaks to us of the complex formation of Mesoamerican civilization and of its unity and diversity. Now we know that the Mexicas did not invent the pillars upon which this civilization was founded but that this group was one of many who inherited it and continued it. With the perspective given to us by the knowledge of Quetzalcoatl's distant origins, we see how the Mexicas adopted this variable figure, how they situated it in their pantheon, and how they transformed it.

Following the traditions of their ancestors, the Mexicas defined their relationship to the cosmos, nature, and ethnic groups through cosmological myths. The available sources indicate that the Mexica myth of the creation of the cosmos is a reworked copy of the cosmogonies of the peoples of the central southern area, with an admixture of conceptions from other regions and the Mexicas' own ideas. Just like the earlier myths, the Mexica myth focuses on the present era. However, unlike the Maya and Mixtec versions, the Mexica myth emphasizes the creation and destruction of four previous eras dominated by four suns or cosmic forces: earth, wind, fire, and water.

Each one of these eras alludes to the primordial forces existing before the creation of the earth. In constant combat, these chaotic forces were each represented by a god with similar attributes and symbols. The earth was represented by the Jaguar, the wind by Ehécatl, fire by Tláloc, and water by Chalchiuhtlicue.[32] The battle between and among these antagonistic forces provokes the destruction of each one of the four suns, whose gods, as the reader may have already noticed, are the most ancient Mesoamerican deities: the Nocturnal Sun Jaguar God of the classical Maya; Tláloc, the old god of rain and celestial fire (lightning); and Ehécatl, the ancient wind god of the peoples of the coast of the Gulf of Mexico, the Mixtecs and the Cholultecos.

In Mexica cosmogony, Ehécatl, the god of the Gulf of Mexico cultures who breathes the winds into the four corners of the cosmos, ranks among the creator gods. His sanctuary was built in front of the Main Temple of Tenochtitlan, and in the codices, paintings, and sculptures, he occupies a place of honor in the Mexica pantheon among the most important gods. He is a creator god because in Nahuatl tradition he participates in the separation of heaven and earth and is one of the supporters of the celestial vault (fig. 4.40). Nevertheless, if one observes the actors who participate in the creation of the Mexica cosmos, one can see that Ehécatl is a secondary figure. In the Mexica cosmogony, Tonatiuh is the creator god of the Fifth Sun, the deity whose birth gives movement and heat to the cosmos, originates time, and creates a new era in the world: the era of the Moving Sun, Ollintonatiuh. This luminous, warlike, and heavenly deity substitutes the ancient fertility gods of the netherworld, incorporating within its symbolism their germinating and ordering powers and exacting a more rigorous tribute upon human beings.

Another feature that distinguishes Mexica religion is its attempts to assimilate outside elements in a syncretic manner. From its beginnings in the highlands of the Valley of Mexico and more forcefully after its victory over the Tepanecas (1426–33), the Mexicas formed an extensive pantheon, integrating gods from the most diverse sources. They began with the small group of ancestral Chichimeca deities. To these, they added the ancient and numerous patrons of the peoples of the Central High Plains with whom they came into contact after settling in these lands. In the period of imperial domination, they appropriated the main Toltec deities and along with them the various titles of Quetzalcoatl and the innumerable gods of the conquering peoples. As Frances Berdan recognizes, instead of a proselytizing

Fig. 4.40. Representation of Ehécatl Quetzalcoatl supporting the sky. As can be appreciated, this drawing is a copy of the same figure that appears in the Vienna Codex (see fig. 1.18). The presence of Ehécatl in the Mexica pantheon and the reproduction in a Mexica codex of a figure represented first in a Mixtec codex are further proof of the highly developed capacity for assimilation on the part of Mexicas enriching their pantheon. Drawing based on the *Códice Borgia,* plate 51.

religion, the Mexicas had developed an inclusive religion. This characteristic is a result of the multiethnic composition of the Mexica state. In proportion to what the Mexicas accepted, they absorbed or conquered other peoples and also incorporated their gods.[33]

The politics of assimilating the belief systems of other peoples is expressed in the construction of the *coateocalli,* the enclosure the Mexicas dedicated to the gods of the conquered provinces.[34] The best-known example of incorporating foreign cults into the idiosyncratic Mexica religion is the magnification of the Toltec kingdom and its elevation as an epitome of civilization. Once Toltec culture was celebrated as the cradle of civilization, the Mexicas were able to make their claim as its rightful heirs. From the reign of Ahuitzotl (1486–1502) until the fall of Tenochtitlan, the Mexicas never ceased publicizing their Toltec lineage. Mexica propaganda obsessively portrayed the Toltecs as sages, artists, and sublime rulers. Through this artifice, they aimed at depriving the ancient peoples of the central and southern areas of Mesoamerica of the prestige as the true creators of civilization.[35]

Whoever takes a look at the multifarious Mexica pantheon experiences a feeling of incredulousness, followed by one of bewilderment. There are so many gods, so many strange, attractive, frightful figures, so many insignias and decorations. Although one's attention is captivated by these magnetic deities, this initial attraction is hampered by the impossibility of comprehending them immediately and by the overgrowth of symbols that, as in the case of the Coatlicue, shroud them in mystery. One characteristic of the Aztec gods is to be interwoven with multiple symbols and meanings, to such a degree that a god seems to represent much more than itself or seems to be a part of a more complex whole.

Nevertheless, behind this perplexing fabric of gods and symbols, there is an order. Even when we lack a complete, rigorous classification of the complicated Mexica pantheon, recent studies indicate the presence of groups of gods integrated around a major deity, or groups of deities related by specific functions. Thus, an ordering of this bevy of gods is possible whereby there are creator gods, heavenly gods, earthly (or tellurian) gods, rain and water gods, fertility and sustenance gods, gods of death and the netherworld, deified ancestors, and so on.[36]

If this classification is observed, we realize that Quetzalcoatl is one of the few Mesoamerican gods who crosses over all categories. It is one of the creator gods, in the Mayan as well as in the Mixtec and Nahuatl pantheons. As Ehécatl (wind god), Tlahuizcalpantecuhtli (Morning Star or god of the dawn), and Evening Star, it is one of the most important celestial deities. For classical-era Maya, it is also a god of the netherworld and thus intimately associated with the gods of rain and water. As Xilonen (tender young corn god), Chicomecóatl (Seven Serpent, corn goddess), and Centeótl (mature corn god), it is the Nahuatl god of corn and vegetation. In the classical period, it is a god of death and resurrection. Finally, it is also a deified ancestor, through antonomasia, the First Father of the classical Maya and the tutelary ancestor of the Toltecs, the divine Ce Acatl Topiltzin Quetzalcoatl, founder of the Toltec dynasty.

The excessive ambitiousness of the Mexica people can be measured in terms of their capacity for absorbing other cultures, especially by means of religious syncretism. The practice of collecting the gods and belief systems of other ethnic groups and the art of blending them with one's own gods were constantly pursued for political purposes. An example is this strategy of conversion whereby the founding warrior of the kingdom of Tula becomes an emblem of Tenochtitlan's dynastic power.

a   *b*

Fig. 4.41. Religious images of Quetzalcoatl: **(a)** sacrificing his own blood and **(b)** bathing at midnight. Drawings based on *Códice Florentino,* bk. 3, plate 19, figs. 9 and 10.

In examining the diverse sources referring to Quetzalcoatl in Tenochtitlan, Eloise Quiñones perceives that the most ancient texts enhance his portrayal as a warrior and conqueror, leader of the migration of his people, and ancestral hero. Quiñones observes that in the texts from the end of the sixteenth century, and in others collected afterwards or drafted by missionaries, this image is supplanted by that of a pious Quetzalcoatl, consecrated to religious duties. The latter is the dominant image in the pictures from the Florentine Codex (fig. 4.41), in the *Historia de las Indias* (History of the Indies) by Friar Diego Durán, and in the history prevalent for years afterwards (fig. 4.42). (See also fig. 2.9.)[37]

In reviewing these images, we come upon another discovery. Many Aztec monuments, instead of representing Quetzalcoatl as a pious, peaceful character, show him as an emblem of dynastic power or participating in rites that legitimize and exalt the rulers. Quiñones suggests that the ancestral archetype represented by Topiltzin Quetzalcoatl of Tula inspired the portraits of the rulers propagated by the Aztecs. In support of her hypothesis, she cites a passage from the *Historia de las Indias* by Friar Durán, who narrates Motecuhzoma Ilhuicamina's decision to erect a monument to memorialize his government. Durán recounts that when the monarch contemplated

Fig. 4.42. Quetzalcoatl in the process of making the blood sacrifice. In the text accompanying this plate in the Codex Vaticano Latino 3738, it is written: "This figure means that Quetzalcoatl was the first inventor of the sacrifices of human blood, among all the other things offered to the gods. And thus he pierced his tongue so that blood would come out of it and his ears and his virile member." Drawing and text taken from Kingsborough, 1964, vol. 3, plate 18.

his sculpted effigy in a hillside rock in Chapultepec (fig. 4.43), he declared that this monument would perpetuate his memory in the same way as with Topiltzin and Quetzalcoatl, who, before leaving on their very last journey, "left their faces sculpted in wood and in stone."[38]

Durán records that Itzcóatl, who governed between 1426 and 1440, had initiated the custom of engraving his and his ancestors' images in stone to perpetuate the memory of the Mexica rulers. It is important to note that the plan of immortalizing Mexica rulers was inspired by the model of Topiltzin Quetzalcoatl of Tula and gains strength during Itzcóatl's government when, after triumphing over the Tepanecas, there was the idea of constructing and propagating a new memory of Mexica power. The images of power which are now disseminated seem to reflect this change in the political scenery in the heart of Mesoamerica.

The effigy of Topiltzin Quetzalcoatl engraved by the Tenochtitlan leaders in the hillside at la Malinche, near Tula de Hidalgo, is very similar to the portraits of the Mexica kings. As in Tula, in Tenochtitlan the most prominent hillside closest to the city was selected in order to present a gallery of rulers. The emblem that in Tula (see figs. 2.2 and 2.3) and in Chichen Itza (fig. 4.44) accompanies those with the highest military and political functions becomes one of the official symbols of Mexica rulers. The undulating body of the Plumed Serpent is transformed into the emblem of those exercising Mexica power. In the representations of the *tlatoani* of Tenochtitlan, the emblem of the Plumed Serpent appears as an indicator of royal power. In the monument called the Acuecuexatl Stone, King Ahuitzotl (1486–1502) celebrates the bloodletting rite in the year 7 Cane (1499), dressed in sacerdotal attire (fig. 4.45). Behind the figure of the *tlatoani*, the emblem of the Plumed Serpent can be identified as it is drawn in a form very similar to the sculptures in the aforementioned la Malinche hillside and building in Tula. In another Mexica monument commemorating the transfer of power from the deceased King Tizoc to Ahuitzotl, both characters appear in priestly attire and pierce their ears with sharpened bones (fig. 4.46).

Two magnificent funerary urns found in the excavations at the Main Temple identify the connection established between the emblem of the Plumed Serpent and the legitimacy of the Mexica rulers. In one of them (fig. 4.47), designed in Toltec style, a highly decorated character carries a lance in his right hand and a bundle of arrows in his left. His costume underscores his military function and the attire of Toltec warriors. Behind this figure, the Plumed Serpent can be seen undulating in the background. The same composition and symbolism are repeated in another urn (fig. 4.48), which is also an imitation of the most appreciated piece of ceramic in the Toltec period. The character represented appears invested with the char-

Fig. 4.43. Motecuhzoma I posing for his portrait. Diego Durán recounts in the *Historia de las Indias* that Motecuhzoma Ilhuicamina wanted his face and Tlacaélel's to be perpetuated in Chapultepec's hillside. Drawing based on Durán, 1984, plate 19.

acteristics of Tezcatlipoca, the protector god of Mexica kings. He, too, is surrounded by the magical figure of the Plumed Serpent.

A new reading of the engraved images in the principal monuments of Tenochtitlan introduces a change in the idea held about Quetzalcoatl. The well-known and influential writings by Friar Bernardino de Sahagún and Friar Diego Durán describe a Topiltzin Quetzalcoatl of Tula dedicated to

Fig. 4.44. The emblem of the Plumed Serpent can be identified in this figure on the mural in the Lower Temple of the Jaguars in Chichen Itza. Drawing based on Coggins and Shane, 1989, 42.

Fig. 4.45. Acuecuexatl's Stone, commemorative monument erected by King Ahuitzotl. In the central section, Ahuitzotl is seen drawing blood with a stake, in front of the emblem of the Plumed Serpent. In the lower section, Ahuitzotl appears with the effigy of the Plumed Serpent behind him. Other figures of plumed serpents undulate in the upper section and on the walls of the monument. Drawing based on Pasztory, 1983, plate 119.

religious duties, absorbed with performing rites and sacrifices, and in anguish over his debilitating transgression of religious norms he himself had established. According to the account given by these and other authors, Topiltzin Quetzalcoatl, afflicted by Tezcatlipoca's successive punishments and overwhelmed by the repeated disgraces with which his people were castigated, finally succumbs to self-sacrifice.

This religious and Christian image of Topiltzin Quetzalcoatl stands in stark contrast to the one widespread in the commemorative monuments erected by the Mexica leaders. In these, the symbols of Toltec dynastic power are exalted to commemorate the triumphant deeds of Topiltzin Quetzalcoatl. It is also helpful to remember that at the height of Tula's and

Fig. 4.46. In the upper section, the Aztec stone shows the transfer
of power from the dead King Tizoc (*left*) to the new *tlatoani*,
Ahuitzotl (*right*). Both are dressed as priests and let blood from their
ears. Drawing based on Nicholson and Quiñones, 1983, 53.

Fig. 4.47. An Aztec funerary urn found in the excavations of the Templo Mayor (the Main Temple) in 1978. An important figure is represented who holds a lance in his right hand and a bunch of arrows in his left hand. An undulating figure can be identified in the background as the Plumed Serpent, emblem of military and political power. The vase is an imitation of the most appreciated ceramic style of the Toltec period. Drawing based on Nicholson and Quiñones, 1983, 94.

Chichen Itza's splendor, the Plumed Serpent celebrated the acts of power and conquest, the same symbolism used in the Tenochtitlan monuments. In this iconography of power, Topiltzin Quetzalcoatl, instead of evoking the archetypal priest, recalls the first leader of the northern tribes who founded a powerful state in the Central High Plains, created the Toltec dynasty, and unified political power with religion.

Fig. 4.48. Representation of a character dressed as the god Tezcatlipoca, the Mexica deity protecting dynastic power, on a funerary urn imitating the Toltec style. Behind the deity's figure, the emblem of the Plumed Serpent can be clearly identified. Drawing based on Nicholson and Quiñones, 1983, 97.

In addition, the images of Quetzalcoatl sacrificing his own blood or bathing at midnight in cold waters (see figs. 4.41 and 4.42), considered in the context of Mexica ceremonials, are actual acts performed by royal personages, not purely religious expressions. The texts describing ceremonies preceding the investiture of a new *tlatoani* mention that the new sovereign must live apart from others for a certain period of time, fast, and then perform the sacrifice of his own blood and make offerings to the gods.³⁹ These are precisely those acts that the hillside monuments of la Malinche (see fig. 2.2), the Acuecuexatl Stone (see fig. 4.45),⁴⁰ and the stele celebrating the transfer of power from Tizoc to Ahuitzotl (see fig. 4.46) commemorate. The style and symbolism of these monuments imitate models from Toltec art. They also celebrate the foundation of the first Nahuatl kingdom in Tula de Hidalgo and perpetuate the emblems of dynastic power established by Topiltzin Quetzalcoatl.

The changes introduced by the Mexicas with regard to the High Plains belief systems are connected to their own interpretations of the myth of the creation of the cosmos, the most central and permanent part of the Meso-american vision of the cosmos. As we have seen, in the version recorded on the Mayan funerary vases of the classical period, Hun Nal Ye travels to the netherworld, penetrates into the mountain of sustenance, and extracts precious corn seeds from the cave inside it. In the cosmogonies engraved in A.D. 690 in the temples of the Cross at Palenque, the main event is the birth of the First Father, Hun Nal Ye, who orders the cosmos, creates human beings, and puts the world in motion. In the Nahuatl tradition, we are familiar with at least three versions of this very ancient myth. The best known of these is the narration of Quetzalcoatl's voyage to the netherworld in search of the bones of lost, ancient humanity. In the text called the Legend of the Suns, after the flood that destroyed the earth, the creator gods resolve to entrust Quetzalcoatl with the task of creating a new humanity:

> Then Quetzalcoatl went to hell (*Mictlan*); he went to see Mictlantecuhtli (the god of the netherworld) and he said: "I have come for the precious bones you are keeping." The regent of the nocturnal region pretended to accede to his demand, but instead of giving him the bones, he un-leashed a series of obstacles to prevent Quetzalcoatl from completing his mission. With cunning similar to that of the Divine Twins in the *Popol Vuh,* Quetzalcoatl comes out victorious against these odds, aided by his sorcerer (*nagual*) who other sources identify as Xólotl (twin). In this way, Quetzalcoatl gathered the bones of men and women and made them into a bundle. But when he was leaving the netherworld, Mictlantecuhtli ordered his messengers to make a hole in the path and Quetzalcoatl fell into it where "he dropped dead and the precious bones fell to the ground where they were bitten and gnawed on by quails. In a little while, Quetzal-

coatl was resuscitated" and began to cry and collect the dispersed bones which he carried to Tamoanchan. There the Mother Goddess Quilaztli ground them up and "threw them into a precious glazed earthenware tub. On top of this, Quetzalcoatl let blood from his penis; and then, all the gods did penance."

Human beings, called "the vassals of the Gods" in the text, wondered what they would eat when they were born. They began the search for basic food. Quetzalcoatl also intervenes in this episode, in which he observes that a red ant was transporting corn kernels. Quetzalcoatl asked him many times where he got the corn, but the ant refused to answer him. Finally, he confessed that he had taken the grains from the Tonacatépetl (the hillside or mountain of sustenance). Transformed into a black ant, Quetzalcoatl followed the red ant, and together they entered into the Tonacatépetl and gathered the precious corn, which Quetzalcoatl brought back to Tamoanchan, where the gods were meeting. There the gods chewed on the corn and put it into the mouths of men and women to make them strong.

Then the gods asked: "What will we do with the Tonacatépetl?" So Quetzalcoatl tied some cords around it and attempted to pull it out of the netherworld, but he could not lift it. The soothsayers, Oxomuco and Cipactonal, predicted that Nanáhuatl (a forerunner of Quetzalcoatl) "would shake the grain from Tonacatápetl by thrashing it about." This occurred in the following manner: the Tlaloques were busy retrieving the different kinds of corn (white, black, yellow, and colored), the bean, wild rushes (amaranth), lime-leafed sage, and the other foodstuffs from inside the Tonacatépetl.[41] As we know, these colors are a reference to the four directions of the cosmos, so that this metaphor alludes to the division Tláloc makes of the corns in the different regions of the world. In this cosmic act, Tláloc repeats the tasks performed by farmers after the harvest: he divides the husks according to grains to be consumed and seeds to be used for the next planting. He then proceeds by taking the grains off the corn cobs, an act symbolizing the division of the grains between consumers and farmers all over the world. Plate 28 of the Borgia Codex illustrates the first of these actions and then shows Tláloc making the precious corn reproduce in the five regions of the cosmos (plate 9).

Another version of this myth recounts that a terrible goddess named Tlaltecuhtli inhabited the primordial waters and her "joints were all filled

with eyes and mouths that bit like a savage beast." The creator gods Quetzalcoatl and Tezcatlipoca said: "It is our duty to make the Earth."

> And in so saying, they both changed into large serpents . . . [and in this
> way] one seized the goddess's right hand and left foot, while the other
> seized her left hand and right foot.
>
> And they squeezed her so tightly that she split in two. From the middle
> of her shoulders, they made the earth, and they sent the other half to the
> heavens. . . .
>
> Then, this done, to compensate the goddess for the damages the gods
> had caused her, all the gods descended to console her and arranged that
> all the fruit necessary for human life would come from her.
>
> In order to do this, they made her hair into trees and flowers and
> herbs; her skin became grass and small flowers; her eyes were turned into
> wells and fountains and small caves; her mouth, rivers and great caverns;
> her nose, valleys and mountains. In this way, all that exists on the surface
> of the earth are parts of Tlaltecuhtli's body.
>
> Sometimes this goddess would cry at night, desirous as she was to eat
> out the hearts of men. She would not be quiet and would not give fruit
> until she was bathed with human blood.[42]

A third Nahuatl version of the origin of corn is also contained in the
"Histoyre du Mechique" (History of Mexico). It goes as follows:

> The grain they eat called corn was made this way:
> The gods all descended into a cavern where the god called Piltzintecutli
> was laying with a goddess named Xochipilli, from whom the god called
> Cinteotl was born.
>
> Cinteotl plunged under the earth and cotton came out of his hair, and
> from one ear, a very good and tasty seed called *huazontli* . . . [and from
> the other ear] another seed.
>
> From his nose, out came another seed called *chien* that is very good to
> drink in summertime. A fruit called *camotli,* which is a very good fruit like
> colewort, came out of his fingers.
>
> Another sort of wide corn, a cereal they eat today, came out of his
> nails. And from the rest of his body, many other fruits came out which
> men plant and harvest.[43]

If some of the details are glossed over, it can be observed that the three Nahuatl stories of the origin of the cosmos and food are strikingly similar to the most ancient Mesoamerican creation myths. In reviewing their narrative structure, one notices that the Mexica myths situate the episode of the origin of human beings and corn after the great flood alluded to in the *Popol Vuh* and in the *Libro del Chilam Balam de Chumayel* (Book of Chilam Balam of Chumayel). The main event of this episode is the creation of human beings, which occurs in the netherworld, in the Mayan Xibalbá or in the Nahuatl Mictlan. The Mayan and Nahuatl stories concur in indicating that the appearance of new humanity is preceded by an intense battle between the celestial emissaries (the Divine Twins, Quetzalcoatl-Xólotl) and the lords of the netherworld, who are against resurrecting human beings, stars, and seeds fallen into Xibalbá-Mictlan.

In the *Popol Vuh,* the battle between the Divine Twins and the Lords of Xibalbá occupies a large part of the narration. In fact, the sequence of strategies, traps, and dangers that the twins manage to elude is the most entertaining part of the narrative. The Nahuatl accounts also allude to this tension and incorporate highly dramatic scenes, such as the one in which the goddess Tlaltecuhtli cries out for human blood. Just as in the Maya's *Popol Vuh,* in the Nahuatl texts claims are also resolved by way of agreements. Henceforth, the netherworld will return human beings, plants, and stars to the surface of the earth on the condition that it retain within it a portion of vital energy. As for the earthly populations, represented in the mythic narration by the Divine Twins, they remain obliged to shed blood periodically on the planted earth and accept their mortal condition as the "vassals of the gods."

In the Nahuatl myth Quetzalcoatl, as Ehécatl, directly participates in the creation of new humanity by watering the corn dough with blood from his sexual organ. This scene is graphically expressed in an earlier monument from the coast of the Gulf of Mexico. In the drawing engraved on the side of a Huasteca conch shell (fig. 4.49), there is a character in the process of making a blood sacrifice from his penis. He stands before a woman who has been identified as the goddess Quilaztli, who, in the Nahuatl myth, is the figure who grinds the corn and makes it into dough. In this drawing, a plate can be seen which holds a kind of dough upon which the sacrificial blood falls.[44]

On one of the walls of the southern ball court in El Tajín, there is also a very expressive representation of human beings (plate 10). In this relief,

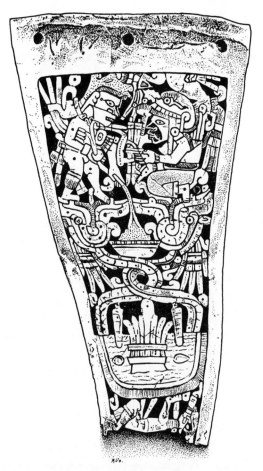

Fig. 4.49. Huasteca ornament made of conch, with a scene depicting the mythical creation of human beings. In the upper section, a masculine character spurts blood from his penis, which falls into a receptacle containing dough or powder. In front of this, a woman, naked to the waist, can be identified as the goddess Quilaztli. In the lower section, a temple emerges from the water inside an enclosure that appears to be a cave. Drawing based on Stresser-Pean, 1971, fig. 2.

a character with the attributes of Tláloc perforates his penis, from which a liquid spurts out, wetting the face of a figure emerging from a pond. This character is wearing a kind of fish mask on his head. Some connect this scene with the Nahuatl myth of how men were changed into fish. In the Huasteca tradition, there are creation myths that recount that before the present humanity men were transformed into fish. In the *Popol Vuh,* there is a similar episode as well.[45]

In comparing Mayan creation myths of the classical period and Huasteca myths, and especially Nahuatl and Mayan myths of the fifteenth and sixteenth centuries, the strong continuity in the Mesoamerican vision of the cosmos is demonstrated. Something deeper is revealed, an essential nucleus: the idea that human beings and food were born in the humid, dark cave within the primordial mountain. This conception affirms that the original matrix is the earth itself, the generating mother of all essential goods.

The obsessive presence of this image in all the cultures and throughout the historical development of Mesoamerica (fig. 4.50) is the best proof of the unity sustaining Mesoamerican thought. For these peoples, primordial creation occurred inside the earth and was the product of the conjunction of the germinating forces of the earth with the fecundating forces of the sky, produced through the sacrifice of gods. The idea of sacrifice is inseparable from primordial creation and, from this first act on, for all creations. Thus, as it is necessary to sacrifice seedlings to mother earth so that corn can sprout each spring, so it is with human beings, who are obliged to sacrifice their blood to compensate the gods for their creation. This conception was translated into all daily actions, through the calendar, rites, and religious ceremonies. The performance of agricultural rites and sacrifices was scrupulously established in the calendar so that in the first days of spring the corn god would emerge victoriously from the depths of the earth (fig. 4.51).[46]

In any case, for the Mesoamerican peoples, the most common way of commemorating the founding moment of creation was the perfect form of the pyramid. In the beginnings of Mesoamerican civilization, the Olmecs established the setting that recorded this moment and defined its rites and symbols. Since then, in the most sacred place, an artificial mound was raised to imitate the First Mountain that emerged from the primordial waters. In being raised, it was oriented toward the four corners of the universe; the primordial mountain centered and circumscribed the terrestrial environment. In Uaxactún, near Tikal, notable examples of symmetric pyramids appear as early as the preclassical period. These connect the netherworld with the surface of the earth and the sky. The first pyramid decorated on all sides with the Plumed Serpent was built in Teotihuacan, in the middle of the second century B.C.E. in the center of the enclosure dedicated to the political government of the city (fig. 4.52). During the postclassical period, the sym-

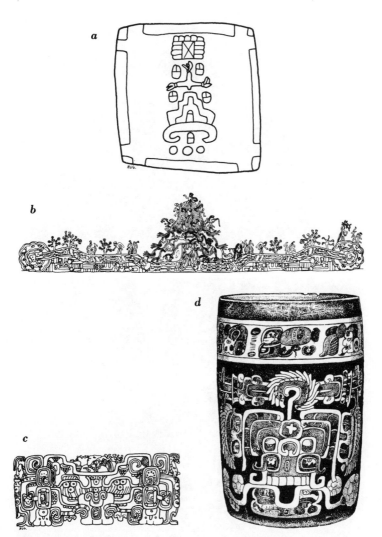

Fig. 4.50. Representations of the First True Mountain: **(a)** in La
Venta; **(b)** on a mural painting in Teotihuacan; **(c)** on a Bonampak
stele; **(d)** on a classical-period Mayan funerary vase. Additional
examples of the First True Mountain can be seen in figures 4.17, 4.18,
1.13, and 4.14.

Fig. 4.51. The Mayan corn god, decorated with husks, emerges dancing inside the earth and represented by the effigy of the First True Mountain, which rose on the day of the creation of the cosmos. Drawing based on a photograph in Kerr, 1992, 32.

memorable interpretation that Marija Gimbutas has made of the archaeological evidence from the Neolithic period in Europe proves that the Mother
Goddess was a principal deity.[2]

During the years between 7000 and 3500 B.C.E., in what is today central
and eastern Europe, the Mother Goddess was an omnipresent deity: earth
goddess and goddess of the fruits of the earth, animals, and the sky. Her dominion in the celestial region controlled the harmonious movement of the
moon, the stars, the rainy season, and the changing of the seasons. She was
a self-created goddess, had no ancestors, and reigned without rivals over the
entire universe. She was adored as the Great Mother of Life, Death, and
Regeneration, Goddess of Animals, and the Lady of the Sea and Fruits of
the Earth.

Everything existing on the earth's surface emanated from this goddess.
In all her manifestations, she was the symbol of the unity of life and nature.
Her power was in water and stone, in animals and birds, in serpents and
fish, in mountains, trees, and flowers. Thus, the overall mythical and poetic
perception is that she was responsible for everything that existed on earth.[3]

The best-known representations emphasize her powers of ordering the
movement of the stars and regeneration in nature, her capacity for producing animals, her kindness in distributing the necessary goods for sustaining
and continuing human life (figs. 5.1, 5.2, 5.3, and 5.4).

The peoples who adored this goddess were hunters, gatherers, and farmers. They were the founders of the early towns where the first ceremonial
centers and sumptuous palaces were built. In these first fixed abodes, inhabited by populations who recognized the lineage of their ancestors, there is
no trace of outer walls or warlike signs. The archaeological evidence suggests
that there was no superiority of men over women. The distribution of goods
in burial sites reveals the existence of a nonpatriarchal and egalitarian society.

In America, much, much later (2000–1000 B.C.E.), various kinds of evidence point to an extended cult of the Mother Goddess in the same period
during which the first agricultural towns were founded. In several regions,
archaeologists have discovered sculptures with the image of the procreating
body of the Mother Goddess, identified by her large breasts and a triangle
representing her sexual organs. Other images represent her with two heads,
one symbolizing life and the other death (figs. 5.5 and 5.6). In the Mesoamerican figures, just as in the European versions, "there is as yet no distinction between the goddess who brings life and the goddess who brings

Fig. 5.1. One of the most ancient representations
of the Mother Goddess, called the Laussel Goddess,
holding the moon in her right hand. Sculpture
dated between 22,000 and 18,000 years B.C.E.
Drawing based on Baring and Cashford, 1993, 44.

death as there was to be in the Bronze Age. . . . For the Neolithic feeling,
like the Paleolithic, was to experience both as a unity through the image of
the Great Mother as the totality of life and death."[4]

In other parts of the American continent—in the Andes, for example—
there are examples of representations of a deity similar to the Neolithic
Mother Goddess or the Mesoamerican Mother Goddess who also possesses
powers of life and death and is the source of vegetal germination and celestial fecundity, giving birth to plants and animals and governing the movements of disappearance and return of the stars. In a famous Peruvian monument, cut in the form of an obelisk, a creation myth is displayed: a pair of

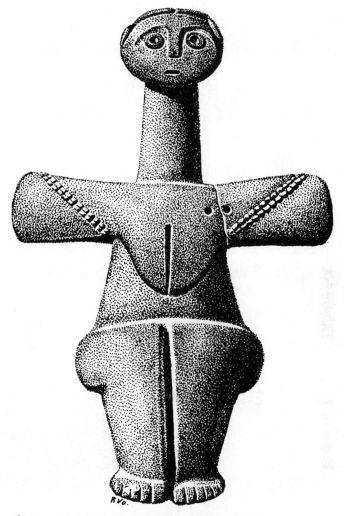

Fig. 5.2. Representation of the Mother Goddess in a sitting position. The center of this sculpture is the feminine triangle in the middle of the figure. This sculpture dates from approximately 3000 B.C.E. Drawing based on Gimbutas, 1989, plate 6.

Fig. 5.3. On the right, the goddess of vegetal regeneration, and on the left another goddess, with serpents in both hands. Both are wearing little skirts made of netting and are surrounded by various animals. Plate from Iraq, 2700–2500 B.C.E. Drawing based on Baring and Cashford, 1993, 189.

Fig. 5.4. Representation of a goddess or priestess from Mycenae with wheat or barley plants in her hands. Fresco from 1300 B.C.E. Drawing based on Baring and Cashford, 1993, 116.

flying caimans, symbols of the reproductive powers of the sky and the earth, are carrying domesticated plants in the lowlands. Likewise, various Peruvian textiles are distinguished by the mask of a supernatural being, composed of plants, serpents, and figures in the form of a dragon, who seems to represent a goddess of the earth (figs. 5.7 and 5.8).[5] It can be said that there are also many other manifestations of the ever present figure of Coatlicue, the

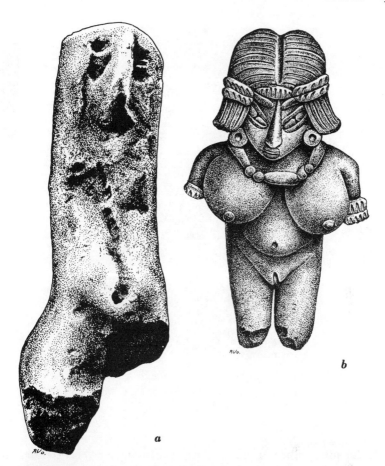

b

a

Fig. 5.5. The Mother Goddess of Mesoamerica. **(a)** The Zohapilco
Mother Goddess. In part of her face, the hollows of her eyes and nose
can be distinguished as very pronounced features. In the lower part,
her bulky midsection and wide hips can be identified. Sculpture dates
from approximately 2300 B.C.E. Drawing based on Niederberger, 1987,
vol. I, fig. 167. **(b)** Feminine figure from the Chupícuaro area with
accentuated breasts and reproductive organs. Drawing based on Piña
Chan, 1977, fig. 12.

Mexica earth goddess in whose overcharged image symbols of vegetal, animal, and cosmic regeneration are blended (plate 12).[6]

Between the years 3500 and 1250 B.C.E., the Bronze Age, according to archaeologists, the Mother Goddess of central Europe and the Near East loses
her position as a principal deity and ceases to be a symbol of the totality

Fig. 5.6. Tlatilco Mask, with a dramatic representation of life (*left*) and death (*right*), 1200–700 B.C.E. Drawing based on Markman and Markman, 1992, 52.

of the life-giving forces of the universe. The multiple powers concentrated in her grandiose effigy begin to be divided into other gods and goddesses, or shared with her sons and daughters. The cause of these changes was the invasion of Aryan and Semitic peoples, nomad and warrior tribes whose traditions were different from those of the sedentary peoples. From the beginning of the fourth century B.C.E., successive waves of Aryan groups descended from the plains of central Europe and from the south of Russia to invade the lands of Anatolia, Mesopotamia, Greece, and the Indus Valley. At the same time, tribes of shepherds and Semitic warriors from the Syrian desert moved toward Mesopotamia and Canaan.

The Aryans were a warrior society. They had learned how to domesticate the horse, and they invented the wheeled, horse-drawn chariot, a machine that spread terror in the farming towns. Wherever they invaded, the warriors left the mark of their devastation and transformed the governing group. In Anatolia, their passage was marked by the sacking and burning of more than three hundred cities, among them the misbegotten city of Troy. In approximately 2100 B.C.E., a Sumerian witness referred to an invasion of a hoard "whose onslaught was like a hurricane" and defined these groups as a people "who had never known a city."[7]

These changes in the political and social scenery were followed by others, which were no less disturbing, in the mythical realm of gods and cosmogonies. All over, in Egypt and in Sumeria as well as in the Mediterranean basin, the ancient goddesses ceded their place to the gods of masculine cults. At the same time that the towns were being transformed into cities, and these were

Fig. 5.7. Representation of caimans, birds, and serpents along with domesticated plants from the lowlands of Peru. The caimans are perceived more clearly when the figure is looked at horizontally. This figure probably dates from 900 to 200 B.C.E. The drawing depicts the images carved in the obelisk at Tello, from Chavín de Huántar, Peru, and based on Townsend, *The Aztecs*, 268.

Fig. 5.8. Earth Goddess, represented in a mask in which plants, serpents, and figures in the form of a dragon converge. Textile from the Ica Valley, Callango, Peru, 900–200 B.C.E. Drawing based on Townsend, *The Aztecs,* 277.

becoming states governed by a king with unlimited powers, religious cults were becoming state religions, centering on the glorification of the king, always identified with the protector god of the kingdom. Then new creation myths emerged in which the Father God usurps the place previously held by the Mother Goddess. In Sumeria and in Egypt, instead of attributing the creation of the world to the ancient Mother Goddess, cosmogonies appeared which introduced a creator god who divides the ancestral cosmic unity into two halves—heaven (or sky) and earth. With this founding division, the god initiates the process of creation. This model will be the basis for later cosmogonies and theological conceptions.[8]

Given the audacity of the conquistadors' ideologies, the priests of the invading peoples destroyed the shrines dedicated to the Mother Goddess and replaced them with altars and temples dedicated to honoring masculine deities. Instead of the creation myth that had the cosmos spring from the breast of the Mother Goddess, in Sumeria and in Egypt the cosmos was divided into three levels: the mountain emerging from the primordial waters into his own temple. From this moment on, Enlil takes over the place previously held by the Mother Goddess as supreme creator of the cosmos.[9]

In Egypt, in the narrow band of desert transformed into fertile earth by the regenerating waters of the Nile, something similar occurred. The First Mountain and the first signs of cosmic vitality spring from the primordial waters. Unlike in Sumeria, however, where these are female, in Egypt they are masculine and are represented by Nun, the First Father. According to the myth of creation of Heliopolis, the god Atum was raised from the primordial waters in the form of the First Mountain. Then Atum created the god Shu, air, which had a masculine nature, and Tefnut, goddess of humidity. Much later, Shu and Tefnut produced Nut, the sky (feminine), and Geb, the earth (masculine). Shu, as in the case of the Sumerian Enlil, performed the following processes of creation: he separated the sky and the earth, thereby producing the duality inaugurating the movement of the creation of the cosmos and human beings.[10]

In the high ziggurats of the Mesopotamian plains, in the temples decorated with cut stones positioned toward the rising of the sun and celebrating the regenerating power of the waters of the Nile, in the beautiful painted palaces in Crete, in the dusty cities of the Near East and in Mediterranean towns, each year, on the first day of the spring equinox, the old myth of the creation of the cosmos was sung out, now shaped by the heroic figures of the gods married with goddesses descended from the ancient Mother Goddess. In the most ancient times, in the Paleolithic period, this had been a myth calibrated according to the phases of the moon. In the Neolithic period, the lunar cycle was combined with the harvest cycle in such a way that the cycles of the stars seemed also to celebrate the renewal of nature and announce the planting season.

From 3500 to 1250 B.C.E., the timeless myth of the origin of the cosmos was joined to the story of how the Mother Goddess separated from her lover (or her brother, or her son), who died in the summer and was buried in the depths of the earth and who, thanks to the determined efforts of his wife and mother, was reborn again in springtime.[11] Such is the distant origin of the myths of Dumuzi-Tammuz, Osiris, Adonis, Persephone, and Quetzalcoatl, all gods of vegetation endowed with powers of fertility previously concentrated in the Mother Goddess figure. In the new creation myths, the Mother Goddess's fragile son suffers attacks from fearsome enemies and is repeatedly persecuted and subjected to terrible trials by the regents of the underworld. Although he dies, he is finally revived and manages to bring precious food to the surface of the earth. Even though the heroes of these myths have different names and their adventures are set in different places, the narration describing their deeds recounts the same story.

Inanna-Istar and Dumuzi-Tammuz's Voyage to the Underworld and the Celebration of Their Return

It is said that "history began" in Mesopotamia. This region is today a hot, desert land where archaeologists have discovered the most ancient historical remains: hundreds of engraved tablets with cuneiform writing date from 3000 B.C.E. Thanks to the deciphering of these writings, we know that in the most ancient times one of the principal gods was indeed the Mother Goddess. Henri Frankfort indicated that the key to understanding this region's resplendent culture was "the Mesopotamian idea that life proceeded from a goddess, that the universe was conceived . . . not engendered; [that] the source of life" is feminine.[12] In the years in which the legendary cities of Ur, Uruk, Eridu, and Lagash were flourishing, the most revered goddess was Inanna.

Inanna, the Egyptian goddess Isis, and the Anatolian Cybele were the great goddesses of the Bronze Age (3500–1250 B.C.E.). For more than five thousand years, the cult of these goddesses forged the archetypal images of the feminine and later influenced the religious tradition that originated the Semitic and Christian goddesses. In this era, the figure of Inanna embodies the different levels of the cosmos. She reigns on earth with the symbols of heaven and has the moon and stars for a crown. She is the goddess of the sky and primordial waters surrounding the earth. She is called the "Green Princess," or "The One of Springtime Green," in reference to the green carpet covering the earth at this time of year. As queen on earth, Inanna was the goddess of the grains and vines, of palm dates, cedar, figs, olives, apple trees, and other fruits that were her other epiphanies (figs. 5.9 and 5.10). From 3500 B.C.E., she was adored as the sovereign of the sky and earth in Sumeria, and two thousand years later, her cult continued in Mesopotamia, where her name was Istar. The marvelous tablets engraved with letters preserved her innumerable honorifics: "Queen of Heaven and Earth," "Priestess of the Sky," "Light of the World," "Morning and Evening Star," "Just Judge," "Pardoner of Sins," "First Daughter of the Moon," "Holder of the Matrix," "Marvel of the Earth."[13]

One of the features that distinguish Inanna is the presence of a masculine character, half god, half human, who appears as her lover, husband, or son on visual representations and in the literature (fig. 5.11). In Sumeria, he received the name Dumuzi, and in the northern territory, where Accadian was spoken, he was called Tammuz. Both names mean "faithful son." Like the Mother Goddess, both are referred to with titles such as "A Green One" or the "First Green." They are gods associated with vegetation and linked to animal reproduction. This is why they are also called "Lord of the Sheep" or "Lord of Livestock." Through their other titles, such as "Lord of Life" or "Lord of the Reeds" or "Shepherd of the People," they are associated with paternity.[14]

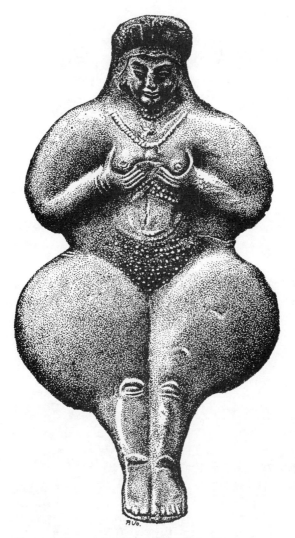

Fig. 5.9. Inanna-Istar as goddess of fertility.
Sculpture from 2000 B.C.E. Drawing based on Baring
and Cashford, 1993, 198.

Fig. 5.10. Cylindrical seal showing Inanna-Istar as goddess of the sky and stars. Drawing based on Baring and Cashford, 1993, 200.

Fig. 5.11. The goddess Inanna, on the right, receives the grain god, who is walking toward her with plants sprouting from its body. Cylindrical seal, 2300–2000 B.C.E. Drawing based on Baring and Cashford, 1993, 208.

Suddenly, in one of the most famous Sumerian stories, Inanna abandons her kingdom and decides to travel to the fearsome region of the underworld. The text does not specify the reasons for this, but the motive appears to be a dispute between the gods of the earth and those of the underworld, since Inanna arrives in this lower region in a belligerent state of mind. She asks the guard at the entrance to open the door of the place of shadows, but instead of having free access to this mysterious region, she encounters one obstacle after another.

Inanna is stopped at the threshold of the seven doors that lead to the underworld and suffers humiliations. Just like the Divine Twins in the *Popol Vuh,* her descent into the humid region is a succession of losses. In each one of these portals, she is stripped of her symbols and decorations, so that when she arrives at the last room, she appears naked and defenseless. Thus, when she encounters Ereskigal, the goddess of the underworld, all Ereskigal has to do is throw her a look and it kills her. For three days, her corpse is hung on a post in the underworld, like Hun Hunahpú's skull in the *Popol Vuh.*

Through the mediation of the god Enki, two celestial emissaries implore Ereskigal to return Inanna's cadaver. They manage to revive Inanna with revitalizing potions. When she returns to life, Inanna asks to leave the lower region, but the regents of the underworld remind her that whoever enters may never leave and return to the world of the living. The only exception to this rule is to leave a substitute. Here begins another chapter of Inanna's Voyage to the Underworld, which culminates with meeting Dumuzi, with whom Inanna is furious because he seems not to have missed her during her absence. She condemns him to reside in the underworld. According to the agreement that the goddesses of the celestial world made with those of the underworld, Dumuzi and his sister, who intervened to have his punishment reduced, would take turns spending half the year in the underworld and the other half on earth.[15] Periodically descending to the underworld (fig. 5.12), Dumuzi repeats a sequence similar to Hun Nal Ye's voyage to Xibalbá. After residing in the humid and cold region, both return triumphantly to the surface of the earth.

Many years after the Inanna tale, the Accadian scribes composed another poem entitled "Istar's Voyage to the Underworld." This was a song repeating the adventures of Inanna and Dumuzi. The poem in Accadian recounts in a clearer and more synthetic fashion the significance of the goddess's descent into the underworld. It relates that the death of Istar and her being

Fig. 5.12. Upon his return from the depths of the underworld, Dumuzi travels by boat, just like the Mayan Hun Nal Ye, accompanied by rowing gods. Plants sprout from the bow of the boat, symbolizing renewal in nature. Sumerian cylindrical seal from 2300–2150 B.C.E. Drawing based on Baring and Cashford, 1993, 223.

retained in the underworld produced disasters causing disorder on earth and disturbing the balance of the cosmos: "Bulls would not couple with cows. . . . No man would copulate with his wives. Everyone slept apart in their own room." During these ominous days, sterility invaded the cosmos, and the inhabitants of the earth did not reproduce.[16] To get rid of this calamity, the heavenly gods sent off their emissaries to the underworld, where they obliged the rulers of the underworld to revive Istar and keep Tammuz inside the earth for half the year. This is the agreement whereby the Mother Goddess receives the mortal remains of earthly humans and in exchange, each year, at the beginning of springtime, she renews nature and produces food. In this way, the ancient cosmic equilibrium, previously governed by the Mother Goddess, was reestablished.

If the poem of the descent of Inanna-Istar to the underworld was transformed into a popular exorcism against barren fields, the populations of Mesopotamia institutionalized a ceremony celebrating the contrary phenomenon: the procreating union of the forces of the earth and heaven. At the beginning of spring, when the god of vegetation returned from his residency in the underworld, the inhabitants of the Sumerian cities celebrated his coupling with Inanna, the goddess of fertility, high up in the main temple. The role of the young god of vegetation, recently released from the underworld, was played by the king of the city, and the role of Inanna was played by the priestess. This ritual was the most important ceremony of the New Year, the great celebration gathering the whole population around the ziggurat, the high temple symbolizing the union of heaven and earth.

The Sumerian and Mesoamerican conceptions of the origin of grains and the place where these were kept are surprisingly similar. In Sumeria, the grains used for food were kept hidden inside a sacred mountain, just like in Mesoamerica. The seeds are extracted in both places by beneficent gods, who give them to human beings. Just like the Maya, the Mesopotamian peoples have a god of grain who literally sprouts from the depths of the earth. In the figures sculpted into the famous cylindrical seal, Dumuzi emerges from inside the earth, assisted by the Mother Goddess and the creator god Enki (fig. 5.13).[17]

The New Year festival is also similar in Mesopotamia, Egypt, and Mesoamerica, where it celebrates the beginning of spring and the renewal of vegetation. In Mesoamerica, the New Year festival celebrating the renewal of nature was symbolized by the sprouting of the young corn god. In Mesopotamia, the union of the forces of heaven and earth were celebrated with the most important public displays. Written tablets have come down to us with emotional poems dedicated to this festival. In those days, the pairing of the regenerating forces of the cosmos was dramatized in the person of the king and the priestess of Inanna. The entire city was then transformed into the stage of the encounter promoting the renewal of nature and the resurgence of food on earth. However, the culminating act of this drama occurred in the most sanctified of places. High up on the ziggurat, the chamber dedicated to the sacred matrimony was richly decorated for the occasion. From this nuptial chamber, transformed into an Eden of abundance, the king, in his role as the young god of vegetation, calls to Inanna:

> My sister, I would go with you to my garden.
> Inanna, I would go with you to my garden.
> I would go with you to my orchard.
> I would go with you to my apple tree.
> There I would plant the sweet, honey-covered seed.

In response to these images of plenty, to this garden of Eden, which we also know of through visual representations (fig. 5.14), Inanna would say:

Fig. 5.13. The sprouting of Dumuzi, god of the grains and the depths of the earth. In this Accadian seal, Dumuzi emerges from the sacred mountain through a U-shaped opening. On the left, the goddess Inanna celebrates his resurrection. On the right, the god of knowledge, Enki, is carrying a dove in his hand. Cylindrical seal in the British Museum. Drawing based on Frankfort, 1988, plate 50.

> He brought me into his garden.
> My brother, Dumuzi, brought me into his garden.
> I strolled with him among the standing trees,
> I stood with him among the fallen trees,
> By an apple tree I knelt as is proper.
> Before my brother coming in song,
> Who rose to me out of the poplar leaves,
> Who came to me in the midday heat,
> Before my lord Dumuzi,
> I poured out plants from my womb.
> I placed plants before him,
> I poured out plants before him,
> I placed grain before him.
> I poured out grain from my womb.

The imagery of fertility permeates other poems:

> At the king's lap stood the rising cedar.
> Plants grew high by their side.
> Grains grew high by their side.
> Gardens flourished luxuriantly.

And Inanna said:

> Bridegroom, dear to my heart,
> Goodly is your beauty, honeysweet.
>
> .   .   .   .
>
> You have captivated me, let me stand tremblingly before you,
> Bridegroom, I would be taken by you to the bedchamber,
> You have captivated me, let me stand tremblingly before you,
> Lion, I would be taken by you to the bedchamber.
> Bridegroom, let me caress you,
> My precious caress is more savory than honey;
> In the bedchamber, honey filled,
> Let us enjoy your goodly beauty,
> Lion, let me caress you,
> My precious caress is more savory than honey.

Another poem celebrates the return of fertility to the land. Inanna sings:

Fig. 5.14. The goddess Inanna, on the left, in front of Tammuz, the young grain god. In between them, a tree bearing fruit, one of the first images of the pair in an earthly paradise. Cylindrical seal, 2500 B.C.E. Drawing based on Baring and Cashford, 1993, 212.

He has sprouted: he has burgeoned;
He is lettuce planted by the water.
He is the one my womb loves best.

My well-stocked garden of the plain,
My barley growing high in its furrow,
My apple tree which bears fruit up to its crown,
He is lettuce planted by the water.

My honey-man, my honey-man sweetens me always.
My lord, the honey-man of the gods,
He is the one my womb loves best.
His hand is honey, his foot is honey,
He sweetens me always.

My eager impetuous caresser of the navel,
My caresser of the soft thighs,
He is the one my womb loves best,
He is lettuce planted by the water.[18]

In these and other images of sacred matrimony, the husband assumes the traits of the farmer, who waters the ground and fertilizes the earth. The woman is equated to the earth, since, in order to conceive, she requires her husband's seed and cultivation. Therefore, it can be said that these texts configure a *hierogamy* (or *hieros gamos*), a wedding of the gods, whose union would produce earthly food to satisfy humanity's appetite.[19]

The Death and Resurrection of Osiris

In Egypt, a vast number of ceremonies celebrated the renewal of nature. Two of these were particularly remarkable. One was the festival that announced the first plants in spring, and the other celebrated the fertilization of the earth in the swell of the river Nile in summer. The cycles of decay and renovation in nature were intimately linked to the phases of the moon, the sun, and the stars. According to this interpretation of the dynamics of the cosmos, everything that happens is part of an uninterrupted succession of the disappearance and return of life, nature, and stars, whose inalterable repetition maintained cosmic vitality. The most popular image of this conception was embodied in the myth of Osiris.

This myth recounts that Nut (the sky) and Geb (the earth) gave birth to Osiris. When he was born, a voice sounded out proclaiming that "the Lord of All advances to the light." Next, other gods and goddesses were born: Horus the elder, Seth, Isis, Nephthys, and Atum, who, along with their predecessors, formed the Ennead, the group of nine gods and goddesses who protected the kingdom. Nephthys married Seth, and Isis married Osiris, who, according to the tradition, had been in love since they were suckling on their mother's breast, if not since inside the womb.

Osiris was transformed into the first king of Egypt and the founder of civilized life. Isis discovered wheat and barley, which grew wild, and Osiris taught how to cultivate them, and people left the wild life behind them. "Osiris was the first to gather fruits from the trees, embower the vines and grow grapes." He then traveled throughout the world, spreading this knowledge, while Isis, his faithful wife, governed the kingdom. Jealous of his brother's knowledge, Seth devised a plan to make him disappear. He built a splendid coffer, exactly the size of Osiris's body, and during a celebration, he promised to give it away to the one who could fit inside it. When Osiris got inside the coffer, seventy-two conspirators hurried to close the top, which they soldered with melted iron, and they then threw the coffer into the Nile. When Isis heard this bad news, she cut off a lock of her hair, went into mourning, and "wandered in her suffering looking everywhere for the corpse." From then on, her pained figure endured as the model for the inconsolable mother.

"A while later, the coffer containing Osiris's body was floating down the river toward the sea, finally running aground in Byblos, a city on the coast of Syria, where suddenly a 'heather tree' sprung up enclosing the box inside its trunk as it grew. The king of the country, admiring the great tree, ordered it cut down to serve as a column in his house," without knowing what it contained. When Isis heard of these events, she hurried off to Byblos to search for her lover. In order not to alarm the kings of this place, she adopted the appearance of a common woman and thus managed to enter into the palace and stood near the tree trunk column enclosing Osiris's body. After many adventures, she revealed her divine nature to the kings and asked that they return the precious timber to her. When she took hold of it, she split the column, opened the coffer, and threw herself on top of Osiris's inert body.

The myth recounts that Horus was born of this union. Horus was a central character in Egyptian mythology who avenges Osiris by transforming himself into Seth's rival. He beats Seth and becomes enthroned as king of Egypt, legitimate heir to Osiris.

On one occasion, Isis had to leave the coffer to go and visit Horus, who was in the city of Buto. Before leaving, she hid the coffer on the riverbank, but it was discovered by the evil Seth. When he recognized the corpse, Seth "cut it in fourteen pieces," which he scattered near and far. The dismemberment of Osiris once again caused Isis to grieve. With her sister Nephthys, she traveled throughout the kingdom searching for the scattered pieces of his body. "The moaning and crying of the grieving sisters was not in vain; feeling pity for their tears, the sun god" sent "Anubis, the god with the jackal's head." Anubis along with Isis and Nephthys, Thoth, and Horus "gathered piece after piece of the dismembered body of the dead god, wrapping it in linen and performing all the rites that Egyptians traditionally perform on the bodies of the dead."

Another account relates that "Isis recovered all the parts of the body except the genitals," which were eaten by a fish. She then made a replica of the phallus and united all the parts of his body and with them "reassembled it as a mummy":

> Isis fanned the dead body again with her wings and Osiris revived to become the Ruler of Eternity. There he enjoys the titles of Lord of the Subterranean World, Ruler of Eternity and King of the Dead. It is there where in the great Hall of The Two Truths, assisted by forty-two accessories, one for each of the main districts of Egypt, he presides as judge of souls of the dead, who solemnly make their confession before him and once their hearts have been weighed on the scales of justice, they receive the gift of virtue in eternal life or the appropriate punishment for their sins.[20] (Fig. 5.15.)

These are, in brief, the essential features of the "most popular of all the Egyptian gods" and one of the most widespread myths of antiquity. Even when this myth went through changes over time, two ancestral themes remained constant: the fertilizing powers of Osiris and his cult as god of the resurrection. From his birth, in his condition as son of Geb (the earth) and Nut (the sky), Osiris incarnates the reproductive forces of the two most important regions of the cosmos, as well as those of the underworld, where he makes his eternal resting place.

Fig. 5.15. Osiris in the underworld, seated on his throne, is receiving the adoration of the scribe Nekht and his wife. Osiris is wearing a white crown and carries the symbols of sovereignty and government in his hands. In the center a rectangle is represented containing the primordial waters of the underworld, from which palm trees, fruit trees, and other plants grow. Drawing based on Budge, 1973, vol. 1, frontispiece and jacket.

The flooding of the Nile, the phenomenon that at the beginning of summer created the miracle of fertility on the once dry fields, was a manifestation of Osiris. In a hymn dedicated to this god, the pharaoh Ramses IV says: "Thou art the Nile. . . . Gods and men live from thy outflow." The idea that Osiris was revealed in the currents of the Nile when the earth and the people most needed it was part of Egypt's traditional beliefs up until its contact with Western culture. Plutarch, the Greek writer who traveled to Egypt in the second century A.D., recounts having been present at a ceremony on the river Nile as it rose. At this time, a multitude of priests and officiators came to the banks of the Nile at night, carrying a little chest and a golden vase. Arriving at the river, they collected some fresh water, poured it in the vase, and jubilantly exclaimed: "Osiris is found!"[21]

Another Greek writer, Pausanias, recorded a tradition that tells of the popular manifestations the swelling of the Nile provoked: "The Egyptians say that Isis bewails Osiris when the river begins to rise; and when it inundates the fields, they say it is the tears of Isis."[22] However, the popular ceremonies that most connect with Osiris were those celebrating the different phases of vegetal renewal, particularly the planting and harvesting of wheat and barley.

The belief that Osiris was reborn in the grains and vegetation was extremely widespread. Over time, it was transformed into one of the dogmas

Fig. 5.16. Osiris dressed in a tunic with a netlike motif with a circle in the center. It is a costume that alludes to the reproductive powers of the humid earth and represents the planted land: each square has a seed in the middle. Drawing based on Budge, 1973, 1:50.

of Egyptian theology. In the text known as Teología Menfita (Memphis Theology), some passages identify Osiris with wheat and barley. One says: "I am [Osiris] who makes barley and wheat to feed the gods . . . [and] living creatures." In another text of the Temple of Dendur, Osiris "made the cereals from the liquid that there is in him in order to feed the nobles and the people." For this, Osiris is called "ruler and lord of food offerings, sovereign and lord of victuals." As a representation of the reproductive power of water, Osiris receives the name "Great Green Thing," and as fertilizer of the earth, he is called "Great Black Thing": the humidity that grows grain. In the sacred city of Memphis, it was said that Osiris was "transformed into the earth," while Isis was called the "Green Goddess, whose green color is like the verdant green of the earth" (fig. 5.16).[23]

Among the many images reproduced in the various episodes of the Osiris myth, there are several that allude to the fertilizing potency emanating from the dead god. Thus, in a painting in which the crocodile god Sebek is seen transporting the mummified body of Osiris, vegetation sprouts both from the crocodile's skin and from the mummy (fig. 5.17). Even more expressive are the images showing how green leaves of barley and wheat sprout from the dead body of the god (fig. 5.18). These are the rebirths of the god in vegetation, as is forcefully indicated in the following song:

> I am the plant of life
> which comes forth from Osiris,
> which grows upon the ribs of Osiris,
> which allows the people to live,
> which makes the gods divine,
> which spiritualizes the spirits,
> which sustains the masters of wealth,

Fig. 5.17. The crocodile god, Sebek, is carrying the mummified body of Osiris on his back. Plants sprout from both bodies. As can be observed, the quadrangular pattern on the crocodile's skin is similar to the pattern on cultivated earth. Above there is a strip of the night sky, with the moon and stars. Drawing based on Budge, 1973, 1:21.

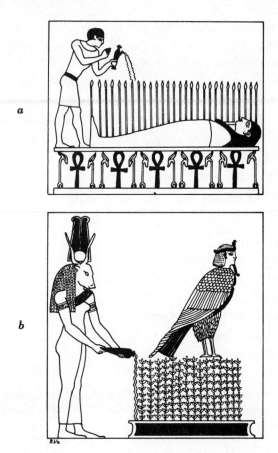

Fig. 5.18. **(a)** Osiris dead. Wheat plants sprout from his body. According to Frazer, the inscription accompanying this image says that Osiris "sprouts from the waters that return." And he adds: "Considering both the drawing and the words together, we believe . . . that Osiris is conceived and represented here as the personification of the grain that sprouts from the fields after being fertilized by irrigation." *The Golden Bough,* 433. Drawing based on Budge, 1973, 1:58. **(b)** Isis, with a cow mask, pours water, making the plants grow. Above the wheat plants sprouting from the ground, we can observe the "soul" of Osiris with a body of a falcon. Drawing based on Budge, 1973, 1:8.

and the masters of substance,
which makes the *pak* cake for the spirits,
which enlivens the limbs of the living.
I live as corn, the life of the living.
I live upon the rib of Geb [the God of Earth],
But the love of me is in the sky, on earth,
on the water and in the fields.
Now Isis is content for her son Horus her god,
She is jubilant in him, Horus her god,
I am life appearing from Osiris.[24]

As in the case of the Quetzalcoatl myth, in the Osiris myth the episodes of the god's death and resurrection correspond to the different phases of the cultivation of grains. In his work on Isis and Osiris, Plutarch recounts that while visiting Egypt he observed that during planting season the farmers, "when they opened the earth with their hands and then covered it up again after having deposited seed in the soil," acted as if they were "burying someone and were in mourning." In one text, the god Horus tells Geb, the earth god, "They have put my father in the earth. . . . We must cry for him." In these passages, it is clear that the planting of the seed was equated with the burial of Osiris.[25] Likewise, when the first stalks were cut, the farmers cried and lamented because they thought of the god's body incorporated with the grain suffering dismemberment. Threshing the grain and the acts connected with grinding the harvest on the threshing floor and separating the grain from the straw constituted the figurative equivalent of the grain god's affliction.[26]

In these manifestations of popular religion, the different times of year corresponding to the phases of cultivating cereals form a dramatic sequence. This drama is accentuated when the farming cycle is transformed into episodes of the life of the grain god. In this way, following the popular rites commemorating the planting, harvest, and transmutation of the grain into food, a cult developed to exalt the death, transfiguration, and resurrection of the god of vegetation.

Some historians believe that the mystery of Osiris resides in this ancient agricultural tradition. Others argue that its origin is connected to the later cults of royal power. In support of the latter thesis, the ceremony of the Great Procession is cited, since this event honored Osiris in Abydos, the city in the south of Egypt on the Nile, where in the origins of the monarchy it was customary to bury kings. Even though the ceremony was dedicated to Osiris, it did not celebrate the rebirth of the grain god but rather the succession of the dead king by his legitimate heir through a ritual reminiscent of the images of the transfer of power engraved by Kan Balam on the temples in Palenque. The ceremony of the Great Procession commemorated the triumph of Horus, the legitimate son of Osiris, over Seth, who cut him to pieces, and the coronation of Osiris as king of the dead. The transfer of power dramatized in the Great Procession thus completed the coronation ceremony referred to in the sacred texts. Coronation legitimized the new ruler's ascent to power, while the Great Procession endowed his father and predecessor with the kingdom of the dead. In this way, the king of upper and lower Egypt assumed the crown symbolizing his power over the kingdom of the living, while his predecessor assumed that of the realm of the dead.[27]

Perhaps the major change the figure of Osiris underwent was his transformation from protector god of the dead pharaohs into a popular god to whom all Egyptians of whatever status entrusted the salvation of their souls. In the beginning of the monarchy, the pharaohs built a necropolis with grandiose tombs where, in addition to exalting their terrestrial passage, they maintained a permanent link between the world of the dead and that of the living. By virtue of this power, commoners believed that their "hope for life in the Hereafter" depended on their relationship with the deceased monarch. Nevertheless, the pharaoh's prestige and power as the intermediary between the realm of the underworld and the people were diminished at the end of the period of the Ancient Kingdom. This uncertain period followed another period of anarchy which sapped the trust the Egyptians had had in their governors. While the power of the king waned and the monarchy lost its legitimacy, the traditional figure of Osiris was maintained. Slowly, but irrevocably, the ancient devotion to fertility was enriched with the cult of the dead to become the most popular Egyptian religion.[28]

Osiris's life and death, his voyage to the underworld, his resurrection, and finally his coronation as king of eternal life become rites celebrated by all Egyptians. The funerary rituals that previously sanctified the burial of kings became commonly used for ordinary burials that "assumed the form of Osirian burial, that is, the archaic burial of the king." Scholars of these cults say that by adopting these rites the Egyptians believed "they were joined to the jubilant circuit of the sun and the stars and the seasons," that they became a part of the "unchanging rhythm of nature,"[29] and that in this way they transcended the troubled frontiers of ephemeral life.

As in Mesoamerica, in death the Egyptians were to travel westward to the region of the dead, which is why Osiris had as his imperial title "Chief of the Westerners." Just as in Mesoamerica, in Egypt the underworld was located in the west because this is obviously the region where the sun and the stars set as well as the mysterious region of darkness and cold where death changes into life. Thanks to Osiris, after their passage on earth, mortals would be incorporated into the group of immortals: along with the sun, the moon, and the stars, they would be a part of the uninterrupted cycle of births and disappearances from life, joined to the immutable rhythm of nature.

Adonis, Baal, and Persephone

At the beginning of this century, James George Frazer studied the common features of the cults of Adonis, Attis, and Osiris, identifying them as gods of vegetation. He observed that all three gods agonized during summer and autumn, that they were reborn triumphantly in spring at (or near) the time of the equinox. Applying a focus that today would be qualified as excessive and simplistic, he noted that all three reflected the stages of growth and decay in vegetation. Today, the understanding and interpretation of these myths have been amplified, but Frazer was still the first to show the importance of the cults of vegetal renewal in myth. Observing the recurrent cycle of decay and regeneration in nature and "the intimate dependency" of human subsistence with respect to this phenomenon, he wrote: "It is no wonder that a phenomenon so important, so striking, and so universal should, by suggesting similar ideas, have given rise to similar rites in many lands."[30]

One of the myths Frazer identified with the vegetal renewal cults was the myth of Adonis. Among the Semites, the name of Adonis was a title signifying a distinguished person. In the Old Testament, he was called Adonai a Yahve. The Greeks changed this title into a proper name, so that by the seventh century B.C.E., Adonis was the beautiful youth for whom Aphrodite, goddess of carnal love, felt an overwhelming passion.

The myth recounts that Adonis was the fruit of the incestuous relationship between the beautiful Myrra and her father, the king of Pafos, a kingdom on the isle of Cyprus. Myrra fell in love with her father and tricked him into having sexual relations with her. When she became pregnant, she asked the gods to protect her son from her father's wrath, which they did by transforming her son into an aromatic myrrh tree. Myrra's pregnancy then became the tree's pregnancy. Ten months later, the tree opened up and Adonis was born, a being both divine and human.

Adonis was so beautiful that when the goddess Aphrodite saw him for the first time, she became dizzy with passion. Obsessed, she wanted to hide him from the others and keep him all to herself. With this in mind, she designed a box in which Adonis could live hidden from the world, and she entrusted him to Persephone, who ruled in the underworld. Driven by curiosity, Persephone opened the box and was herself overtaken by the beauty of Adonis to such a degree that she decided to keep him in her kingdom. Aphrodite became angry and fought with the other goddess over the possession of this youth with disturbing features.

Going against the established rules, Aphrodite descended to the underworld in search of Adonis, but it was all in vain. Persephone refused to return him. The furious dispute between the goddess of love and the goddess of the underworld disrupted the harmony of the cosmos and led to Zeus's mediation. Zeus prudently decided that Adonis would live with Persephone in the underworld for part of the year and with Aphrodite on earth the rest of the year. Nevertheless, this wise decision did not save Adonis from his unfortunate destiny. One day while he was hunting, he was killed by a wild boar, a tragedy that caused Aphrodite's inconsolable lamentations.[31] Including this myth within his group of gods of vegetation who die in autumn and are revived in spring, Frazer wrote: "Again, the story that Adonis spent half, or according to others a third of the year in the lower world and the rest of it in the upper world, is explained most simply and naturally by supposing that he represented vegetation, especially the corn, which lies buried in the earth half the year and reappears above ground the other half." Frazer, in noting that the god the Greeks called Adonis, and the Jews and Assyrians call Tammuz, was celebrated in ceremonies each year, remarks that the god is lamented when he dies and then the cause for rejoicing when he returns to life. Frazer interprets Adonis as the symbol of the seeds of the earth, which are mourned when they are planted but cause for joy for the farmers when they grow and mature.[32]

The battle between Baal, the Canaanite god of fertility, and Mot, the god of sterility, is another version of the myth of death and regeneration in nature. The narratives referring to this myth are in the form of a short theatrical script or libretto, with scenes organized in a dramatic way, for what could have been a play performed on memorable occasions. This play was perhaps performed on the New Year celebrated at the beginning of the agricultural year. However, unlike the previously discussed myths, the cycle of death and resurrection in nature was not seasonal but rather sabbatical. A succession of seven years of abundance followed by seven years of deprivation is described. This is therefore an antecedent to the famous cycle of seven years of fat cows followed by seven years of lean cows in the Old Testament.

One commentary on these myths explains that in Canaan what was feared above all was not the loss of a year's harvest but rather a succession of droughts and the prolonged absence of fertility in winter and the repeated invasion of destructive locusts that devastated the fields. In order to combat this horrible cycle of years of bad harvests, the major catastrophe that could afflict the Canaanites, the rulers came up with the cycle of alternating triumphs between Baal and Mot. In accordance with this cycle, after seven years of residency in the underworld, Baal was reborn and would spread agricultural abundance for the following period of seven consecutive years. On the clay tablets where Baal's victories and defeats are recounted, one of the most dramatic episodes is when Mot convinces him to descend into the underworld. One text specifies that when Baal hears this imperious call he is frightened into a state of panic. After greeting the king of the underworld with humility, Baal responds to him: "I am your slave, I am yours forever." Against this capitulation of her brother, the fertility god, Anat, goddess of life, famous for her battles against destructive forces, takes her revenge. In a way similar to Isis's reaction after being informed of Osiris's death, when Anat learns of Baal's death, she sets off traveling around the world, in pain and suffering, searching for his corpse. When she finds it, she proceeds to bury it with ceremonies and sacrifices. Then, she avenges her brother. When she finds Mot, she beats him and destroys him. In this account, the destruction of Mot seems to be, step by step, the process of transforming harvested grain into seed for the next year. Anat overpowers Mot and cuts his body up with a sword. Then, just as one does when spreading grain to air-dry it, she spreads his pieces out with a rake. Afterwards, she burns them in a fire and puts them through the mill. Finally, she plants his remains in the field.

The narration continues further with another scene in which Baal reappears, full of vitality, endowed with new force to proceed with the following agricultural cycle.[33]

Masculine deities of vegetation dominated the Mediterranean basin, but goddesses of fertility continued to be adored as well. In Greece, where powerful Zeus reigned over the rest of the immortals high up on Olympus, the earth goddesses (Gaia, Hera, and Demeter) continued to be important (fig. 5.19). In the pantheon of the classical period, Demeter's and Persephone's figures embodied the powers of fertility and the new myths and cults of vegetal renewal.

Demeter was the goddess of the cultivated earth and the golden wheat harvest. Like Inanna of Sumeria, she is called the "First Green," the "Bearer of Fruits," and is represented with apple trees, grains, and bunches of wheat in her hands (fig. 5.20). Like the ancient goddesses of fertility, she is connected to the inside of the earth, the place where grains germinate and sprout. In classical Greece, Demeter is the wife of Zeus, by whom she gives birth to Persephone.

In Greek mythology, the maiden Persephone is equivalent to the gods of vegetation protected by Inanna, Isis, or Aphrodite. Like Dumuzi, Osiris, and Adonis, Persephone is the image of vegetal renewal: wheat grain, the seed of life. If her mother represents cultivated soil, she is the renewal that sprouts from the earth with springtime.

Like her predecessors, Persephone lived happily in the kingdom of light until an unexpected event changed her life. The myth recounts that one day she was picking flowers in a field and was attracted by the presence of a narcissus with many buds. When she bent down to pick it, the earth suddenly opened up, and Hades, god of the underworld, emerged from this opening in his golden carriage. Hades grabbed Persephone by the arm, and despite her struggling against him and calling out to Zeus for help, she was quickly swept away to the subterranean world, where Hades married her and kept her hidden (fig. 5.21). When Demeter realized that her daughter was missing, she began to search throughout the earth, heartbroken, inquiring as to her whereabouts. Finally, the goddess Hecate confessed to her that no one other than Zeus himself was responsible for Persephone's loss, since he himself had given her to Hades, his brother, as his bride. From then on, Hades kept Persephone in the underworld.

Demeter was even more upset when she found out the details of how

Fig. 5.19. Hera, crowned, raises her hands in a triumphal gesture. Her dress simulates the surface of the earth when the fields are labored and seeds planted in each of the divisions made. Two priestesses flank her and care for her magnificent dress. Ceramic from Tebas, dated between 680 and 670 B.C.E. Drawing based on Baring and Cashford, 1993, 312.

Fig. 5.20. Demeter, the Greek goddess of the harvest, with bunches of wheat in each of her hands. Relief on a vase from Magna Grecia, approximately 300 B.C.E. Drawing based on Baring and Cashford, 1993, 117.

Fig. 5.21. Persephone and Hades in the underworld, with wheat stalks and symbols of fertility in their hands. Votive plaque from Locri, Italy, dated 480–450 B.C.E. Drawing based on Baring and Cashford, 1993, 373.

Persephone was captured. Furious with Zeus, she abandoned Olympus and shunned contact with the other deities. She disguised herself as an old woman and traveled among mortals from town to town. As with Isis, the owners of the royal house offered her a place to stay and asked her to nurse the smallest of their children. With her divine powers, Demeter made the child grow and wanted to turn him into an immortal, which she did by burning his mortal flesh on a slow fire. When the child's mother surprised her at this task, the mother was horrified and had Demeter detained. Irritated, Demeter then revealed her true condition and demanded that a temple be built in her honor on a hill called Eleusis. When the temple was completed, Demeter enclosed herself within it. Isolated and pained by the loss of her daughter, she condemned mortal human beings to the worst of punishments imaginable: she decreed that the earth would become sterile. As a result of hunger, "the human lineage almost perished completely," and the gods, too, were deprived "of the honor of offerings and sacrifices."

Alarmed by the disgraceful condition that had befallen humanity and the punishment inflicted on the immortals' lineage, Zeus ordered Demeter to be called up to Olympus. His messengers were refused, one after the other, by the grief-stricken goddess, who intransigently declared that she would not go up to "perfumed Olympus nor would she permit the fruits of the earth to go up until she saw her beautiful daughter again." When Zeus found this out, he ordered his celestial emissaries to the underworld to ask Hades to return Persephone from the darkness "to carry her into the light . . . , so that her mother could see her with her own eyes and shed her anger." Hades agreed and brought Persephone to meet with her mother. However, before leaving the region of darkness, Hades gave her some pomegranate seeds to eat, so that she would not stay on the earth's surface forever. Because of these magic seeds, Persephone (like Tammuz, Adonis, Baal, Osiris, and Quetzalcoatl) remained obliged to live a part of the year in the underworld and the other part of the year in the luminous world in the company of the immortals. Thus, each year, according to a hymn dedicated to the goddess of fertility, "when the earth sprouts her perfumed spring flowers of all kinds [Persephone will go up] again from the shadowy darkness, a marvel for the gods and mortal men" (fig. 5.22).

Once this pact was agreed to between the gods of the heavenly region and those of the underworld, Demeter allowed the "fruit of the fertile fields" to emerge, and "the whole wide earth was full of leaves and flowers."

Fig. 5.22. The goddess of vegetation emerges from inside the earth. Plants sprout beside her. Cylindrical seal from Boetia, ca. 1500 B.C.E. Drawing based on Baring and Cashford, 1993, 115.

Along with the wonderful blessing of fertile earth, Demeter bestowed on the mortals an even more appreciated gift: she taught them to "administer the sacred ceremonies, and taught them her mysteries." From then on and for more than two thousand years, the peoples of the different Greek provinces would make a pilgrimage to Demeter's temple in Eleusis, where they performed the rites that conveyed the deep meaning of life and death.[34]

Of all the myths focusing on deities of vegetation which celebrate the birth of life and show its origin in the inalterable cycle of death and regeneration in nature, none managed to present this process with more mystic intensity than the cults of Eleusis. The voyage to Eleusis was the equivalent of a voyage to the underworld, and the ritual practiced in its temple represented the rebirth of life, symbolized by the intense contemplation of a sprig of wheat.

The objective of the "mysteries of Eleusis" was to initiate the participants in the knowledge of a cult that would impart an enlightening vision, a true revelation. Perhaps this is why its name means "place of the happy arrival." The Eleusian rituals began at the end of winter with some ceremonies called "minor mysteries," which included the sacrifice of a deer, rites of purification, and the ingestion of food and drink made from cereals. The "major mysteries" took place in autumn and welcomed the participation of initiates from the entire Hellenic world. Like the passageway to the underworld, the road to Eleusis had barriers and dangerous passages that the pilgrims managed to traverse by using exorcisms and public, ritual prayers. On the border between Athens and Eleusis, the procession would be mocked by masked characters who would rid themselves of the old and celebrate the new. After the crossing of a water barrier, the procession finally arrived at the area surrounding the divine temple where Demeter had lamented the loss of Persephone.

As with Demeter's anguished lament in this place, the pilgrims would arrive at the temple and submit themselves to harsh rituals of atonement and purification. After crossing through the doorways of the enclosed courtyard of the sanctuary, they celebrated a ceremonial dance. The final rites took place in the Telesterion, the sanctuary or final boundary: a rectangular building that could hold multitudes of people. There the initiates participated in a ceremony reenacting the scenes of Persephone's capture and confinement in the underworld and Demeter's desperate search. They would set up a doorway to represent the entrance to the underworld and use torches to light up the surrounding darkness throughout the ceremony dramatizing this passage.

Afterwards, in an act filled with emotion, the supreme priest would present the faithful with sacred objects whose significance could not be revealed without suffering the most severe punishment. While the initiates would be sitting, waiting anxiously on the steps in back of the temple walls, a secret ceremony was taking place in the main half-lit area. Some believe that this ceremony was a repetition of an ancient sacred marriage rite between the forces of heaven and earth, represented by two hierophants. Suddenly, the silence and anticipation were broken by the striking of a percussion instrument which reproduced the sound of thunder. The doors were opened to the underworld, and from the depths of the earth Persephone emerged. A light illuminating the temple showed the splendid figure of Persephone suspended above the floor with a child in her arms. The supreme priest sung out: "The great goddess has brought forth a divine child." Then, amid deep silence, he held up a stalk of wheat for all to see.

The crowd exploded after this mystic climax. The temple's patio was transformed into a gigantic stage for music and dance. When the bull was sacrificed, the people would break their fast. Finally, a priest filled two vases with liquor, and raising one to the west and the other to the east, he poured their contents into the earth. Then, the multitudes would join together to gaze at the sky and exclaim: "Rain!" Then, they would look to the ground and cry: "Conceive!" Thus the mysteries of Eleusis were completed with the repetition of the most ancient prayers and chants ever spoken by agricultural peoples.[35]

Fig. 5.23. Demeter, on the left, offers wheat to Triptolemos, who is carrying a plough, while Persephone illuminates the scene with torches, on a painted Greek vase. Drawing based on Baring and Cashford, 1993, 387.

The sacred matrimony between the underworld and the sky, and the product of this union, the appearance of grain in the earth, were the two great rites that were played out in Eleusis, as they had previously been commemorated in Egypt and Mesopotamia through the cults of Osiris and Dumuzi-Tammuz. Another version of these ancient Near Eastern and African cults can be found in the legend of Triptolemos, which was spread throughout classical Greece and was connected to the cults of Eleusis. In various texts from this period, and in numerous vases and paintings, this character is represented as a beautiful youth, in the company of Demeter and Persephone (fig. 5.23). In these scenes Demeter offers a stalk of wheat to him while Persephone is illuminating this event with her torches. Other paintings and texts present Triptolemos as a son or protégé of the goddesses of fertility. Like Osiris, Triptolemos was responsible for spreading the gospel on how to cultivate plants. Another series of pictures shows Triptolemos mounted on a splendid carriage, ready to travel the world to propagate the secrets of cultivation and agricultural techniques.[36]

The Defeat of the Mother Goddess

As we have seen, even if Demeter and Persephone are not the principal goddesses of the Greek pantheon, they rank significantly among the gods and goddesses. They are symbols of the ancient religious conception holding that there were divergent forces animating the cosmos which, although different, did not oppose or exclude each other. In this conception, the fertile forces of the sky were just as esteemed as the procreating forces within the earth. Before being considered opposing forces, these forces were viewed as complementary. The underworld was not yet the infernal region but rather the site where forces regenerating nature would flow together and from whose depths plants would grow. It was a conception in which the creator and its creations constituted a universal source from which innumerable forms of life would sprout, develop, die, and return again to the original source. According to Ann Baring and Jules Cashford, this conception fed the myth of the great Mother Goddess: the goddess who created the world from herself, in such a way that everything that existed was part of her divine substance and was animated by the sacred, through and through. Thus, there was no distinction between "spirit" and "nature," or "thought" and "matter," or "body" and "soul," because humanity and nature shared a common identity. This myth, perhaps the longest-lived myth in the history of humanity, was substituted by the myth of the Father God, the one, exclusive warrior god whose beginnings date from the Iron Age (1200 B.C.E.). The prototype of this new conception is the Babylonian creation myth.[37]

In Babylon, between 1700 and 1580 B.C.E., when the kings of this city were imposing their domination over the other kingdoms of Mesopotamia, a new creation epic began to be recounted. The Enuma Elish is the name given to this epic because these are the first words of the story, which begins with the creation of the gods by the first mother, Tiamat, and the first father, Apsu. In a series of creations, the primordial couple gave forth a pair of gods, then a second pair, and, later, another pair, called Anu and Ea. It so happened that this new generation of gods bothered Apsu by making too much noise. The creator god then consulted his minister, Mummu, and they resolved to destroy them. When Apsu informed Tiamat of this decision, the goddess protested and asked him: "Why should we destroy those we have created?" Nevertheless, Apsu and his minister drew up a plan to get rid of the new gods.

The young gods heard of this plan and counterattacked. The god Ea, who assumed control, created a magic circle of protection, killed Apsu, and took Mummu prisoner. Ea established his residency over the fresh waters that Apsu used to dominate, and with his wife, Damkina, they begat Marduk. From his early childhood, Marduk showed that he was a powerful and fearsome leader. He radiated with the light of ten suns, "like a majesty inspiring terror." The presence of this champion provoked desire for vengeance from Tiamat's side, because Ea had assassinated her husband. The gods that surrounded Tiamat also pushed her to destroy the young gods. Driven to act, Tiamat called upon her talents as a universal creator and conceived a monstrous army, populated by deformed, half-formed, hybrid, frightening beings.

News of the formation of this formidable army reached Ea's camp. To face this threat, Ea's allies proposed various candidates to head up their forces, until this task finally fell to the young Marduk. Invested with the insignias of royalty, fortified with religious talismans, and endowed with military authority, Marduk goes off in search of Tiamat and her terrifying army. When he eventually found her, he sent a conflagration of winds against her which sent her flying and paralyzed her. Surprised, Tiamat opened her mouth, and Marduk immediately filled it with other winds that silenced her. At this point, Marduk impaled her with his sword and drained from her the blood that had given him life, which he carefully hid in an inaccessible place. Once this task was completed, he divided the great body of the goddess in half; the upper part became the sky, and the lower part became the earth's surface.

Thus, in a way that differed from the established tradition, Marduk initiated a new creation of the cosmos from the bloodless body of the overthrown goddess. He divided the cosmos into different regions and built a splendid sanctuary in the highest part of the sky. He then proceeded to establish the temporal cycles and give life to the stars whose movement originated days, months, and years. He next created the race of human beings and delegated to them the task of producing food and goods on earth. Because this task was formerly the responsibility of the gods, this meant that the deities would thereafter live in lazy opulence. The last part of the text celebrates the coronation of Marduk as king of the gods and culminates with his glorification. The apotheosis of Marduk's glorification is the recitation of a catalogue of more than fifty epithets that embody his vast creative powers, his sovereign authority, his absolute preeminence, his incomparable force, the justice and knowledge emanating from each of his acts, his devotion to the gods, and his kindness toward mortals, as well as his infinite virtue and so on.[38]

For a thousand years, this new war song of creation was recited in Babylon on the day the spring equinox was celebrated. As has been noted by other commentators, it shows the appearance of a priestly ideology oriented to invert the ancient religious values completely, in such a way as to transform the divinities of the previous period into demons while the new gods were raised to the rank of supreme divinities.

The defeat of the Mother Goddess, represented by the dragon-serpent Tiamat, signals the end of a culture and the imposition of a new conception of the cosmos, nature, and human existence. Baring and Cashford note that in this war song of creation

> there is already the germ of three principal ideas that were to inform the age to come: the supremacy of the father god over the mother goddess; the paradigm of the opposition implicit in the deadly struggle between god and goddess; and the association of light, order and good with the god, and of darkness, chaos and evil with the goddess. . . . When this opposition was crudely expressed, as it often was, the "male" aspect of life became identified with spirit, light, order and mind, which were good; and the "female" aspect of life became identified with nature, darkness, chaos and body, which were evil.[39]

The victory of the solar god over the tellurian goddess originated new images of religious cults and inaugurated new social paradigms. Heaven and the solar god became supreme values. Thus, just as there is only one sun, it was thought there would have to be only one savior, the god of gods, one to occupy the highest place in the sky and reign alone. According to this new conception, the feminine was equated with the dragon-serpent goddess, the earth and the moon, obscurity and chaos, spiritless nature. On the other hand, the masculine was identified with the sky god, the sun, light, order, the liberated spirit of nature.[40]

The magnification of the warrior's importance was another of the purposes inherent in the Babylonian epic sung to celebrate the coronation of kings. On this occasion, the song recalled that the most celebrated act of the king-god was the conquest of foreign peoples. The ascent of Marduk's cult coincided with the glorification of war and the annihilation of populations who attempted to resist the conquerors' attacks. As Joseph Campbell observed, the Iron Age was dominated by a mythology of war whose ideal was the conquering hero: Hammurabi, Dario, Agamemnon, and Alexander are the prime examples. Major literary works like *The Iliad* and the Old Testament focus on wars and military conflicts. The archetype of the king is

Fig. 5.24. Persecution and conquest of the Mother Goddess Tiamat by the god Marduk on a cylindrical seal dating from approximately 700 B.C.E. Drawing based on Baring and Cashford, 1993, 273.

no longer the "Shepherd of the People," or the ruler-sage who follows the evolution of the stars to predict the good and bad harvests, but rather the conquering warrior.[41]

The visual and literary images, the political language, and the religious chants and songs center on victory in war and the confrontation between the solar god and the dragon of obscurity and chaos (fig. 5.24). The rise of heavenly father gods endowed with unbeatable arms can be traced to Anatolia, Persia, Canaan, and Greece. "These gods were originally the sky gods of the Aryan invaders. Their weapons were fire, wind, and storm, the lightning bolt and the thunder's roar. Marduk, Assur, El, Baal, Yahweh and Zeus" personified these gods: in their representations, they are seen "armed with the great sky powers of nature. The supremacy of sky gods is assured by a male priesthood, in India, Persia and Hebrew Canaan, as later in Christian and Islamic cultures."[42]

EPILOGUE

⊂⎯⎯⎯⎯⎯⎯⎯⎯⎯⎯⎯⊃

> A world created by us can be understood by us, as Vico
> said. We are not simply groping in the darkness. The
> beam which illuminates the dark spots of our past is the
> reflector of our consciousness.
>
> Agnes Heller, *A Theory of History*

As can be observed at this point, even the briefest analysis of the Mesopotamian and Mediterranean vegetation gods shows how they share features in common with Quetzalcoatl, the Mesoamerican corn god. If the comparison is pursued, even more interesting similarities appear with regard to the main divisions of the cosmos for agricultural peoples as well as the temporal and narrative structure of myth and its functions in these societies.

The first aspect linking Quetzalcoatl to the Mediterranean gods of vegetation is that in both the resurrection of the grain god is identified with the creation of the cosmos. In Mesoamerica, the celebration of the rebirth of the corn god at the spring equinox was a rite marking the beginning of the agricultural year and the reappearance of green leaves in the corn plant on the surface of the earth. Nonetheless, above all, from the Maya of the classical period, the myth of the resurrection of corn was joined with rites commemorating the primordial creation, the ordering of the cosmos, and the birth of human beings. Also in the temples of Mesopotamia, during the equinox, a series of rites celebrated the beginning of the year with ceremonies in which the reigning king would appear as the incarnation of the god of vegetation in order to depose the goddess of the earth. The union of the two celebrated the beginning of the fertile season. The rites culminated with the song narrating the first creation of the cosmos, which in Babylon was attributed to the prodigious powers of Marduk, and to the local god in other Sumerian cities. The religious and symbolic link between the resurrection of the god of vegetation and the first creation of the cosmos shows that in these societies the cult of the appearance of plants was one of the most important public ceremonies.

The myths that narrate the adventures of the vegetation god in Egypt, Mesopotamia, Greece, and Mesoamerica relate their principal episodes to the temporal and spatial division of the cosmos which determined the cycles of its death and resurrection and the precise place where they occurred. In the stories of the appearances and disappearances of the god of vegetation, the former occurred in spring and the latter in autumn. The significance of this is that this temporal cycle was also linked to the three regions of the cosmos: heaven, earth, and the underworld. As we have seen, the disappearance of the vegetation gods in autumn and winter was equated with their descent to the depths of the underworld. Conversely, their resurrection occurs in spring and is extended throughout the summer, a period during which the grain remains on the surface of the earth, fed by farmers and used as seed for the next crop.

In the Sumerian myths of the voyage of Inanna or Istar into the underworld, the vegetation god's residency in the underworld is dramatically emphasized. In these, just as in the Greek myth of Persephone, the gods of fertility do not have to remain long in this cold and humid area, since prolonging their stay could cause sterility in the fields, hunger, and destruction of the terrestrial order. In this conception, the idea was that the myth would imitate the rhythm of nature. The gods of vegetation had only to remain part of the year (fall-winter) in the depths of the earth, so that the rest of the year (spring-summer) they would dispense their goods on the surface, as exemplified by the archetypal cases of Dumuzi-Tammuz, Persephone, and Quetzalcoatl. The cosmogonies and the religious ritual aimed at producing this alteration through many ceremonies throughout the year.

In the cosmogonies of agricultural peoples, the ordering of the cosmos was only possible when the creator gods were successful in placating the sky's fury (flooding, for example) and regulating the insatiable appetite of the regents of the underworld. Only when an agreement was reached with these powers was the beginning of the creation of the cosmos and its ordering possible. In the same way, only the union of the fertile forces of the sky and the germinal powers of the earth could produce the miracle of the gestation of grains and ensure the abundance of earthly goods. In mythical thought, the verification of these principles determines the functioning of the universe and the continuous regeneration of nature which sustains human life.

With the recitation of the cosmogonies during the spring equinox, the performance of ceremonies celebrating the union of the sky with the earth, and the accomplishment of rites to produce rain and exorcise sterility, the peoples thought of ways to maintain the regularity of these directing principles, established at the time of the first primordial creation. The highest ambition of peoples subject to unpredictable changes in climate and in nature consisted in duplicating or reenacting the harmony that founded the cosmos. In this way, the similarity we perceive in the temporal cycles that direct the movements of the vegetation gods, or in the voyages that these gods make to different regions of the cosmos, provides a cosmological conception common to different agricultural peoples.

The myths are written or spoken stories with a characteristic narrative structure. The story recounted has a linear sequence including a beginning, a middle, and an end, and its conservation and diffusion depend largely on its narrative qualities. Nevertheless, those myths with the death and resurrection of plants as themes differ from other myths in that they are characterized by a narrative structure that faithfully follows the critical phases of their cultivation, as I believe to have demonstrated for the Quetzalcoatl myth.

The main episodes of the Quetzalcoatl myth are related to the phases of the planting, gestation inside the earth, rebirth, and harvest of grain. With varying emphases, these episodes are the same as those recounted in the myths of Dumuzi-Tammuz, Baal, Osiris, and Persephone: the culminating moments are the descent of the seed into the underworld (planting), the resurrection of the grain from the depths of the earth, and the harvest. Mesopotamian, Egyptian, Greek, and Mesoamerican myths all follow a narrative sequence that repeats the temporal structure of the biological process of plant growth, with the variations belonging to the different types of climate and cultivation.

When the myth is joined to ritual, the narration acquires greater drama, and the description of different episodes is enriched with the enhancements of scenery, song, music, dance, and religious liturgy. The songs and chants recited at the spring equinox in the ziggurats of Mesopotamia celebrated the marriage of the gods of heaven and earth; the elaborate ceremonies that in Egypt accompanied the death and resurrection of Osiris, or the hymns that celebrated the return of Persephone from the depths of the netherworld, are examples of the dramatic and literary force that the myths of the death and resurrection of nutritious grains had acquired. Probably, in the most ancient times, the different episodes of the drama of death and resurrection of the vegetation god were celebrated separately. However, from the beginning of the Neolithic period, the different tasks implied the cultivation of plants integrated into a dramatized narration, and following the rhythm of the phases of cultivation and climax was the sprouting of the first plants in the sunny days at the beginning of spring.

When the different phases of growing wheat were integrated into the narration describing the adventures of the god of vegetation, these passages also formed the nucleus of the liturgical dramas that in the Hellenic world celebrated the voyage to the underworld and the triumphal appearance of the first renewals in the spring equinox. As discussed, the mysteries of Eleusis were a symbolic representation of the dramatic voyage made by the seeds inside the earth, whose reappearance was the revelation of birth in the grain of wheat. At the end of the ceremony, it was customary to make a presentation to the faithful of the portentousness embodied in the seed of grain, with waves of incense and a great collective expectation that exploded in a religious climax. In the mysteries of Eleusis, the presentation of the wheat seed acquired the sense of a unique revelation, aimed at a privileged group of people. The liturgical process transformed the seed, step by step, into a sacred object, and the faithful discovered that the ultimate meaning of the cereals was to become the flesh of human beings.

The Mesoamerican cult closest in religious tenor to the mysteries of Eleusis was performed each year at the appearance of the corn plant in the Mayan city of Copán on the shores of the Motagua River. On the heights of the acropolis dominating the city, in a magnificent temple whose lower section symbolized the heart of the earth, each year the resurrection of the corn god was celebrated during the spring equinox. The entrance of the temple was the doorway to the netherworld, the sacred region where essential regenerations took place. In this hidden space imitating the form of a cave, the specific day of the equinox began with a solemn rite that climaxed when the supreme ruler presented the first sprouts of the corn plant. The upper section of the temple was a glorious representation of this joyous moment, since its façade was decorated with beautiful sculptures of the young corn god sprouting from the earth.[1] In other words, in a more dramatic way than in Eleusis, in Mesoamerica the grain was transformed into a god with human appearance.

The annual repetition of the ceremony was one of the features that defined these rites and reaffirmed the value and significance of the myth.[2] Each year, with the symbolic representation of the resurgence of the grains from the earth, the myth confirmed the regularity of a biological phenomenon transformed into religious mystery through the power of the priests and rulers. As we have seen, the commemoration of this event in the New Year's festival was a rite common to cities in Mesopotamia, upper and lower Egypt, the Greek world, and Mesoamerica. This annual actualization through an emotion-laden religious festival, which ended in a collective celebration, confirmed the idea held by the population that their rulers enjoyed the protection of the gods. In Teotihuacan, where the paintings on the temples, palaces, and common houses celebrate the union of the fertile forces of the sky with the germinal forces of the earth, the equinox festivity in spring had to have been one of the most emotional and best-attended festivals. One can imagine what these collective celebrations might have been like by observing the crowds that still come to Chichen Itza today to contemplate the image of the Plumed Serpent's prodigious descent from heaven to earth at the spring equinox.

Among the various purposes attributed to myths, one of the most immediate is to ratify the customs supporting the life of peoples, conserving the memory of their traditions, and acquiring for them prestige and authority. In this sense, the annual resurrection of the gods of vegetation—manifest in the sprouting of the plants—was the most visible demonstration of the privilege the gods gave the chosen people, a sort of legitimacy for their fortunate destiny.

The myths of the origin of cereals also support two central ideas belonging to the ancient agricultural peoples' view of the cosmos: the identity between the beginning of agriculture and the dawn of civilization, and the concept of ethnic identity. The myths of creation dealing with cultivating plants gave a sense of cosmic foundation to the birth of cereals and transformed the origin of agriculture into the inaugural moment of civilized life. Thus, the myths, songs, and ceremonies as well as painting, sculpture, architecture, ceramics, and the other arts celebrating the origin of cultivated plants exalted the values belonging to agricultural society. The birth of agriculture coincides with the ordering of the cosmos and in the cosmogonies preceded the appearance and multiplication of human beings.

Consequently, agriculture was synonymous with wealth and civilized life. Its symbols were an abundance of goods, sumptuous temples, magnificent cities, and the splendor that shone from the image of the gods. The origin of agriculture was considered such a decisive part of the development of humanity that in the myths the gods and rulers fought over getting credit for having created it and spread it among mortals. Likewise, the origin of the cultural hero is linked to the proliferation of agricultural knowledge. In Egypt, Osiris was revered as the propagator of agriculture and precious knowledge; in Mesopotamia, the invention of agriculture was equated with the beginning of civilized life and was also an attribute of the creator gods; in classical Greece, agriculture was a gift of the goddesses of the earth, but a cultural hero, Triptolemos, was entrusted with spreading knowledge about it among different peoples.

In the same way, in Mesoamerica the corn god is synonymous with civilized life. Hun Nal Ye is the Mayan creator god and cultural hero who transports food to human beings. In other words, the Mesoamerican corn god is at once the creator of the present era of the world and the incarnation of the food that nourishes humankind. The god Nine Wind, the Mixtec equivalent of the Mexica Quetzalcoatl, is one of the creator gods and the divine intermediary who generates civilized life and founds the first dynasties. Later, even when the Mexicas attempted to add the virtues of the ancient creator gods to their national god, they took on Quetzalcoatl as their greatest cultural hero: creator god of corn and new humanity, the inventor of writing, astronomy, the arts, and the sciences.

In addition, the creation myths identifying the origin of grains with the birth of civilized life carried the message that human beings and plants were born in the same earth; both were indigenous products of the region. Similarly, the creation myths from the European Neolithic period and the most ancient Mesoamerican myths of the cosmos and human life both had their origin in the earth: in both, humanity emerged from the hidden cave in the primordial hillside. In turn, myths exalting the valor of the locality founded the relationships of social identity through this beginning. The highest values corresponded to the earth itself, the place of birth and the place of the ancestors. In the most ancient times, these beliefs were assumed by the

Olmecs and, later on, by the classical Maya, the Zapotecas, and the people of Teotihuacan, as can be seen in their myths and visual arts.

Symbolically, the Mesoamerican creation myths refer to a world comprising the whole of the cosmos and in whose center the sky, the earth, and the underworld were in contact with one another. Nevertheless, on a day-to-day basis, this expanded environment was restricted to the limited geography of the kingdom, marked in its four spatial corners by the colors of local birds and in its center by the emblematic tree of the region. Thus, local character was accentuated in the creation myths and specific emblems of the region, just as the cosmos, gods, and rulers appear invested with the symbols of the flora and fauna of the place, illuminated by local colors and animated by powerful indigenous forces. This obsession of exalting one's own produced strong ties of identity in the small kingdoms of the classical period. An identity so strongly tilted toward one's own kind fatally led to confrontations with nearby peoples with different ethnicities, languages, and traditions.

The objective so earnestly pursued by the creation myths was to infuse the community with a notion of stability, duration, and continuity according to the fundamental cycles of human and natural life. The commemoration of the creation of the cosmos and of the origin of cereals and civilized life, dramatized in the festivals of the spring equinox and the beginning of the agricultural year, confirmed the population's conviction that the gods were keeping their pact with mortals by renewing the order and harmony established on the first day of creation.

Even when myth glorified continuity, it also evidenced the impact of historical change. As Ann Baring and Jules Cashford recall: "Myths are not history, yet . . . they manifest in time and create history and so are clothed in the language of becoming and change."[3] Therefore, although the creation myths of Mesopotamia and Crete narrate the same story of the origin of the world throughout the centuries, the gods and symbols that participate in this act differ according to each period. The transformation that occurred between the Neolithic period and the Iron Age was evidenced by the ancient Mother Goddess losing her omnipotent powers and becoming a secondary deity alongside new masculine gods.

The Mesoamerican Mother Goddess also ceded her position to powerful gods. Later, when the kingdoms of the classical period were disintegrating and the turbulent postclassical period was beginning, the fertility gods were gradually displaced in favor of heavenly gods of thunder and lightning. In these transitional years, the myths glorifying the indigenous origin of peoples were substituted by myths exalting warrior peoples from distant, foreign lands. The Mayan god Hun Nal Ye changed his name, and sometimes his symbols and cults, where he was called Nine Wind, Ehécatl, Kukulcán, the Plumed Serpent, Ce Acatl Quetzalcoatl, and Hun Hunahpú. On many occasions, his name and cult were mixed in with those of other gods, and the cult of the ancient god of corn was in turn influenced by new gods and cults. The myth of Quetzalcoatl, by gathering up these transformations in its stories and symbols, was itself transformed into historical testimony. Thus, Quetzalcoatl stands as a complex accumulation of multiple meanings, without ever losing anything of his essentially mythic condition.

Male flower, the stamen producing 25 million grains of pollen.

Female flowering, the ear of corn, situated at the end of the branch, containing up to more than a thousand fertile flowers, or potential grains.

The corn plant can develop branches in each axilla of the leaf and stalk, under which it produces the main spike. The ears of corn produced in the other branches often do not attain the same size as the main ear. Some prolific varieties produce more than one ear.

The typical habits of the plant change according to the variety or species and the planting conditions. Here it is shown with only one stem. The primary and seminal roots sustain the plant as it develops. The root system is fundamentally adventitious, originating from the base of the basal roots.

Drawing based on the original by Walton C. Galinat.

Morphology of the corn plant

NOTES

Introduction

1. Campbell, *Hero with a Thousand Faces.*

2. Michael Coe notes that Karl Taube, Constance Cortez, and Gareth W. Lowe all independently identified the presence of the Divine Twins in Izapa's monuments. See Coe, "Hero-Twins," 163 and figs. 1 and 2.

3. On the conception of the earth as a devouring monster, see Tomkins, *This Tree Grows out of Hell,* 35–38; and on the fertility cults during the classical period, see Pasztory, "Artistic Traditions of the Middle Classic Period," 129–30.

Chapter 1: The Diverse Manifestations of the Divinity

1. See Caso and Bernal, *Urnas de Oaxaca,* 114; Coe, "Religion and the Rise of Mesoamerican States," 168; and Taube, "The Temple of Quetzalcoatl," 82–83.

2. For various interpretations of the Plumed Serpent in Teotihuacan, see Millon, "Last Years of Teotihuacan Dominance"; López Austín, López Luján, and Sugiyama, "El Templo de Quetzalcoatl en Teotihuacan." See also Cabrera, Sugiyama, and Cowgill, "Templo de Quetzalcóatl Project at Teotihuacan"; Cowgill, "Toward a Political History of Teotihuacan"; and Pasztory's book *Teotihuacan.*

3. See Florescano, *Memoria mexicana,* ch. 4, and "Mitos mesoamericanos"; Caso, "El paraíso terrenal de Teotihuacan"; Pasztory, *Murals of Tepantitla* and *Teotihuacan;* and Berlo, "Icons and Ideologies at Teotihuacan."

4. In this connection, Pasztory observes: "Many of the myths of the agricultural cycle, the ball game and the warrior cult deal with the theme of transformation through death and rebirth. The primary metaphor for all transformation was the diurnal cycle of the sun. The sun was believed to die every night at sunset as it descended into the underworld, and to be reborn every morning as it emerged from the earth." See Pasztory, "Artistic Traditions of the Middle Classic Period," 130.

5. Šprajc, "Venus, lluvia y maíz," 120, 166–68, 170; Aveni, *Skywatchers of Ancient Mexico,* 82–86, 184–95; Aveni, *Empires of Time,* 225; Aveni, "Real Venus-Kukulcan." See also Coe, "Hero-Twins."

6. Šprajc, "Venus, lluvia y maíz," 27–28, 87, 120.

7. Šprajc, based on Tedlock, observes the following: "Given the Venus table in

the *Dresden Codex,* the Ahau days represent one of the series of canonical days during which the helical settings of the star were expected in the east, it is probable that it is the same Hun Hunahpú that Vucub Hunahpú personifies in the morning aspect of Venus (Tedlock, *Popol Vuh,* 234). His descent into the netherworld corresponds to the invisibility during the superior conjunction, whereas his fatal confrontation with the Lords of Xibalbá, Hun Camé, and Vucub Camé (One Death and Seven Death) signifies the reappearance of Venus in the Western sky, given that in the Dresden Codex the Cimí days begin the first period of evening visibility after the morning period that begins with the Ahau days. The severed head of Hun Hunahpú represents the afternoon star." Ŝprajc, "Venus, lluvia y maíz." 85.

8. Schele and Freidel, *Forest of Kings,* 145–49 and n. 45, 443–44; Stone, "Disconnection, Foreign Insignia, and Political Expansion," 156–58.

9. Recent studies document that the famous war scenes painted on the walls of Bonampak have an astronomical relationship to the dates that correspond to the appearance of Venus, and that the war victories and the sacrifice that were celebrated are propitious acts for the designation of the legitimate heir to the throne. The Cacaxtla murals also depict scenes of war and present similar associations with the great star, in addition to symbols proclaiming the importance of the blood sacrifice and its connection to the legitimacy of royal power. Lounsbury, in his study "Astronomical Knowledge and Its Uses at Bonampak," was the first to observe that Mayan military actions were governed by the movements of Venus; see also Miller, *Murals of Bonampak,* 44–51; Schele and Miller, *Blood of Kings,* 217. On Cacaxtla, see Baird, "Stars and War at Cacaxtla," 114–19.

10. Other studies show abundant representations of Venus in Chichen Itza. In the monuments and sculpted columns of this city a kind of military order was discovered which wore armor plating with a star shape on the breastplate. Another series of warriors wore a helmet in the form of a star; and other columns and buildings have representations of stars beaming rays and anthropomorphic figures decorated with arrows, lances, skeletons, and skulls alluding to war and sacrifice and directly linked to Venus. See Miller, "Star Warriors at Chichen Itza," 287–305.

11. Brundage, *Phoenix of the Western World,* 45, 218–23.

12. Baudez, "Solar Cycle and Dynastic Succession," 125–48.

13. A synthesis of the importance of Venus for the Maya is found in Aveni's *Empires of Time,* 220–32.

14. Seler, *Comentarios al Códice Borgia,* 1:264–65, 2:11, 41, 238.

15. Dütting, "Astronomical Background of Mayan Historical Events," 269.

16. *Códice Chimalpopoca,* 11. See Seler's interpretation cited in note 14, which is based on the analysis of Venus's movements through the netherworld up to its culminating appearance as the Morning Star or Lord of the Dawn. Alfonso Caso considers these astronomical movements of the sun and Venus as the basis of the myth about the flight of Quetzalcoatl and the prophecy of his return: "Also Que-

tzalcoatl's escape from Tula, for the mythic Tlillan Tlapallan, the land of black and red, and his promise to return by the east in the year of his name, 'Ce Acatl,' is nothing more than a way of explaining in mythic form the death of the planet, that is, its concealment by the west, in the place where black and red are joined, day and night, and the prediction that he will return to emerge in the east, transformed into the Morning Star and preceding the Sun." Caso, *El pueblo del sol,* 39.

17. Closs, Aveni, and Crowley, "Planet Venus and Temple 22 at Copan," 221–47.

18. See Freidel, Schele, and Parker, *Maya Cosmos,* 146–52, and figures 3.18 and 3.24. The religious and architectonic symbolism of this building was analyzed by Larios, Fash, and Stuart in "Architectural History and Political Symbolism of Temple 22 at Copan." See other relationships between Venus and the city of Copán, its monuments, and its governors in Schele, Larios, and Villela, "Some Venus Dates on the Hieroglyphic Stair"; Schele, Fash, and Villela, "Venus and the Reign of Smoke-Monkey"; Schele and Villela, "Venus and the Monuments of Smoke-Imix-God K."

19. See Kelley, "Birth of the Gods at Palenque"; Lounsbury, "Identities of the Mythological Figures"; Schele and Freidel, *Forest of Kings,* 246–51; Tate, *Yaxchilan,* 51–55, 101; Schele, *Notebook for the Sixteenth Maya Hieroglyphic Workshop,* 151–60.

20. Caso, *Reyes y reinos de la mixteca,* 2:61; Jansen, "Huisi Tacu," 140–253; Anders, Jansen, and Pérez, *Origen e historia,* 90–93.

21. Caso, *Reyes y reinos de la Mixteca,* 2:61–62; Furst, *Codex Vindobonensis Mexicanus,* 108–12, 129–42, 179, 219–20; Jansen, "Huisi Tacu," 206–17, 218–22; and Anders, Jansen, and Pérez, *Origen e historia,* 129.

22. Furst, *Codex Vindobonensis Mexicanus,* 103–4; Jansen, "Huisi Tacu," 143–46. See the analysis of the representations of Ehécatl as singer, poet, and writer in King, "Hearing the Echoes of Verbal Art," 105–8, fig. 2.

23. Nicholson, "Ehécatl Quetzalcoatl vs. Topiltzin Quetzalcoatl," 36–38; "The Deity 9 Wind," 61–92.

24. Furst, *Codex Vindobonensis Mexicanus,* 219–20; Jansen, "Huisi Tacu," 425–40; Anders, Jansen, and Pérez, *Origen e historia.*

Chapter 2: Ce Acatl Topiltzin Quetzalcoatl

1. "Historia de los mexicanos por sus pinturas," 35.

2. Sahagún, *Historia general de las cosas de Nueva España,* 1:278–79.

3. Ibid., 3:184–89.

4. Ibid., 2:185; Nicholson, "Topiltzin Quetzalcoatl of Tollan," 303–4, 318, 324. The best historical study of Tula and the Toltecs is *The Toltecs,* by Nigel Davies.

5. *Códice Chimalpopoca,* 5, 7.

6. On the dating of the relief on the Malinche hillside, see Nicholson, "Topiltzin Quetzalcoatl of Tollan," 294; and on the sculpted figure in the Tula altar, see

Acosta, "Resumen de los informes de las exploraciones arqueológicas," 77–80 and plates 28–29.

7. Graulich, *Quetzalcóatl y el espejismo de Tollan,* 222–24.

8. The facts about Ce Acatl Topiltzin Quetzalcoatl which are considered the most genuine are found in the following texts: "Historia de los mexicanos por sus pinturas," the *Relaciones* by Juan Cano, the "Histoyre du Mechique," the *Leyenda de los soles,* Sahagún's work, and the *Anales de Cuauhtitlán.* The best analysis of these sources and the bulk of testimony referring to the legend and history of Quetzalcoatl is Nicholson's thesis, "Topiltzin Quetzalcoatl of Tollan." Graulich's study *Quetzalcóatl y el espejismo de Tollan* contains a minute compilation of the majority of the texts about Quetzalcoatl and his connection to Tollan. An analysis of the multiple problems connected to the figure of Ce Acatl Topiltzin and his magnificent kingdom can be consulted in the previously cited work by Davies, *The Toltecs.* See also Healan, *Tula of the Toltecs.*

9. Diehl, "Tula," 279–80, 293.

10. *Relaciones geográficas del siglo XVI: Tlaxcala, II,* 128–32; Nicholson, "Topiltzin Quetzalcoatl of Tollan," 136–39.

11. García, *Origen de los indios,* 327–29; Nicholson, "Topiltzin Quetzalcoatl of Tollan," 201–6; and Flannery and Marcus, *Cloud People,* 213–15, 358–59.

12. See Scholes and Roys, *Maya Chontal Indians,* 115–45, and Thompson, *Maya History and Religion,* 4–72. In this work, Thompson affirms that around the year 800, "other Putun groups, probably from Potonchan, at the mouth of the Grijalva River, established a trading base at the strategic site of the Altar de los Sacrificios, where the Pasión and Chixoy rivers meet to form the Usumacinta. . . . From the Altar de los Sacrificios, the invaders, pushing farther up the Pasión conquered Seibal (ca. A.D. 850), an important Classic-period site and pushed on to Ucanal, almost on the British Honduras border and in the Belize River drainage" (4). Fox's work, *Maya Postclassic State Formation,* 18, 19, 37, 60–63, 66–67, 260–64, presents new evidence on the center of irradiation which pushed the Itza, Xiu, Canil, Chan, and other group immigrations toward the Yucatan and Guatemala.

13. Lincoln, "Chronology of Chichen Itza," 152–60, 183–86; Wren and Schmidt, "Elite Interaction during the Terminal Classic Period," 212–14, 224–25; Culbert, "Maya Political History and Elite Interaction," 327; Schele and Freidel, *Forest of Kings,* 354–67.

14. Jiménez Moreno, "Tula y los toltecas," 79–83, and Lincoln, "Chronology of Chichen Itza," 151–55.

15. See Landa, *Relación de las cosas de Yucatán,* 12–13; Nicholson, "Topiltzin Quetzalcoatl of Tollan," 269–70, 272.

16. Another text, also from the Yucatan province, states that "the Mexicans entered into [this province] and took possession of it. [There was] a captain, called Quetzalcoatl in the Mexican language, which means in our language snake plumage

and among them this name is given to the serpent because they say it has feathers; and this captain with this name introduced idolatry into this land and the use of idols for gods, which were made with sticks and mud clay and stone, which he had them adore and make offerings of hunted game and traded goods and especially of blood from the nose and ears and hearts of those who sacrificed in his honor." Both quotes come from Nicholson, "Topiltzin Quetzalcoatl of Tollan," 276–77.

17. Landa, *Relación de las cosas de Yucatán,* 13–14; Nicholson, "Topiltzin Quetzalcoatl of Tollan," 272–73.

18. *Popol Vuh,* 142–43, 149–50; Nicholson, "Topiltzin Quetzalcoatl of Tollan," 229, 233–34. See also Fox, *Maya Postclassic State Formation,* 60–63.

19. *Memorial de Sololá;* Nicholson, "Topiltzin Quetzalcoatl of Tollan," 236–40.

20. *Memorial de Sololá;* Nicholson, "Topiltzin Quetzalcoatl of Tollan," 245–67; Stone, "Disconnection, Foreign Insignia, and Political Expansion," 166–68.

21. An attempt to explain these multiple manifestations of Quetzalcoatl can be read in Brundage, *Phoenix of the Western World,* and in Quiñones Keber, "Topiltzin Quetzalcoatl in Texts and Images," and by the same author, "The Aztec Image of Topiltzin Quetzalcoatl." With regard to the Aztec pantheon, Marcus, relying on Zantwijk, states that they incorporated into their own pantheon gods of the various ethnic groups they conquered. And he adds: "The continual incorporation of these foreign gods, combined with those who were deified royal ancestors, led to the growth of a pantheon unlike any other in Mesoamerica. The Aztec case is an extremely interesting example of the effect social and political policy can have on religion." Marcus, *Mesoamerican Writing Systems,* 261, 270.

22. *Códice Chimalpopoca,* 163–64.

23. See Brundage, *Phoenix of the Western World,* 140–44.

24. *Códice Chimalpopoca,* 121.

25. "Histoyre du Mechique," 106–7.

26. Caso, *El pueblo del sol,* 34–35.

27. Brundage, *Phoenix of the Western World,* 102–10; Carrasco, *Quetzalcoatl and the Irony of Empire,* 64–65, 78–80, 174.

28. Durán, *Historia de las Indias,* 1:61–67.

29. Ibid., 1:65–66, and Brundage, *Phoenix of the Western World,* 110–17.

Chapter 3: Interpretations

1. The main proponents of the first interpretation have been Daniel G. Brinton, Eduard Seler, K. Th. Preuss, Lewis Spence, George C. Vaillant, David H. Kelly, and, in recent years, Michel Graulich. The following are among those who support the historical existence of Ce Acatl Topiltzin Quetzalcoatl: George Bandelier, Desiré Charnay, Alfredo Chavero, Manuel Gamio, Herbert J. Spinden, Wigberto Jiménez Moreno, and Laurette Séjourné. For an evaluation and analysis of these

interpretations, see the much cited thesis by Nicholson, "Topiltzin Quetzalcoatl of Tollan," 292–328, and the book by Alfredo López Austin, *Hombre-Dios*, 13–34.

2. The analytical separation of the principal components of the myth of Quetzalcoatl was initiated with studies by Pedro Armillas, "La Serpiente Emplumada," and Nicholson, "Topiltzin Quetzalcoatl of Tollan," 327–29. See also Piña Chan, *Quetzalcóatl*, and Brundage, *Phoenix of the Western World*, 287–93. In his analysis of Ce Acatl Topiltzin Quetzalcoatl, López Austin introduced the thesis that the forces of different gods were present in figures who received the name Quetzalcoatl, or other divine names, since these were incarnated in human beings selected by the divinities. See his work, *Hombre-Dios*.

3. Nicholson, "Topiltzin Quetzalcoatl of Tollan," 324. Recently, new studies have been published on the sacrificial practices of these peoples which specify their antiquity and analyze their meaning in different cultures. See Boone, *Ritual Human Sacrifice in Mesoamerica;* Schele and Miller, *Blood of Kings;* and Clendinnen, *Aztecs.*

4. Caso notes that the character Eight Stag of the Tilantongo dynasty travels to Tula in the year 1045, where the king of this city "perforates the septum in his nose and makes him *tecuhtli.*" Caso, *Reyes y reinos de la Mixteca,* 79, 81. Nevertheless, it is improbable, given the dates, geography, and political circumstances, that the Mixtec rulers proceeded to Tula de Hidalgo to ratify their investitures. It is far more probable, as noted in the *Relación de Cholula,* that provincial governors were confirmed in their regional capital, in this case, in Tullam Cholullam. See *Relaciones geográficas del siglo XVI: Tlaxcala, II,* 128–32.

5. On the identification of Hun Nal Ye with the Mayan corn god of the classical period, see Taube, "Classic Maya Maize God." An innovative analysis of the origin of the Mayan cosmos and its relation to the corn god can be found in the book by Freidel, Schele, and Parker, *Maya Cosmos.* As for the identification of Pakal with the Evening Star, see Dütting, "Astronomical Background of Mayan Historical Events," 269.

6. Coe, "Hero-Twins," 162–64.

7. Michael Coe was the first to describe the characteristics of the netherworld and propose a new interpretation of this region, its characters, and symbols. See *Maya Scribe and His World,* and by the same author, *Lords of the Underworld;* Benson, *Death and the Afterlife in Pre-Columbian America;* Robicsek and Hales, *Maya Book of the Dead;* and Schele and Miller, *Blood of Kings,* 265–88.

8. See Hellmuth, "Iconography of the Early Classic Peten Maya," *Surface of the Underwaterworld,* and *Monster und Menschen,* 356–60; and Reilly, "Enclosed Ritual Spaces and the Watery Underworld."

9. See Taladoire, *Terrains de jeu de balle,* and Scarborough and Wilcox, *Mesoamerican Ballgame.*

10. Baudez, "Solar Cycle and Dynastic Succession," 137–43.

11. See Taube, *Major Gods of Ancient Yucatan;* Pasztory, *Teotihuacan.*

12. Seler, *Comentarios al Código Borgia;* Brundage, *Phoenix of the Western World,* 214–24; Gillespie, "Ballgames and Boundaries," 319; Cohodas, "Ballgame Imagery of the Maya Lowlands," 255.

13. Pasztory, *Murals of Tepantitla,* 209–10.

14. The reference on the previous interpretations of the netherworld can be found in Gillespie, "Ballgames and Boundaries," 321. The most recent interpretations are those in Freidel, Schele, and Parker, *Maya Cosmos,* ch. 2; Schele and Freidel, "Courts of Creation," 289–315; Schele, "Creation and Cosmology in the Maya World"; and Gutiérrez, "Ballcourts," 1–3.

15. Spero, "Beyond Rainstorms." On the relations between the cave and the underworld, see Heyden, "Interpretation of the Cave," 131–47; Bassie-Sweet, *Mouth of the Dark Cave,* chs. 3 and 4; and Taube, "Iconography of Toltec Period."

16. For an analysis of these images, see Joralemon, *Study of Olmec Iconography;* Fields, "Iconographic Heritage of the Maya Jester God," 168–71; and Freidel, "Jester God."

17. Fields, "Iconographic Heritage of the Maya Jester God," 173; Grove, "Olmec Altars and Myths"; Grove and Gillespie, "Chalcatzingo Portrait Figurines." Grove and Gillespie observe that "this depiction of the chiefs seated at the entrance of the underworld displays their pivotal position in the cosmos as mediators between society and the supernatural forces associated with rain and fertility, over which they were believed to have influence. In other words, the chief was figuratively positioned at a critical point within the general order of existence—linking humanity and divinity—as shown by the position of this portrait at the juncture between the earth's surface and the underworld. This meaning was reinforced by the fact that the 'altar' is really a throne, the ruler's direct means of contacting the supernatural infraworld; when seated on the throne, he seated himself at that cosmological threshold." Grove and Gillespie, "Formative Period in Mesoamerica," 26–27.

18. This is the meaning that Carolyn Tate and Joanne M. Spero attribute to Cauac or the earth monster. The Cauac "was a place, the earth or ancestral abode, for the transformation of matter into energy." See Spero, "Beyond Rainstorms," 186. This conception is the same as that of Maya in Guatemala today. See Carlsen and Prechtel, "Flowering of the Dead."

19. New studies on the netherworld, dead, skeletons, and skulls have modified the interpretation previously given to these representations. For example, Furst notes: "The apparent contradiction between fertility, generation and rebirth, on one hand, and bones, on the other, is a perfectly comprehensible thing in the general context of the native Mesoamerican ideology, in that skeleton remains were . . . considered the essential basis of vital force, and the metaphoric seed from which the individual, whether animal, human or plant, was reborn." See Furst, *Codex Vindobonensis Mexicanus,* 318. This is a very similar interpretation to the one Westheim proposed, *Ideas fundamentales,* 59–70. Ancient and present-day Mixtecs have

a very similar conception. See King, *Mixtec Political Ideology,* 163–65, 418–21, and Monaghan, "We Are People Who Eat Tortillas," 481–85.

20. Stross, "Maize and Blood," 82–107. See a present-day version of this ancient belief in the myths of Maya from Guatemala, studied by Carlsen and Prechtel, "Flowering of the Dead," 28.

21. Stross, "Maize and Blood," 102.

22. Joraleman, *Olmec Iconography.*

23. See Taube, "Iconography of Toltec Period," 171–81; Taube showed that the "young lord" recognized by Hellmuth on various Mayan vases was the corn god. He identified the glyph of this god's name as the number one, combined with the head of the corn god. See Schele, *Notebook for the Sixteenth Maya Hieroglyphic Workshop,* 127, and by the same author, "Creation and Cosmology in the Maya World."

24. Coe, *Lords of the Underworld,* 83.

25. Taube, "Iconography of Toltec Period," 177.

26. Hellmuth, "Primary Young Lord," cited by Taube, "Iconography of Toltec Period," 174.

27. Taube, "Iconography of Toltec Period," 180, and Stross, "Maize and Blood," 99.

28. See Freidel, Schele, and Parker, *Maya Cosmos.*

29. In the *Popol Vuh,* the mountain cat, the coyote, the parakeet (*cotorra*), and the raven are animals who indicate the location of the white and yellow ears of corn to the creator gods: "These four animals gave them notice of the white and yellow ears of corn, they told them that they should go to Paxil and they taught them the road to Paxil." *Popol Vuh,* 103.

30. On these scenes, see the previously cited studies by Coe, Robicsek and Hales, and Schele and Miller. See also Foncerrada and Lombardo, *Vasijas pintadas mayas,* 128. The outstanding book by Justin Kerr, *The Maya Vase Book,* should be added to the list, for it includes a major selection of excellent photographs of vases and painted Mayan plates. The corn god's dance before his resurrection is the subject of an iconographic study by Hellmuth, "Holmul Dancer"; (see also, by the same author, *Monster und Menschen,* 362; Reents-Budet, "'Holmul Dancer' Theme"); and by Houston, Stuart, and Taube, "Image and Text in the 'Jauncy Vase.'" The most complete study and explanation of this dance can be found in Freidel, Schele, and Parker, *Maya Cosmos,* ch. 6.

31. "Enough data have been presented, I hope, to confirm my thesis that the pictorial ceramics of the Classic Maya, and the glyphic texts painted upon them, deal exclusively with death and the Underworld. . . . There is enough congruence in this material to suggest that the artist who was responsible for painting funerary vases . . . was drawing upon an already existing corpus of written and painted material in Codex form. It is not beyond the bounds of possibility that there was a real Book of the Dead for the Classic Maya, akin to the Book of the Dead of ancient Egyptians,

which contained ritual text and pictures describing the long and terrifying journey of the dead man's soul to its final resting place." Coe, *Maya Scribe and His World*, 22.

32. Coe states: "Pictorial ceramics, whether painted or carved, are to be ranked among the finest artistic creations of the Classic Maya civilization. However, the subject matter of this pottery, and the hieroglyphic texts painted or inscribed upon it, have been generally ignored by archaeologists and art historians. This neglect of one aspect of Maya culture is unfortunate since it can be demonstrated that these remarkable vessels describe a strange and esoteric world which is barely alluded to in the stone monuments and in the surviving books." Ibid., 11. In another work, he cautions: "But much of the iconography cannot be explained by anything in the *Popol Vuh*, probably because the Xibalba episode in the book is only a tiny fragment of a far more extensive chthonic myth or myth cycle that may have been known over the entire Maya area." *Lords of the Underworld*, 13.

33. *Códice Chimalpopoca*, 121. A very rich and innovative analysis of the resurrection of the Mayan corn god can be found in Freidel, Schele, and Parker, *Maya Cosmos*, ch. 6. In the early 1950s, Westheim interpreted the resurrection of the Mexica corn god, Cintéol, as follows: "He is the grain of corn hidden in the earth. And in hiding himself in the subterranean world, he dies and is transformed into the god of death for having performed this miracle which is the resurgence of the corn plant." See *Ideas fundamentales*, 73, 76 and 79. On the tortoise shell as a symbol of the earth floating in primordial waters, see Taube, "Prehispanic Maya Katun Wheel," 195–99.

34. See Freidel, Schele, and Parker, *Maya Cosmos*, for an extraordinary astronomical interpretation of the creation of the cosmos by the First Father, Hun Nal Ye.

35. Most works cited in this essay are representative of studies in the past few years, with the support of a rich earlier tradition of scholarship, which have modified our comprehension of the history of the ancient Maya. In order to appreciate the diversity and depth of these changes, other works should be consulted as well: Coe, *Breaking the Maya Code*; Clancy and Harrison, *Vision and Revision in Maya Studies*; Danien and Sharer, *New Theories on the Ancient Maya*; Miller and Taube, *Gods and Symbols of Ancient Mexico and the Maya*. The anthropological bibliography is quite extensive, but the following studies can be cited with specific reference to the Maya area: Vogt, *Tortillas for the Gods*; Tedlock, *Time and the Highland Maya*; Gossen, *Los chamulas en el mundo del sol*; Bricker, *Indian Christ, the Indian King*; and Earle, "Metaphor of the Day in Quiche."

36. In the *Popol Vuh*, when the masters of Xibalbá hear this noise over their heads, they exclaim: "What are they doing on the earth? Who is making it tremble and making so much noise? Let us go and call them! Let them come and play ball here, where we will beat them!" *Popol Vuh*, 50.

37. The idea that in clearing the land the peasants would be intruding upon and disturbing the forces dwelling inside the earth is a very widespread belief among

the peoples of Mesoamerica. A large part of agricultural ritual in antiquity was dedicated to making offerings and performing ceremonies and propitious acts before the gods of the earth, rain, and sustenance. Recently, Linda Schele recorded the existence of a cult of some Masters of the Earth in a cave near Utatlán (in Guatemala) and the custom among neighbors of the region who solicit permission from these masters in order to be allowed to disturb the earth at corn-planting season. In the cave, she found the remains of a sacrificed chicken that the inhabitants explained was an offering the farmers had given to the Masters of the Earth. See Freidel, Schele, and Parker, *Maya Cosmos,* ch. 4. Tedlock, in his excellent English edition of the *Popol Vuh* (1972, 244), refers to other metaphors of agricultural life. Westheim, following Seler, was one of the first to observe the relationship between biological processes, agricultural labors, and corn myths. See the chapters "El fenómeno de la muerte" and "Muerte y resurrección de la planta," in *Ideas fundamentales.* For both the ancient and present-day Mixtecs, the myth of sacrifice to the gods of the earth is necessary for the presence of life. King, following Monaghan, observes that in this region sacrifice is the structural basis of the myth of creation and refers to an ancient pact between human beings and the earth. This is expressed in the proverb "We eat the earth and she in turn eats us." This means that in exchange for the damage caused to the earth by agricultural labors, the farmers will go into the earth at death. See King, *Mixtec Political Ideology,* 163–64, and Monaghan, *We Are People Who Eat Tortillas,* 481–85.

38. *Popol Vuh,* 101–2.

39. Freidel, Schele, and Parker, *Maya Cosmos,* 60. See also Schele, "Creation and Cosmology in the Maya World."

40. See Reilly, "Enclosed Ritual Spaces and the Watery Underworld."

41. Heyden, "Interpretation of the Cave"; Taube, "Teotihuacan Cave of Origin," 76.

42. Pasztory, *Teotihuacan,* ch. 6.

43. See Taube, "Iconography of Toltec Period," 19–20, and by the same author, "Teotihuacan Cave of Origin," 59, fig. 16.

44. See Taube, "Teotihuacan Cave of Origin." On the myths of the origin of corn in the southwestern United States, see Sebag, *L'invention du monde;* Walters, *Libro de los hopis;* and Zolbrod, *Diné Bahané.*

45. Coe, "Hero-Twins," 161.

46. Furst, "Jaguar Baby or Toad Mother."

47. See Baudez, "Solar Cycle and Dynastic Succession."

48. Independently, Karl Taube arrived at this same interpretation. After reading a version of this essay, he indicated a chart in his study *Major Gods of Ancient Yucatan* which identifies the image of Pakal on the sarcophagus as that of the corn god. Taube notes that this was the original interpretation proposed by Ruz Lhuillier. On page 225 in his book *El Templo de las Inscripciones,* Ruz writes: "The flesh of man

is made from corn. Man and corn are the same thing, given that they both participate in the same substance and have to have the same destiny: like the buried grain, man deposited into the earth after death will germinate and spring to life again."

49. The relationship of the netherworld with the rebirth of life, the corn god, and the solar cycle was a generalized belief by the postclassical period. Pasztory writes: "In Postclassic Mesoamerican belief, the sun descended to the underworld where he married the earth goddess. The god of maize was born of this union. The god of maize, however, was not really and entirely a separate deity, since he was the sun reborn in new aspect. The sun god had two facets: during the dry season he was a deity of the sky and the day; during the rainy season he was a deity of the underworld and the night. As the night sun, the god was associated with water and fertility. He was believed to die in the underworld and to be reborn as the god of maize. He was, therefore, associated with symbols of death and sacrifice as well as with symbols of birth and fertility. As the night sun, the deity was associated with the jaguar. As the day, or sometimes the descending sun, he was associated with a reptorial bird." Pasztory, "Artistic Traditions of the Middle Classic Period," 132.

50. *Popol Vuh*, 103–7.

51. See Florescano, *Tiempo, espacio y memoria*, 9–45.

52. For another consideration of the unity of the Mesoamerican cosmovision and a different model of the mythical-historical sequence of the origin and development of these peoples from the one expounded herein, see López Austin, *Mitos del tlacuache*, 55–74 and table 2, 68.

Chapter 4: Toward a New Interpretation of the Myth of Quetzalcoatl

1. In the following quotations, I follow the Spanish version of the *Popol Vuh* by Adrián Recinos, published by the Fondo de Cultura Económica in 1961. In the interpretation of the text, I rely on studies of this work by Edmonson, *Book of Counsel*, and Tedlock, *Popol Vuh*. From the excellent English translation by Tedlock, a Spanish version has recently been published by Editorial Diana. [The English translation provided here is a translation of the Spanish edition used by the author. *Trans.*]

2. In addition to the *Popol Vuh*, the following cite this episode of the flood: *El libro de los libros del Chilam Balam*, the *Anales de los Cakchiqueles*, and other Mayan texts collected since the Spanish Conquest. For an account of this tradition, see Thompson, *Historia y religión de los mayas*, 397–446. Taube, in *Ancient Yucatecan New Year Festival*, 135–52, analyzes the myth of the flood in the Yucatecan texts and in the Mayan codices. The most comprehensive analysis of the flood in the Mesoamerican cosmogonies is by Fernando Horcasitas, "Analysis of the Deluge Myth in Mesoamerica."

3. See Taube, *Ancient Yucatecan New Year Festival*, 138–41.

4. Coe, "Hero-Twins," 63–64.

5. See Reilly, "Cosmos and Rulership," and Schele, "Olmec Mountain and the Tree of Creation."

6. For these interpretations, see Chapter 3 of this book; Koontz, "Aspects of Founding Central Places," and Schele, "Olmec Mountain and the Tree of Creation."

7. On this Mayan cosmogony from the classical period, see Freidel, Schele, and Parker, *Maya Cosmos,* 69–72. See Taube, "Classic Maya Maize God," 171–81, and his book *Major Gods of Ancient Yucatan,* 41–50, for the identification of Hun Nal Ye as the corn god of the classical period.

8. Coe, "Hero-Twins," 175–76.

9. See Freidel, Schele, and Parker, *Maya Cosmos.* This work presents an innovative astronomical interpretation of the creation of the cosmos by the First Father, Hun Nal Ye.

10. Years ago, Ruz Lhuillier announced the idea that the stone on Pakal's sarcophagus represented the resurrection of the king transformed into a god; see *El Templo de las Inscripciones,* 225. This ancient conception of the reincarnation of life after death has also been verified among present-day Maya by ethnologists. See Carlsen and Prechtel, "Flowering of the Dead," 26, 28–35.

11. See a description of this account in Estrada Monroy, *El mundo K'echi' de la Verapaz,* and also Coe, "Hero-Twins," 161–62.

12. Tedlock, *Popol Vuh,* 31.

13. Cited by Recinos in the introduction of his edition of the *Popol Vuh,* 11.

14. Armillas, "Serpiente Emplumada," 170–71.

15. Clendinnen, *Aztecs,* 228.

16. Ibid., 217. On this same page, Clendinnen transcribes a magnificent description of this bird, given by the ornithologist Alexander Skutch: "The whole head and the upper part of its plumage, the gullet and breast, are an intense, brilliant green. The lower part of the breast, the stomach and lower tail feathers are the brightest shade of scarlet red. . . . The dark, middle tail feathers are completely hidden by the much larger upper feathers which are golden green with iridescent shades of blue or purple, and have smooth, soft tufts. As the middle portion of the plumage is the most extended and much wider than the whole body of the bird, it extends much beyond the end of the tail which is of normal proportions. Soft and delicate, the feathers interlace at the tail and from here, separating bit by bit, form a wide, gracefully curved tail that hangs down below the bird when it rests on a branch and floats visibly behind it when in flight. The outside feathers of the tail are absolutely white and contrast with the scarlet color of the belly. . . . Completing the splendor of its finery, blue and violet reflections shine off the bright metallic plumage of the back and head, when observed in a favorable light."

17. Armillas, "Serpiente Emplumada," 77; Caso and Bernal, *Urnas de Oaxaca,* 113; Jiménez Moreno, "Síntesis de la historia pretolteca," 1071; Taube, "Temple of

Quetzalcoatl," 82–83; Pasztory, *Teotihuacan*. See a complete study of the meanings of the serpent in Garza, *Universo sagrado de la serpiente*.

18. Armillas, "Serpiente Emplumada," 175.

19. See Palacios, *Cintura de serpientes*, 242–43.

20. See this text in the *Leyenda de los soles*, contained in the *Códice Chimalpopoca*, 126.

21. Schele and Graube, "Peten Wars," 149, 152; Yadeun, *Toniná*, 74–80.

22. Nagao, "Art of Cacaxtla and Xochicalco," 99–100; Hirth, "Militarism and Social Organization at Xochicalco."

23. Oral testimony gathered by the archaeologists Norbert Gonzalez and Augusto Molina, February 1994.

24. Sáenz, *Quetzalcóatl*, 75–80.

25. Pasztory, "Xochicalco Stelae," 185–215.

26. Wilkerson, "And Then They Were Sacrificed," 45–71, and by the same author, "In Search of the Mountain of Foam"; and Brüggemann, "Juego de pelota," 85–97.

27. On the ball game in Mesoamerica, see the studies cited in note 26 as well as Scarborough and Wilcox, *Mesoamerican Ballgame;* Taladoire, *Terrains de jeu de balle*. Angel García Cook is presently working on the results of these excavations. It appears that the city of Cantona flourished between A.D. 700 and 900, according to García Cook.

28. See Chapter 2.

29. This type of state, which was highly developed in Chichen Itza and Tula, is already present at the end of the classical period in Xochicalco. Hirth states that "perhaps the most important characteristic of Xochicalco and the other conquering States of the Epiclassical era is that they had the ability to conquer, integrate and administer political areas that extended beyond the borders of their own geographical regions." See Hirth, "Militarism and Social Organization at Xochicalco," 77, 79.

30. On the conception of Tollan as a symbol of the ideal metropolis, see Florescano, "Mito e historia en la memoria nahua," 607–32.

31. Sahlins, *Historical Metaphors and Mythical Realities*. In the same sense, Zuidema signals that "history almost disappears in incorporating myth, at the same time that myth attempts to present itself as history." See Zuidema, *Reyes y guerreros*, 221.

32. Florescano, *Memoria mexicana*, ch. 1.

33. Berdan, *Aztecs of Central Mexico*, 124–30; Zantwijk, *Aztec Arrangement*, 18–21; Nicholson, "Religion in Pre-Hispanic Central Mexico."

34. Durán, *Historia de las Indias*, 1:439; Townsend, *The Aztecs*, 108.

35. León-Portilla, *Toltecáyotl;* Davies, *Toltec Heritage*, chs. 11 and 12; Duverger, *Origen de los aztecas*, 232–58; Klein, "Ideology of Autosacrifice," 298–304.

36. See Nicholson, "Religion in Pre-Hispanic Central Mexico"; Carrasco, "So-

ciedad mexicana antes de la Conquista"; and Townsend, *The Aztecs,* ch. 7 and 110–11.

37. Quiñones Keber, "Aztec Image of Topiltzin Quetzalcoatl," 330–31. See also the following studies by the same author: "Topiltzin Quetzalcoatl in Texts and Images" and "From Tollan to Tlapallan."

38. Quiñones Keber, "Aztec Image of Topiltzin Quetzalcoatl," 331; Durán, *Historia de las Indias,* 2:246.

39. Frances F. Berdan describes the ceremonial preceding ascension to the throne as follows: "The critical events surrounding the coronation of a Mexica ruler were deeply religious, but also cleverly political. The initial series of events was religious. High priest summoned the new ruler and presented him before a group of nobles congregated at the temple of Huitzilopochtli. The ruler was dressed in priestly garb and was taken by the priest to the idol of Huitzilopochtli. There he offered the god incense while the populace looked on and shell trumpets were blown. The new ruler's four advisers were also religiously dressed and offered incense. Then all five were led down the 120 steps of the temple and taken to a house of fasting. Here, dressed in 'fasting capes,' with a design of bones, they fasted and did penance for four days. At the end of this period, the priests came for them and they repeated the incense rite at the temple of Huitzilopochtli. Finally, they ate and again ascended the steps of the great temple. There, by piercing the fleshy parts of their bodies, they offered blood, and again incense. Descending from the temple and bathing, they fasted for an additional four days, again offering incense and blood after their fast. The ruler was then escorted to his palace, while his four councilors were led to their homes." Berdan, *Aztecs of Central Mexico,* 101. A more detailed description of the ceremonies preceding the investiture of Mexica rulers can be found in Townsend, *The Aztecs,* 201–7, and in the article by the same author, "Coronation at Tenochtitlan," 371–440.

40. See Quiñones Keber, "Aztec Image of Topiltzin Quetzalcoatl," and by the same author, "Quetzalcoatl as a Dynastic Patron," 149–55. A recent article by Quiñones Keber reaffirms her previous interpretations and supports the hypothesis expounded herein. See "Quetzalcoatl as a Dynastic Patron."

41. *Códex Chimalpopoca,* 120–21. Another simplified version of this episode can be found in the "Histoyre du Mechique," in Garibay, *Teogonía e historia de los mexicanos,* 106.

42. This story is contained in the "Histoyre du Mechique" (see Garibary, *Teogonía e historia de los mexicanos,* 108), and in Castellón Huerta, "Mitos cosmogónicos de los nahuas antiguos," 129–30.

43. Garibay, *Teogonía e historia de los mexicanos,* 110.

44. As for this interpretation, see Delhalle and Luykx, "Nahuatl Myth of the Creation," 117–21 and fig. 3.

45. See Stresser-Pean, "Ancient Sources on the Huasteca"; Delhalle and Luykx, "Nahuatl Myth of the Creation"; Wilkerson, "And Then They Were Sacrificed," 68–70.

46. Durán states that the figures and dates marked in the sacred calendar (Tonalámatl) served "these nations so that they would know the days on which they had to plant and harvest, work and cultivate the corn, weed, gather, take the corn off the cob and preserve it in pits, plant beans, lime-leaved sage, keeping track of which month after which holiday, which day and which figure, all organized in a superstitious order that if planting of squash was not done on a certain day and corn on another, etc. that in not following a certain order and count of these days they would experience loss and misfortune of whatever they planted outside that order." *Historia de las Indias,* 1:226. The calendar of the eighteen festivals associated with the solar year of 365 days was centered around "three types of ceremonies: those directed toward mountains and water to ensure rain; those directed toward the earth, the sun and corn, to ensure fertility and abundant harvests; and those directed toward special deities, particularly to those patrons of different groups or the community." Townsend, *The Aztecs,* 128. The festivals dedicated to corn were as follows. "The first, *Huey Tzoztli,* was celebrated at the height of the dry season when the dry corn husk was consecrated by the goddess Chicomecóatl in order to favor the next plantings. Chicomecóatl, 'Seven Serpent,' was the Aztec deity of dry corn. The second festival was called *Huey Tecuilhuitl* and took place toward the middle of the rainy season. The central figure was the feminine deity called Xilonen whose name derives from the word *Xilotl,* meaning the stringy hair of green corn. This term was also applied to the first sweet corn appearing during the plant's growth. Xilonen represented youth and was the central figure in the ritual offering of first fruits. The last of the corn festivals was called *Ochpaniztli,* which brought together a series of ceremonies represented by the deities of the earth and corn and signaled the harvest and the beginning of the dry season. It also announced the approaching war season. . . . The last four days of this festival were particularly dramatic because their final scenes mixed agricultural acts with warlike acts. . . . The final episodes were marked by the return of the priestesses of Chicomecóatl who scattered white, yellow, black and red corn seeds, mixed with squash seeds. All the attendees would fight to get one of these seeds for the next planting." Townsend, *The Aztecs,* 142. See Broda, in particular, "La fiesta azteca de los dioses de la lluvia," and the study by the same author, "Sacred Landscape."

47. Broda, "La fiesta azteca de los dioses de la lluvia," 246, "Provenience of the Offerings," 246–48, and "Templo Mayor as Ritual Space," 93–94, 98, 105–7. See also Townsend, "Coronation at Tenochtitlan," 375–91, 405–7.

48. León-Portilla, "Ethnohistorical Record for the Huey Teocalli," 78–81 and fig. 1.

49. Molina, "Templo Mayor Architecture," 99–100.

50. See the studies contained in Boone, *Aztec Templo Mayor,* and in Broda, Carrasco, and Matos, *Great Temple of Tenochtitlan.*

51. Broda, "Templo Mayor as Ritual Space," 105; see also her study "Provenience of the Offerings," 246–47.

52. The picture of the *altepetl* is from the Borbonic Codex, plate 24. In this codex, the picture refers to the festival called Tozoztontli, celebrated when the corn is already born and the plants are "knee high." See Anders, Jansen, and Reyes, *Libro del ciuacoatl,* 198–200; Paso y Troncoso, *Descripción, historia y composición,* 100–103. A description of this festival is given by Durán, *Historia de las Indias,* vol. 1, ch. 7.

Chapter 5: The Children of the Mother Goddess

1. Frazer, *Golden Bough,* chs. 46 and 59. An exception to this tendency is the exceptional work done by Campbell. See in particular the four volumes in the series *The Masks of God: Primitive Mythology, Oriental Mythology, Occidental Mythology,* and *Creative Mythology.*

2. The results of Gimbutas's investigations are resumed in the following works: *Goddesses and Gods of Old Europe, Language of the Goddess,* and *Civilization of the Goddess.*

3. Gimbutas, *Language of the Goddess,* 321; see also Baring and Cashford, *Myth of the Goddess,* 107.

4. Baring and Cashford, *Myth of the Goddess,* 57.

5. Burger, "Sacred Center of Chavin de Huantar."

6. Fernández, *Coatlicue.* Among the first studies on the symbolism and iconography of the Mesoamerican gods, see those by Joralemon, *Study of Olmec Iconography;* Lathrap, "Our Father the Cayman, Our Mother the Gourd"; and Stocker, Meltzoff, and Armsey, "Crocodilians and Olmecs."

7. Quotation is from Stuart Piggot's *Prehistoric India,* cited in Baring and Cashford, *Myth of the Goddess,* 156.

8. Baring and Cashford, *Myth of the Goddess,* 153–54; Bonnefoy, *Greek and Egyptian Mythologies,* 215–18.

9. Baring and Cashford, *Myth of the Goddess,* 145.

10. Frankfort, *Reyes y dioses,* 305.

11. Baring and Cashford, *Myth of the Goddess,* 145.

12. Frankfort, *Reyes y dioses,* 305.

13. Baring and Cashford, *Myth of the Goddess,* 176, 194–95.

14. Ibid., 207.

15. The most complete and faithful version available of the poem relating Inanna's voyage to the underworld is presented by Jean Bottéro and Samuel Noah Kramer in *Lorsque les dieux,* 202–307. See also Baring and Cashford, *Myth of the Goddess,* 216–24.

16. Bottéro and Kramer, *Lorsque les dieux,* 322–33, 327–29.

17. On the origin of grains and where they are kept, see Frankfort, *Reyes y dioses,* 335–37, 340–43, 421; Bottéro and Kramer, *Lorsque les dieux,* 512–17.

18. Baring and Cashford, *Myth of the Goddess,* 211–15. Another Sumerian poem cited by Berger in *Goddesses Obscured,* 11, reads as follows:

> Smooth, big Earth made herself resplendent, beautified her body joyously,
> Wide Earth bedecked her body with precious metal and lapislazuli
> Adorned herself with diorite, chalcedony, and shiny carnelian,
> Heaven arrayed himself in a wig of verdure, stood up in princeship,
> Holy Earth, the virgin, beautified herself for Holy Heaven,
> Heaven, the lofty god, planted his knees on Wide Earth,
> Poured the semen of the heroes Tree and Reed into her womb,
> Sweet Earth, the fecund cow, was impregnated with the rich semen of
>   Heaven,
> Joyfully did Earth tend to the giving birth of the plants of life,
> Luxuriantly did Earth bear the rich produce, did she exude wine and honey.

19. Gordon, "Canaanite Mythology," 214–95.

20. During the three or more centuries in which this myth was current in Egypt, there was no complete narration of it, perhaps because it was the most popular myth and its means of transmission was mainly oral. The most coherent version of it was given by the Greek Plutarch in his famous treatise on Isis and Osiris. Here I have used the edition by C. Froidefond: *Oeuvres morales: Isis et Osiris.* The best-known narration of this myth was disseminated by Frazer in the original version of *The Golden Bough,* also the work that first studied the interpretation of the different meanings of this myth. Among the modern studies of this myth, we mention the following: Budge, *Osiris and the Egyptian Resurrection;* Frankfort, *Reyes y dioses;* Griffiths, *Origins of Osiris and His Cult;* Baring and Cashford, *Myth of the Goddess,* 228–72.

21. Plutarch, *Oeuvres morales: Isis et Osiris,* 212 (hereafter cited as *Isis et Osiris*); Frankfort, *Reyes y dioses,* 212–13.

22. Baring and Cashford, *Myth of the Goddess,* 233–34. Frankfort, *Reyes y dioses,* 214.

23. Frankfort, *Reyes y dioses,* 207; Baring and Cashford, *Myth of the Goddess,* 236–37. Plutarch recounts that the Egyptians "globally call 'Osiris' the humidifying principle and power in and of itself, considering them the cause of generation and the substance of all seed. . . . Osiris . . . according to their myths, was black, because water makes everything it penetrates black." *Isis et Osiris,* 205. [Translated from the French. *Trans.*]

24. See Frankfort, *Reyes y dioses,* 207–8. The song to Osiris is taken from Baring and Cashford, *Myth of the Goddess,* 238; see also Frazer, *Golden Bough.* In relation to fertility, Frazer points out that "hymns addressed to Osiris contain allusions to this

important side of his nature. In one of them it is said that the world waxes green in triumph through him; and another declares, 'Thou art the father and mother of mankind, they live on thy breath, they subsist on the flesh of thy body.' *Golden Bough*, 6:112–13.

25. Plutarch, *Isis et Osiris*, 239; Frankfort, *Reyes y dioses*, 208–9.

26. Frazer, *Golden Bough*, "Adonis, Attis, Osiris"; Baring and Cashford, *Myth of the Goddess*, 238; Frankfort, *Reyes y dioses*, 150.

27. See Frankfort, *Reyes y dioses*, 225–28 ("La Gran Procesion") and ch. 11 ("El Misterio de la Sucession").

28. Ibid., 228–29.

29. Ibid.

30. Frazer, *Golden Bough*, 229.

31. See the text of the myth contained in Frazer, *Golden Bough*, ch. 30. See also Detienne, "Adonis and the Adonia," in Bonnefoy, *Greek and Egyptian Mythologies*, 134–36.

32. Frazer, *Golden Bough*, 284, "The Gardens of Adonis," and Detienne, "Adonis and the Adonia," 134. Frazer's interpretation of the myth of Adonis has been substantially revised in recent years, as has his view of the offerings made and gardens planted in the god's honor in various regions of the Near East and the Mediterranean. For example, Detienne believes that "the Adonis of the Athenians could have been the opposite of the god of vegetation. The miniature gardens, planted in pots and fragile containers, grew during the hottest days of summer. The young plant sprouts became green for brief periods and were then dried under the heat of the sun. . . . This negation of true cultivation was also confirmed by the mythological tradition of the Greeks, who emphasize the seductive aspects of myrrh. . . . Irresistibly seductive, Adonis awakens desire in both Aphrodite and Persephone. As the seducer of opposite goddesses, for the Greeks Adonis is neither the figure of the husband nor a baronial lord. He is nothing more than an effeminate lover whose followers, as Plutarch notes, were women and androgynous beings." "Adonis and the Adonia," 134. Detienne develops this thesis fully in *Jardins d'Adonis*.

33. This reading of Canaanite myths comes from the clay tablets with cuneiform writing which were found in the Assyrian city of Ugarit in 1928. See Gordon, "Canaanite Mythology," 183–218. The quotations come from this study. See also Hooke, *Middle Eastern Mythology*, 79–94.

34. The famous *Homeric Hymn* to Demeter is the principal source of the myth of Demeter and Persephone. A complete version of this can be seen in the work of Wasson, Hofmann, and Ruck, *Camino a Eleusis*, 95–120. The quotations cited above come from this text. Among the more recent interpretations of this myth, see Baring and Cashford, *Myth of the Goddess*, 364–77; and Detienne, "Demeter," and Bonnefoy, *Greek and Egyptian Mythologies*, 152–56.

35. The most recent studies of the mysteries of Eleusis are those by Kereny,

Eleusis, and Goblet d'Alviella, *Mysteries of Eleusis.* Baring and Cashford, in their much cited work *Myth of the Goddess,* 377–85, present an abbreviated version. See also Wasson, Hofmann, and Ruck, *Camino a Eleusis.*

36. Baring and Cashford, *Myth of the Goddess,* 386–88; Wasson, Hofmann, and Ruck, *Camino a Eleusis,* 70, 169.

37. One of the first to propose this interpretation was Campbell, *Occidental Mythology,* 79–88; Baring and Cashford, *Myth of the Goddess,* chs. 7 and 16.

38. See the complete text of the creation epic of Marduk in Bottéro and Kramer, *Lorsque les dieux,* 604–53.

39. Baring and Cashford, *Myth of the Goddess,* 282–83.

40. Ibid., 285.

41. Campbell, *Myths to Live By,* 140; Baring and Cashford, *Myth of the Goddess,* 285–90.

42. Baring and Cashford, *Myth of the Goddess,* 297. The extraordinary history of the progressive rise of the masculine god and the parallel demise of the Mother Goddess can be read in the following works: Patai, *Hebrew Goddess;* Warner, *Alone of All Her Sex;* and Berger, *Goddesses Obscured.*

Epilogue

1. My interpretation of this ceremony is based on Freidel, Schele, and Parker, *Maya Cosmos,* 146–55. See also the description of this building given by Baudez in *Maya Sculpture of Copán,* 200–217.

2. See Kirk, *Myth.*

3. Baring and Cashford, *Myth of the Goddess,* 305.

BIBLIOGRAPHY

Acosta, Jorge R. "Resumen de los informes de las exploraciones arqueológicas en Tula, Hidalgo, durante las VI, VII y VIII temporadas 1946–1950." *Anales del Instituto Nacional de Antropología e Historia* 8, no. 37 (1954): 37–115.

Anders, Ferdinand, Maarten Jansen, and Gabina A. Pérez. *Origen e historia de ls reyes mexicas: Libro explicativo del llamado Códice Vindobonense.* Mexico City: Fondo de Cultura Económica, 1992.

Anders, Ferdinand, Maarten Jansen, and Luis Reyes García. *El libro del ciuacoatl: Homenaje para el año del Fuego Nuevo: Libro explicativo del llamado Códice Borbónico.* Mexico City: Fondo de Cultura Económica, 1991.

Armillas, Pedro. "La Serpiente Emplumada, Quetzalcóatl y Tláloc." *Cuadernos Americanos,* year 6, vol. 31 (1947): 161–78.

Aveni, Anthony F. *Skywatchers of Ancient Mexico.* Austin: University of Texas Press, 1980. (Spanish edition: *Observadores del cielo en el México antiguo.* Mexico City: Fondo de Cultura Económica, 1992.)

———. "The Real Venus-Kukulcan in the Maya Inscriptions and Alignments." In *Sixth Palenque Round Table,* compiled by Merle Greene Robertson, 309–21. Norman: University of Oklahoma Press, 1986.

———. *Empires of Time: Calendars, Clocks, and Cultures.* New York: Basic Books, 1989.

Baird, Ellen T. "Stars and War at Cacaxtla." In *Mesoamerica after the Decline of Teotihuacan: A.D. 700–900,* compiled by Richard Diehl and Janet Berlo, 105–22. Washington: Dumbarton Oaks Research Library and Collection, 1989.

Barba, Beatriz, and Román Piña Chan. "La metalurgia mesoamericana: Purépechas, mixtecas y mayas." In *Orfebrería prehispánica,* 105–216. Mexico City: Corporación Industrial San Luis, 1989.

Baring, Ann, and Jules Cashford. *The Myth of the Goddess.* London: Penguin Books, 1993.

Bassie-Sweet, Karen. *From the Mouth of the Dark Cave: Commemorative Sculpture of the Late Classic Maya.* Norman: University of Oklahoma Press, 1991.

Baudez, Claude F. "Solar Cycle and Dynastic Succession in the South-East Maya Zone." In *The Southeast Classic Maya Zone,* compiled by Elizabeth Boone and Gordon Willey, 195–222. Washington: Dumbarton Oaks Research Library and Collection, 1988.

————. *Maya Sculpture of Copán: The Iconography.* Norman: University of Oklahoma Press, 1994.

Benson, Elizabeth P., comp. *Death and the Afterlife in Pre-Columbian America.* Washington: Dumbarton Oaks, 1975.

Berdan, Frances F. *The Aztecs of Central Mexico: An Imperial Society.* New York: Holt, Rinehart and Winston, 1982.

Berger, Pamela. *The Goddesses Obscured: Transformation of the Grain Protectress from Goddess to Saint.* Boston: Beacon Press, 1985.

Berlo, Janet. "Icons and Ideologies at Teotihuacan: The Great Goddess Reconsidered." In *Art, Ideology, and the City of Teotihuacan,* compiled by Janet Berlo, 129–68. Washington: Dumbarton Oaks Research Library and Collection, 1992.

Berrin, Kathleen, comp. *Feathered Serpents and Flowering Trees: Reconstructing the Murals of Teotihuacan.* San Francisco: Fine Arts Museum of San Francisco, 1988.

Berrin, Kathleen, and Esther Pasztory, comps. *Teotihuacan: Art from the City of the Gods.* San Francisco: Fine Arts Museum of San Francisco, 1993.

Bonnefoy, Yves, comp. *Greek and Egyptian Mythologies.* Chicago: University of Chicago Press, 1992.

Boone, Elizabeth Hill, comp. *The Codex Magliabechiano and the Lost Prototype of the Magliabechiano Group.* 2 vols. Berkeley: University of California Press, 1983.

————, comp. *Ritual Human Sacrifice in Mesoamerica.* Washington: Dumbarton Oaks Research Library and Collection, 1984.

————, comp. *The Aztec Templo Mayor.* Washington: Dumbarton Oaks Research Library and Collection, 1987.

Boone, Elizabeth Hill, and Walter D. Mignolo, comps. *Writing without Words: Alternative Literacies in Mesoamerica and the Andes.* Durham, N.C.: Duke University Press, 1994.

Bottéro, Jean, and Samuel Noah Kramer. *Lorsque les dieux faisaient l'homme.* Paris: Gallimard, 1989.

Bricker Reifler, Victoria. *The Indian Christ, the Indian King: The Historical Substrate of Maya Myth and Ritual.* Austin: University of Texas Press, 1981. (Spanish edition: *El Cristo indígena, el rey nativo: El sustrato histórico de la mitología del ritual de los mayas.* Mexico City: Fondo de Cultura Económica, 1991.)

Broda, Johanna. "La fiesta azteca de los dioses de la lluvia." *Revista Española de Antropología Americana* 6 (1971): 243–327.

————. "La fiesta azteca del fuego nuevo y el culto a las pléyades." In *La antropología americanista en la actualidad: Homenaje a Raphael Girard,* 283–304. Mexico City: Editores Mexicanos Unidos, vol. 2, 1980.

————. "Templo Mayor as Ritual Space." In *The Great Temple of Tenochtitlan: Center and Periphery in the Aztec World,* compiled by Johanna Broda, David Carrasco, and Eduardo Matos, 61–123. Berkeley: University of California Press, 1987.

————. "The Provenience of the Offerings: Tribute and Cosmovision." In *The*

Aztec Templo Mayor, compiled by Elizabeth Boone, 211–56. Washington: Dumbarton Oaks Research Library and Collection, 1987.

———. "The Sacred Landscape of Aztec Calendar Festivals: Myth, Nature, and Society." In *To Change Place: Aztec Ceremonial Landscape,* compiled by David Carrasco, 74–120. Niwot: University of Colorado Press, 1991.

Brüggemann, Jürgen. "El juego de pelota." In *El Tajín,* 85–97. Mexico City: Citibank, 1992.

Brundage, Burr C. *The Phoenix of the Western World: Quetzalcoatl and the Sky Religion.* Norman: University of Oklahoma Press, 1982.

Budge, E. A. Wallis. *Osiris and the Egyptian Resurrection.* 2 vols. New York: Dover Publications, 1973.

Burger, Richard L. "The Sacred Center of Chavin de Huantar." In *The Ancient Americas,* compiled by Richard F. Townsend, 265–78. Chicago: Art Institute of Chicago, 1992.

Cabrera Castro, Rubén, Saburo Sugiyama, and George L. Cowgill. "The Templo de Quetzalcoatl Project at Teotihuacan." *Ancient Mesoamerica* 2 (1991): 77–92.

Cacaxtla. Mexico City: Citicorp, 1987.

Campbell, Joseph. *El héroe de las mil caras: Psicoanálisis del mito.* Mexico City: Fondo de Cultura Económica, 1959.

———. *The Hero with a Thousand Faces.* Princeton: Princeton University Press, 1972.

———. *Myths to Live By.* London: Souvenir Books, 1973.

———. *Creative Mythology: The Masks of God.* New York: Penguin Books, 1976.

———. *Occidental Mythology: The Masks of God.* New York: Penguin Books, 1976.

———. *Oriental Mythology: The Masks of God.* New York: Penguin Books, 1976.

———. *Primitive Mythology: The Masks of God.* New York: Penguin Books, 1976.

Campos, Julieta. *Bajo el signo de Ix Bolon.* Mexico City: Gobierno del Estado de Tabasco–Fondo de Cultura Económica, 1988.

Carlsen, Robert S., and Martin Prechtel. "The Flowering of the Dead: An Interpretation of Highland Maya Culture." *Man* 6, no. 1 (1991): 23–42.

Carrasco, David. *Quetzalcoatl and the Irony of Empire: Myths and Prophecies in the Aztec Tradition.* Chicago: University of Chicago Press, 1982.

Carrasco, Pedro. "La sociedad mexicana antes de la Conquista." In *Historia general de México,* 165–288. Mexico City: El Colegio de México, 1977. Vol. 1.

Caso, Alfonso. "El paraíso terrenal de Teotihuacan." *Cuadernos Americanos,* no. 6 (1942): 27–136.

———. *El pueblo del sol.* Mexico City: Fondo de Cultura Económica, 1975.

———. *Reyes y reinos de la Mixteca.* Mexico City: Fondo de Cultura Económica, 1977 (vol. 1), 1979 (vol. 2).

Caso, Alfonso, and Ignacio Bernal. *Urnas de Oaxaca.* Mexico City: Instituto Nacional de Antropología e Historia, 1952.

Castellón Huerta, Román. "Mitos cosmogónicos de los nahuas antiguos." In *Mitos cosmogónicos del México indígena,* coordinated by Monjaraz-Ruiz, 125–76. Mexico City: Instituto Nacional de Antropología e Historia, 1987.

Clancy, S. Flora, and Peter D. Harrison, comps. *Vision and Revision in Maya Studies.* Albuquerque: University of New Mexico, 1990.

Clendinnen, Inga. *Aztecs: An Interpretation.* Cambridge: Cambridge University Press, 1991.

Closs, Michael, A. Aveni, and Bruce Crowley. "The Planet Venus and Temple 22 at Copan." *Indiana* 9 (1984): 221–47.

Codex Borgia: A Full-Color Restoration of the Ancient Mexican Manuscript. Compiled by Gisele Díaz and Alan Rodgers, introduction and commentary by Bruce E. Byland. New York: Dover Publications, 1993.

Codex Vindobonensis Mexicanus I. Edition by Ferdinand Anders, Maarten Jansen, and Gabina Aurora Pérez Jiménez. Mexico City: Fondo de Cultura Económica, 1992.

Códice Azcatitlán. Edited facsimile by Robert Barlow. *Journal de la Societé des Américanistes,* new ser. (1949): vol. 38, 101–35.

Códice Borbónico. Mexico City: Siglo XXI, 1980.

Códice Borgia. Mexico City: Fondo de Cultura Económica, 1993.

Códice Chimalpopoca: Anales de Cuauhtitlán y Leyenda de los soles. Edited and translated by Primo Feliciano Velázquez. Mexico City: Universidad Nacional Autónoma de México, Instituto de Investigaciones Históricas, Primera Serie Prehispánica, 1945.

"Códice Fejérváry-Mayer." In Kingsborough, *Antigüedades de México,* edition and interpretation by José Corona Núñez, 4:185–275. Mexico City: Secretaría de Hacienda, 1967.

Códice Florentino. Manuscript 218–220 of the Colección Palatina de la Biblioteca Medicea Laurenziana, edited facsimile. 3 vols. Mexico City: Secretaría de Gobernación, Archivo General de la Nación, 1979.

Coe, Michael D. *The Maya Scribe and His World.* New York: Grolier Club, 1973.

———. *Lords of the Underworld: Masterpiece of Classic Maya Ceramics.* Princeton: Princeton University Press, 1978.

———. "Religion and the Rise of Mesoamerican States." In *The Transition to Statehood in the New World,* compiled by Grant D. Jones and Robert R. Kautz, 155–77. Cambridge: Cambridge University Press, 1981.

———. *Old Gods and Young Heroes: The Pearlman Collection of Maya Ceramics.* Photographs by Justin Kerr. Jerusalem: Israel Museum, Maremont Pavilion of Ethnic Arts, 1982.

———. *Rediscovered Masterpieces of Mesoamerica: México-Guatemala-Honduras.* Bolonia: Editions Arts, 1985.

———. "The Hero-Twins: Myth and Image." In *The Maya Vase Book,* compiled by Justin Kerr, 1:161–84. New York: Kerr Associates, 1989.

———. *Breaking the Maya Code.* New York: Thames and Hudson, 1992.

Coggins, Clemence, and Orrin C. Shane III. *El cenote de los sacrificios.* Mexico City: Fondo de Cultura Económica, 1989.

Cohodas, Marvin. "Ballgame Imagery of the Maya Lowlands: History and Iconography." In *The Mesoamerican Ballgame,* compiled by Vernon L. Scarborough and David R. Wilcox, 251–87. Tucson: University of Arizona Press, 1991.

Covarrubias, Miguel. *Arte indígena de México y Centroamérica.* Mexico City: Universidad Nacional Autónoma de México, 1961.

Cowgill, George L. "Toward a Political History of Teotihuacan." In *Ideology and Pre-Columbian Civilizations,* compiled by Arthur A. Demarest and Geoffrey W. Conrad. Santa Fe: School of American Research Press, 1992.

Culbert, T. Patrick. "Maya Political History and Elite Interaction: A Summary Review." In *Classic Maya Political History: Hieroglyphic and Archaeological Evidence,* compiled by T. Patrick Culbert, 311–46. Cambridge: Cambridge University Press, 1991.

Danien, Elin C., and Robert J. Sharer, comps. *New Theories on the Ancient Maya.* Philadelphia: University Museum–University of Pennsylvania, 1992.

Davies, Nigel. *The Toltecs.* Norman: University of Oklahoma Press, 1977.

———. *The Toltec Heritage: From the Fall of Tula to the Rise of Tenochtitlan.* Norman: University of Oklahoma Press, 1980.

De la Fuente, Beatriz. "Toward a Conception of Monumental Olmec Art." In *The Olmec and Their Neighbors,* compiled by Elizabeth P. Benson, 83–94. Washington: Dumbarton Oaks Research Library and Collection, 1981.

Delhalle, Jean Claude, and Albert Luykx. "The Nahuatl Myth of the Creation of Humankind: A Coastal Connection?" In *American Antiquity* 51, no. 1 (1986): 117–21.

Detienne, Marcel. *Les jardins d'Adonis.* Paris: Gallimard, 1972.

———. "Adonis and the Adonia." In *Greek and Egyptian Mythologies,* compiled by Yves Bonnefoy, 134–36. Chicago: University of Chicago Press, 1992.

———. "Demeter." In *Greek and Egyptian Mythologies,* compiled by Yves Bonnefoy, 152–56. Chicago: University of Chicago Press, 1992.

Diehl, Richard A. "Tula." In *Supplement to the Handbook of Middle American Indians,* 277–95. Austin: University of Texas Press, 1981.

Durán, Fray Diego. *Historia de las Indias de Nueva España e islas de tierra firme.* 2 vols. Edited by Ángel Ma. Garibay. Mexico City: Editorial Porrúa, 1984.

Duverger, Christian. *El origen de los aztecas.* Translated by Carmen Arizmendi. Mexico City: Grijalbo, 1987.

Dütting, Dieter. "On the Astronomical Background of Mayan Historical Events." In *Fifth Palenque Round Table, 1983,* compiled by Merle Greene Robertson, 261–74. San Francisco: Pre-Columbian Art Research Institute, 1985.

Earle, Duncan M. "The Metaphor of the Day in Quiche: Notes on the Nature of the Everyday Life." In *Symbol and Meaning beyond the Closed Community: Essays in Mesoamerican Ideas,* compiled by Gary H. Gossen, 155–72. New York: Institute for Mesoamerican Studies, 1986.

Edmonson, Munro S. *The Book of Counsel: The Popol Vuh of the Guatemala Quiche.* Orleans: Middle American Research Institute Publication, 35, 1971.

Estrada Monroy, Agustín. *El mundo K'echi' de la Verapaz.* Guatemala City: Editorial del Ejército, 1979.

Fernández, Justino. *Coatlicue: Estética del arte indígena antiguo.* Mexico City: Universidad Nacional Autónoma de México, 1959.

Fields, Virginia M. "The Iconographic Heritage of the Maya Jester God." In *Sixth Palenque Round Table,* compiled by Merle Greene Robertson, 167–74. Norman: University of Oklahoma Press, 1986.

———. "The Origins of Divine Kingship among the Lowland Classic Maya." Doctoral thesis, Ann Arbor, University Microfilms International, 1989.

Flannery, Kent, and Joyce Marcus, comps. *The Cloud People: Divergent Evolution of the Zapotec and Mixtec Civilizations.* New York: New York Academic Press, 1983.

Florescano, Enrique. "Mito e historia en la memoria nahua." *Historia Mexicana* (Colegio de México) 39 (1990): 607–61.

———. *Tiempo, espacio y memoria histórica entre los mayas.* Tuxtla Gutiérrez: Gobierno del Estado de Chiapas, 1992.

———. *El mito de Quetzalcóatl.* 1st ed. Mexico City: Fondo de Cultura Económica, 1993.

———. *Memoria mexicana.* Mexico City: Fondo de Cultura Económica, 1994.

———. "Mitos mesoamericanos: Hacia un enfoque histórico." *Vuelta,* no. 207 (February 1994): 25–35.

Foncerrada de Molina, Marta, and Sonia Lombardo de Ruiz. *Vasijas pintadas mayas en contexto arqueológico.* Mexico City: Universidad Nacional Autónoma de México, 1979.

Fox, John W. *Maya Postclassic State Formation: Segmentary Lineage Migration in Advancing Frontiers.* Cambridge: Cambridge University Press, 1987.

Frankfort, Henri. *Reyes y dioses.* Madrid: Alianza Editorial, 1988.

Frazer, James George. *The Golden Bough.* London: Macmillan, 1966.

———. *La rama dorada.* Mexico City: Fondo de Cultura Económica, 1961.

Freidel, David. "The Jester God: The Beginning and End of a Maya Royal Symbol." In *Vision and Revision in Maya Studies,* compiled by Flora S. Clancy and Peter D. Harrison, 67–78. Albuquerque: University of New Mexico Press, 1990.

Freidel, David, Linda Schele and, Joy Parker. *Maya Cosmos: Three Thousand Years on the Shaman's Path.* New York: William Morrow and Co., 1993.

Furst, Jill Leslie. *Codex Vindobonensis Mexicanus I: A Commentary.* Albany: Institute for Mesoamerican Studies–State University of New York, 1978.

Furst, Peter T. "Jaguar Baby or Toad Mother: A New Look at an Old Problem in Olmec Iconography." In *The Olmec and Their Neighbors,* compiled by Elizabeth P. Benson, 149–62. Washington: Dumbarton Oaks Research Library and Collection, 1981.

Fussell, Betty. *The History of Corn.* New York: Alfred A. Knopf, 1992.

Gamio, Manuel. *La población del Valle de Teotihuacan.* 5 vols. Mexico City: Instituto Nacional Indigenista, 1979.

García, Gregorio. *Origen de los indios del Nuevo Mundo.* Mexico City: Fondo de Cultura Económica, 1981.

Garibay, Ángel Ma., comp. *Teogonía e historia de los mexicanos.* Mexico City: Editorial Porrúa, 1965.

Garza, Mercedes de la. *El universo sagrado de la serpiente entre los mayas.* Mexico City: Universidad Nacional Autónoma de México, 1984.

Gay, Carlo T. E. *Chalcatzingo.* Graz, Austria: Akademische Druckv. Verlagsanstalt Graz, 1971.

Gendrop, Paul, and Doris Heyden. *Arquitectura mesoamericana.* Madrid: Aguilar Ediciones, 1975.

Gillespie, Susan D. "Ballgames and Boundaries." In *The Mesoamerican Ballgame,* compiled by Vernon L. Scarborough and David R. Wilcox, 317–45. Tucson: University of Arizona Press, 1991.

Gimbutas, Marija. *Civilization of the Goddess.* San Francisco: Harper San Francisco, 1991.

———. *The Language of the Goddess.* San Francisco: Harper San Francisco, 1989.

———. *The Goddesses and Gods of Old Europe.* Berkeley: University of California Press, 1992.

Goblet d'Alviella, Eugéne. *The Mysteries of Eleusis: Mystery Tradition.* Wellingborough: Northants Aquarian Press, 1981.

Gordon, Cyrus H. "Canaanite Mythology." In *Mythologies of the Ancient World,* compiled by Samuel Noah Kramer, 181–218. New York: Anchor Books, 1961.

Gossen, Gary H. *Los chamulas en el mundo del sol: Tiempo y espacio de una tradición oral maya.* Mexico City: Instituto Nacional Indigenista, 1979.

———, comp. *Symbol and Meaning beyond the Closed Community: Essays in Mesoamerican Ideas.* New York: Institute for Mesoamerican Studies, 1986.

Graulich, Michel. *Quetzalcóatl y el espejismo de Tollan.* Antwerp: Instituut voor Amerikanistick, 1988.

Griffiths, J. Gwyn. *The Origins of Osiris and His Cult.* Leiden: E. J. Brill, 1980.

Grove, David C. *The Olmec Paintings of Oxtotitlan Cave, Guerrero, Mexico.* Washington: Dumbarton Oaks Research Library and Collection, 1970.

———. "Olmec Altars and Myths." *Archaeology,* no. 26 (1973): 128–35.

———, comp. *Ancient Chalcatzingo.* Austin: University of Texas Press, 1987.

———. "Chalcatzingo and Its Olmec Connection." In *Regional Perspectives on the*

Olmec, compiled by David Sharer and David C. Grove. Cambridge: Cambridge University Press, 1989.

Grove, David C., and Susan D. Gillespie. "Chalcatzingo Portrait Figurines and the Cult of the Ruler." *Archaeology* 4, no. 37 (1984): 27–33.

———. "Formative Period in Mesoamerica." *Ideology and Pre-Columbian Civilizations,* compiled by Arthur A. Demarest and Geoffrey W. Conrad, Santa Fe: School of American Research Press, 1992.

Gutiérrez, Mary E. "Ballcourts: The Chasm of Creation." *Texas Notes on Precolumbian Art, Writing and Culture,* no. 53 (1993): 1–3.

Healan, Dan M., comp. *Tula of the Toltecs.* Iowa City: University of Iowa Press, 1989.

Heller, Agnes. *Teoría de la historia.* Mexico City: Fontamara, 1982.

———. *A Theory of History.* London: Routledge & Kegan Paul, 1982.

Hellmuth, Nicholas. "The Primary Young Lord." In *Abstracts, 44th International Congress of Americanists,* Manchester, England, 1982.

———. "The Holmul Dancer and the 'Principal Young Lord' in Maya Art." Manuscript, 1982.

———. "The Iconography of the Early Classic Peten Maya Underwater Cosmos." In *Preliminary Notes in Maya Iconography,* 1982–84, no. 4, Culver City, Calif.: Foundation for Latin American Anthropological Research.

———. *Monster und Menschen in der Maya-Kunst.* Graz, Austria: Akademische Druckv. Verlagsanstalt Graz, 1987.

———. *The Surface of the Underwaterworld: Iconography of the Gods of Early Classic Maya Art in Peten, Guatemala.* Vol 2. Culver City, Calif.: Foundation for Latin American Anthropological Research, 1987.

Heyden, Doris. "An Interpretation of the Cave underneath the Pyramid of the Sun in Teotihuacan, Mexico." *American Antiquity,* no. 40 (1975): 131–47.

Hirth, Kenneth G. "Militarism and Social Organization at Xochicalco, Morelos." In *Mesoamerica after the Decline of Teotihuacan: A.D. 700–900,* compiled by Richard Diehl and Janet Berlo, 69–81. Washington: Dumbarton Oaks Research Library and Collection, 1989.

"Historia de los mexicanos por sus pinturas." See Ángel Ma. Garibay, comp., *Teogonía e historia de los mexicanos.*

"Histoyre du Mechique." See Ángel Ma. Garibay, comp., *Teogonía e historia de los mexicanos.*

Hooke, Samuel Henry. *Middle Eastern Mythology.* Aylesbury: Penguin Books, 1963.

Horcasitas, Fernando. "An Analysis of the Deluge Myth in Mesoamerica." In *The Flood Myth,* compiled by Alan Dundes. Berkeley: University of California Press, 1988.

Houston, Stephen, David Stuart, and Karl Taube. "Image and Text in the 'Jauncy

Vase.'" In *The Maya Vase Book,* compiled by Justin Kerr, 3:498–512. New York: Kerr Associates, 1992.

Jiménez Moreno, Wigberto. "Tula y los toltecas según las fuentes históricas." *Revista Mexicana de Estudios Antropológicos* (1941): 79–84.

———. "Síntesis de la historia pretolteca en Mesoamérica." In *Esplendor del México Antiguo,* 2 vols., compiled by Raúl Noriega, Carmen Cook, and Julio Rodolfo Moctezuma, 2:1019–1108. Mexico City: Centro de Investigaciones Antropológicas de México, 1959.

Joralemon, Peter D. *A Study of Olmec Iconography.* Washington: Dumbarton Oaks, 1971.

———. "The Olmec Dragon: A Study in Pre-Columbian Iconography." In *Origins of Religious Art and Iconography in Preclassic Mesoamerica,* compiled by Henry B. Nicholson, 27–71. Los Angeles: University of California at Los Angeles, Latin American Center Publications, 1976.

Juan Cano, Relaciones de. *Relación de la genealogía y linaje de los señores que han señoreado esta tierra de la Nueva España; Origen de los mexicanos: Nueva Colección de documentos para la historia de México.* Edited by Joaquín García Icazbalceta. Mexico City: Editorial Chávez Hayhoe, 1941.

Kelley, David. "The Birth of the Gods at Palenque." *Estudios de Cultura Maya,* no. 5, Universidad Nacional Autónoma de México (1965): 93–134.

Kereny, Carl. *Eleusis: Archetypal Image of Mother and Daughter.* Princeton: Princeton University Press, 1967.

Kerr, Justin. *The Maya Vase Book: A Corpus of Rollout Photographs of Maya Vases.* 3 vols. New York: Kerr Associates, 1989–92.

King, Mark Bernard. "Mixtec Political Ideology: Historical Metaphors and the Poetics of Political Symbolism." Doctoral thesis, Ann Arbor, UMI Dissertation Services, 1988.

———. "Hearing the Echoes of Verbal Art in Mixtec Writing." In *Writing without Words: Alternative Literacies in Mesoamerica,* compiled by Elizabeth H. Boone and Walter D. Mignolo, 102–36. Durham, N.C.: Duke University Press, 1994.

Kingsborough, Lord Edward King. *Antigüedades de México.* 4 vols. Edited by José Corona Núñez. Mexico City: Secretaría de Hacienda y Crédito Público, 1964–67.

Kirk, G. S. *El mito: Su significado y funciones en las distintas culturas.* Barcelona: Barral Editores, 1973.

———. *Myth: Its Meaning and Functions in Ancient and Other Cultures.* Berkeley: University of California Press, 1970.

Klein, Cecelia F. "The Ideology of Autosacrifice at the Templo Mayor." In *The Aztec Templo Mayor,* compiled by Elizabeth H. Boone, 293–370. Washington: Dumbarton Oaks Research Library and Collection, 1987.

Koontz, Rex. "Aspects of Founding Central Places in Post-Classic Mesoamerica."

In *The Briefing Book for Cosmology and Natural Modeling among an Aboriginal American Peoples*. Austin: University of Texas Press, Art Department and College of Fine Arts, 1993.

Kramer, Samuel Noah, comp. *Mythologics of the Ancient World*. New York: Anchor Books, 1961.

———. *Sumerian Mythology*. Philadelphia: University of Pennsylvania Press, 1972.

Landa, Fray Diego de. *Relación de las cosas de Yucatán*. Mexico City: Editorial Porrúa, 1982.

Larios, Rudi, William Fash, and David Stuart. "Architectural History and Political Symbolism of Temple 22, Copan." Presentation given at the Seventh Palenque Round Table, 1989.

Lathrap, Donald W. "Our Father the Cayman, Our Mother the Gourd: Spinden Revisited, or a Unitary Model for the Emergence of Agriculture in the New World." In Charles A. Reed, *Origins of Agriculture*, 713–52. The Hague: Mouton Publishers, 1977.

León y Gama, Antonio de. *Descripción histórica y cronológica de las dos piedras que con ocasión del nuevo empedrado que se está formando en la plaza principal de México se hallaron en ella el año de 1730*. Mexico City: Imprenta del Ciudadano Alejandro Valdés, 1832; facsimile ed., Instituto Nacional de Antropología e Historia, 1990.

León-Portilla, Miguel. *Quetzalcóatl*. Mexico City: Fondo de Cultura Económica, 1968.

———. *Toltecáyotl: Aspectos de la cultura náhuatl*. Mexico City: Fondo de Cultura Económica, 1981.

———. "The Ethnohistorical Record for the Huey Teocalli of Tenochtitlan." In *The Aztec Templo Mayor*, compiled by Elizabeth H. Boone. Washington: Dumbarton Oaks Research Library and Collection, 1987.

Lincoln, Charles. "The Chronology of Chichen Itza: A Review of the Literature." In *Late Lowland Maya Civilization: Classic to Postclassic*, compiled by Jeremy Sabloff and Wyllys Andrews, 141–96. Albuquerque: University of New Mexico Press, 1986.

López Austin, Alfredo. *Hombre-Dios: Religión y política en el mundo náhuatl*. Mexico City: Universidad Nacional Autónoma de México, 1973.

———. *Los mitos del tlacuache*. Mexico City: Editorial Patria, 1990.

López Austin, Alfredo, L. López Luján, and S. Sugiyama. "El Templo de Quetzalcóatl en Teotihuacan: Su posible significado ideológico." Manuscript, 1991.

Lounsbury, Floyd G. "Astronomical Knowledge and Its Uses at Bonampak, Mexico." In *Archaeoastronomy in the New World*, compiled by Anthony Aveni, 143–68. New York: Cambridge University Press, 1982.

———. "The Identities of the Mythological Figures in the Cross Group Inscriptions of Palenque." In *Fourth Palenque Round Table*, compiled by Merle Greene Robertson, 45–58. San Francisco: Pre-Columbian Art Research Institute, 1985.

Maarten, Evert. "Huisi Tacu." Doctoral thesis, Escuela Nacional de Antropología, Mexico City, 1976.

Marcus, Joyce. *Mesoamerican Writing Systems: Propaganda, Myth, and History in Four Ancient Civilizations.* Princeton: Princeton University Press, 1992.

Markman, Roberta, and Peter Markman. *Masks of the Spirit: Image and Metaphor in Mesoamerica.* Berkeley: University of California Press, 1989.

———. *The Flayed God: The Mythology of Mesoamerica.* New York: Harper, 1992.

Marquina, Ignacio. *El Templo Mayor de México.* Mexico City: Instituto Nacional de Antropología e Historia, 1960.

———. *Arquitectura prehispánica.* Mexico City: Instituto Nacional de Antropología e Historia, 1981.

Martínez Donjuán, Guadalupe. "Teopantecuanitlán, Guerrero: Un sitio olmeca." *Revista Mexicana de Estudios Antropológicos,* no. 28 (1982): 128–33.

Maudslay, Alfred P. *Biologia Centrali-Americana; or, Contributions to the Knowledge of the Flora and Fauna of Mexico and Central America.* 6 vols. London: 1889–1902; ed. facsimile Francisco Robicsek, New York: Milpatron Publishing Corp., 1974.

Memorial de Sololá: Anales de los Cakchiqueles. Translation, introduction, and notes by Adrián Recinos. Mexico City: Fondo de Cultura Económica, 1950.

Miller, Arthur. *The Mural Painting of Teotihuacan.* Washington: Dumbarton Oaks Library and Collection, 1973.

Miller, Mary E. *The Murals of Bonampak.* Princeton: Princeton University Press, 1986.

Miller, Mary E., and Karl Taube. *The Gods and Symbols of Ancient Mexico and the Maya.* New York: Thames and Hudson, 1993.

Miller, Virginia. "Star Warriors at Chichen Itza." In *Word and Image in Maya Culture: Explorations in Language, Writing, and Representation,* compiled by William Hanks and Don Rice, 287–305. Salt Lake City: University of Utah Press, 1989.

Millon, Rene. "The Last Years of Teotihuacan Dominance." In *The Collapse of Ancient State and Civilizations,* compiled by Yoffee Norman and George Cowgill, 102–64. Tucson: University of Arizona Press, 1988.

Molina Montes, Augusto F. "Templo Mayor Architecture: So What's New?" In *The Aztec Templo Mayor,* compiled by Elizabeth H. Boone. Washington: Dumbarton Oaks Research Library and Collection, 1987.

Monaghan, John Desmond. "We Are People Who Eat Tortillas." In "Household and Community in the Mixteca," doctoral thesis, Ann Arbor, UMI Dissertation Services, 1987.

Morris, Earl H. *The Temple of the Warriors.* New York: Charles Scribner's Sons, 1931.

Nagao, Debra. "Public Proclamation in the Art of Cacaxtla and Xochicalco." In *Mesoamerica after the Decline of Teotihuacan: A.D. 700–900,* compiled by Richard A. Diehl and Janet Catherine Berlo, 83–104. Washington: Dumbarton Oaks Research Library and Collection, 1989.

Nicholson, Henry B. "Topiltzin Quetzalcoatl of Tollan: A Problem in Mesoamerican Ethnohistory." Doctoral thesis, Harvard University, 1957.

————. "Religion in Pre-Hispanic Central Mexico." In *Handbook of Middle American Indians,* 10:395–445. Austin: University of Texas Press, 1971.

————. "Ehécatl Quetzalcoatl vs. Topiltzin Quetzalcoatl of Tollan: A Problem in Mesoamerican Religion and History." In *Actes du XLIIe Congrés International des Américanistes,* vol. 6. Paris: Société des Américanistes, 1976.

————. "The Deity 9 Wind 'Ehecatl-Quetzalcoatl' in the Mixteca Pictorials." *Journal of Latin American Lore* 4, no. 1 (1978): 61–92.

Nicholson, Henry B., and Eloise Quiñones Keber. *Art of Aztec Mexico: Treasures of Tenochtitlan.* Washington: National Gallery of Art, 1983.

Niederberger Betton, Christine. *Paleopaysage et Archéologie pré-urbaine du bassin de México.* Mexico City: Centre d'Etudes Mexicaines et Centramericaines, 1987.

Palacios, Enrique. *La cintura de serpientes en la pirámide de Tenayuca.* Mexico City: Talleres Gráficos del Museo Nacional de Arqueología, Historia y Etnografía, 1935.

Paso y Troncoso, Francisco del. *Descripción, historia y composición del Códice Borbónico.* Edited facsimile, commentary by E. T. Hamy. Mexico City: Siglo XXI, 1979.

Pasztory, Esther. "The Xochicalco Stelae and a Middle Classic Deity Triad in Mesoamerica." *Actas del XXIII Congreso Internacional de Historia del Arte* (1973): 185–215.

————. *The Murals of Tepantitla, Teotihuacan.* New York: Garland, 1976.

————. "Artistic Traditions of the Middle Classic Period." In *Middle Classic Mesoamerica: A.D. 400–700,* 131–32. New York: Columbia University Press, 1978.

————. *Aztec Art.* New York: Abrams, 1983.

————. *Teotihuacan: Art from the City of the Gods.* New York: Thames and Hudson, 1993.

Patai, Raphael. *The Hebrew Goddess.* Detroit: Wayne State University Press, 1990.

Piña Chan, Román. *Quetzalcóatl, Serpiente Emplumada.* Mexico City: Fondo de Cultura Económica, 1977.

Popol Vuh. Translation, introduction, and notes by Adrián Recinos. Mexico City: Fondo de Cultura Económica, 1961.

Plutarch (Plutarco). *Oeuvres morales: Isis et Osiris.* Translated by Christian Froidefond. Paris: Les Belles Lettres, 1988.

Quiñones Keber, Eloise. "Topiltzin Quetzalcoatl in Texts and Images." Master's thesis, Columbia University, 1979.

————. "From Tollan to Tlapallan: The Tale of Topiltzin Quetzalcoatl in the Codex Vaticanus A." *Latin American Indian Literatures Journal* 3, no. 1 (1987): 76–94.

————. "The Aztec Image of Topiltzin Quetzalcoatl." In *Smoke and Mist: Meso-*

american Studies in Memory of Thelma D. Sullivan, compiled by Kathryn Josserand and Karen Dakin, 329–43. Oxford: Bar, 1988.

———. "Quetzalcoatl as a Dynastic Patron: The 'Acuecuexatl Stone' Reconsidered." In *The Symbolism in the Plastic and Pictorial Representations of Ancient Mexico,* compiled by Jacqueline Durand de Forest and Marc Erisinger, 149–55. Amsterdam: Estudios Americanistas de Bonn, 1993.

Reents-Budet, Dorie. "The 'Holmul Dancer' Theme in Maya Art." In *Sixth Palenque Round Table,* compiled by Merle Greene Robertson, 217–32. Norman: University of Oklahoma Press, 1986.

———. *Painting the Maya Universe: Royal Ceramics of the Classic Period.* Durham, N.C.: Duke University Press, 1994.

Reilly, F. Kent, III. "Enclosed Ritual Spaces and the Watery Underworld in Formative Period Architecture: New Observations of the Function of La Venta Complex A." Mimeograph, Austin, University of Texas at Austin, Institute of Latin American Studies, 1989.

———. "Cosmos and Rulership: The Function of Olmec Style Symbols in Formative Period Mesoamerica." In *Paper Prepared for the First Sibley Family: Symposium on World Traditions of Culture and Art. April 18–21.* Austin: University of Texas Press, 1992.

Relaciones geográficas del siglo XVI: Tlaxcala, II. Edited by René Acuña. Mexico City: Universidad Nacional Autónoma de México, 1985.

Robertson, Merle Greene. *The Sculpture of Palenque.* Vol. 1, *The Temple of Inscriptions.* Princeton: Princeton University Press, 1983.

———. *The Sculpture of Palenque.* Vol. 2, *The Early Buildings of the Palace and the Wall Paintings.* Princeton: Princeton University Press, 1985.

Robicsek, Francis, and Donald M. Hales. *The Maya Book of the Dead: The Ceramic Codex.* Charlottesville: University of Virginia Art Museum, 1981.

Ruz Lhuillier, Alberto. *El Templo de las Inscripciones: Palenque.* Mexico City: Fondo de Cultura Económica, 1973.

Sáenz, César. *Quetzalcóatl.* Mexico City: Instituto Nacional de Antropología e Historia, 1962.

Sahagún, Bernardino de. *Historia general de las cosas de Nueva España.* 4 vols. Mexico City: Editorial Porrúa, 1956.

Sahlins, Marshall. *Historical Metaphors and Mythical Realities: Structure in the Early History of the Sandwich Islands Kingdom.* Ann Arbor: University of Michigan Press, 1990.

Scarborough, Vernon L., and David R. Wilcox, comps. *The Mesoamerican Ballgame.* Tucson: University of Arizona Press, 1991.

Schele, Linda. *Notebook for the Sixteenth Maya Hieroglyphic Workshop at Texas.* Austin: University of Texas Press, 1992.

———. "Creation and Cosmology in the Maya World." In *The Briefing Book for*

Cosmology and Natural Modeling among Aboriginal People. Austin: Art Department and College of the Fine Arts, 1993.

——. "The Olmec Mountain and the Tree of Creation in Mesoamerica Cosmology." Manuscript, 1994.

Schele, Linda, Barbara Fash, and Khristaan Villela. "Venus and the Reign of Smoke-Monkey." *Copan Mosaic Project: Copán Note 100* (September 1991): 1–5.

Schele, Linda, and David Freidel. *A Forest of Kings: The Untold Story of the Ancient Maya*. New York: William Morrow and Co., 1990.

Schele, Linda, and David Freidel. "The Courts of Creation: Ballcourts, Ballgames, and Portals to the Maya Other World." In *The Mesoamerican Ballgame*, compiled by Vernon L. Scarborough and David R. Wilcox, 289–315. Tucson: University of Arizona Press, 1991.

Schele, Linda, and Nicolai Graube. "The Peten Wars 8.17.0.0.0–9.15.13.0.0." In *Notebook for the Eighteenth Maya Hieroglyphic Workshop*. Austin: Department of Art and History, 1994.

Schele, Linda, Rudi Larios, and Khristaan Villela. "Some Venus Dates on the Hieroglyphic Stair at Copan." *Copan Mosaic Project: Copan Note 99* (September 1991): 1–8.

Schele, Linda, and Mary Ellen Miller. *The Blood of Kings: Dynasty and Ritual in Maya Art*. Fort Worth: Kimbell Art Museum, 1986.

Scholes, France V., and Ralph L. Roys. *The Maya Chontal Indians of Acalan-Tixchel: A Contribution to the History and Ethnography of the Yucatan Peninsula*. Norman: University of Oklahoma Press, 1968.

Sebag, Lucien. *L'invention du monde chez les indiens pueblos*. Preface by Claude Lévi-Strauss. Paris: François Maspero, 1971.

Séjourné, Laurette. *Arquitectura y pintura en Teotihuacan*. Mexico City: Siglo XXI, 1966.

Seler, Eduard. *Comentarios al Códice Borgia*. 2 vols. Mexico City: Fondo de Cultura Económica, 1963.

Smith, Virginia G. *Izapa Relief Carving: Form, Content, Rules for Design, and Role in Mesoamerican Art History and Archaeology*. Washington: Dumbarton Oaks Research Library and Collection, 1984.

Soustelle, Jacques. *Los olmecas*. Mexico City: Fondo de Cultura Económica, 1992.

Spero, Joanne M. "Beyond Rainstorms: The Kawak as an Ancestor, Warrior, and Patron of Witchcraft." In *Sixth Palenque Round Table*, compiled by Merle Greene Robertson, 184–93. Norman: University of Oklahoma Press, 1986.

Šprajc, Ivan. "Venus, Iluvia y maíz: Simbolismo y astronomía en la cosmovisión mesoamericana." Master's thesis, Escuela Nacional de Antropología e Historia, Mexico City, 1982.

Stocker, Terry, Sara Meltzoff, and Steve Armsey. "Crocodilians and Olmecs: Further Interpretations in Formative Period Iconography." *American Antiquity* 45, no. 4 (1980): 740–58.

Stone, Andrea. "Disconnection, Foreign Insignia, and Political Expansion: Teoti-huacan and the Warrior Stelae." In *Mesoamerica after the Decline of Teotihuacan: A.D. 700-900,* compiled by Richard Diehl and Janet Berlo, 153–72. Washington: Dumbarton Oaks Research Library and Collection, 1989.

Stresser-Pean, Guy. "Ancient Sources on the Huasteca." In *Handbook of Middle American Indians: Archaeology of Northern Mesoamerica,* compiled by Robert Wauchope, vol. 11, pt. 2, pp. 582–602. Austin: University of Texas Press, 1971.

Stross, Brian. "Maize and Blood: Mesoamerica Symbolism on an Olmec Vase and a Maya Plate." *RES* 22 (1992): 82–107.

Taladoire, Eric. *Les terrains de jeu de balle (Mésoamérique et Sud-ouest des Etats-Unis).* Mexico City: Misión Arqueológica y Etnológica Francesa en México, 1981.

Tate, Carolyn A. *Yaxchilan: The Design of a Maya Ceremonial City.* Austin: University of Texas Press, 1992.

Taube, Karl. "The Classic Maya Maize God: A Reappraisal." In *Fifth Palenque Round Table,* compiled by Merle Greene Robertson, 171–81. San Francisco: Pre-Columbian Art Research Institute, 1985.

———. "The Teotihuacan Cave of Origin: The Iconography and Architecture of Emergence Mythology in Mesoamerica and the American Southwest." *RES* 12 (1986): 51–82.

———. "A Prehispanic Maya Katun Wheel." *Journal of Anthropological Research* 44, no. 2 (1988): 183–203.

———. "The Ancient Yucatecan New Year Festival: The Liminal Period in Maya Ritual and Cosmology." Doctoral thesis, Yale University, 1988.

———. "The Temple of Quetzalcoatl and the Cult of Sacred War at Teotihuacan." *RES* 21 (1992): 53–87.

———. *The Major Gods of Ancient Yucatan.* Washington: Dumbarton Oaks Research Library and Collection, 1992.

———. "The Iconography of Toltec Period: Chichen Itza." Forthcoming.

Tedlock, Barbara. *Time and the Highland Maya.* Albuquerque: University of New Mexico Press, 1992.

Tedlock, Dennis. *Popol Vuh: The Definitive Edition of the Maya Book of the Dawn of Life and the Glories of God and Kings.* New York: Simon and Schuster, 1985.

Thompson, Eric S. *Historia y religión de los mayas.* Mexico City: Siglo XXI, 1975.

———. *Maya History and Religion.* Norman: University of Oklahoma Press, 1970.

———. *Un comentario al Códice de Dresde.* Mexico City: Fondo de Cultura Económica, 1988.

Tompkins, Ptolemy. *This Tree Grows out of Hell: Mesoamerica and the Search for the Magical Body.* New York: Harper Collins Publishers, 1990.

Townsend, Richard F. "Coronation at Tenochtitlan." In *The Aztec Templo Mayor,* compiled by Elizabeth H. Boone, 371–440. Washington: Dumbarton Oaks Research Library and Collection, 1987.

———. *The Aztecs.* New York: Thames and Hudson, 1992.

————, comp. *The Ancient America*. Chicago: Art Institute of Chicago, 1992.

Umberger, Emily. "Antiques Revivals and References to the Past in Aztec Art." *RES* 13 (1987): 62–105.

Uriarte, María Teresa. *El juego de pelota en Mesoamérica: Raíces y supervivencia*. Mexico City: Siglo XXI, 1992.

Villa Rojas, Alfonso. "Los conceptos de espacio y tiempo entre los grupos mayas contemporáneos." In *Tiempo y realidad en el pensamiento maya*, compiled by Miguel León-Portilla, 119–67. Mexico City: Universidad Nacional Autónoma de México, 1986.

Vogt, Evon Z. *Tortillas for the Gods: A Symbolic Analysis of Zinacanteco Ritual*. Cambridge: Harvard University Press, 1976.

Walters, Frank. *El libro de los hopis*. Mexico City: Fondo de Cultura Económica, 1992.

Warner, Marina. *Alone of All Her Sex: The Myth and the Cult of the Virgin Mary*. New York: Vintage Books, 1993.

Wasson, Robert G., Albert Hofmann, and Carl A. Ruck. *El camino a Eleusis: Una solución el enigma de los misterios*. Mexico City: Fondo de Cultura Económica, 1980.

Westheim, Paul. *Ideas fundamentales del arte prehispánico en México*. Mexico City: Fondo de Cultura Económica, 1957.

Wilkerson, Jeffrey K. "In Search of the Mountain of Foam: Human Sacrifice in Eastern Mesoamerica." In *Ritual Human Sacrifice in Mesoamerica*, compiled by Elizabeth Benson and Elizabeth H. Boone, 101–29. Washington: Dumbarton Oaks Research Library and Collection, 1984.

————. "And Then They Were Sacrificed: The Ritual Ballgame of Northeastern Mesoamerica through Time and Space." In *The Mesoamerican Ballgame*, compiled by Vernon L. Scarborough and David Wilcox, 45–71. Tucson: University of Arizona Press, 1991.

Wren, Linnea, and Peter Schmidt. "Elite Interaction during the Terminal Classic Period: New Evidence from Chichen Itza." In *Classic Maya Political History: Hieroglyphic and Archaeological Evidence*, compiled by T. Patrick Culbert, 199–225. Cambridge: Cambridge University Press, 1991.

Yadeun, Juan. *Toniná: El laberinto del inframundo*. Mexico City: Gobierno del Estado de Chiapas, 1992.

Zantwijk, Rudolf van. *The Aztec Arrangement: The Social History of Pre-Spanish Mexico*. Prologue by Miguel León-Portilla. Oklahoma City: University of Oklahoma, 1985.

Zolbrod, Paul G. *Diné Bahané: The Navaho Creation History*. Albuquerque: University of New Mexico Press, 1984.

Zuidema, R. Tom. *Reyes y guerreros: Ensayos de cultura andina*. Lima: Fomciencias, 1989.

INDEX

Page numbers in *italics* refer to illustrations.
Those in **boldface** refer to tables.

Library of Congress Cataloging-in-Publication Data

Florescano, Enrique.

    [Mito de Quetzalcóatl. English]

    The myth of Quetzalcoatl / Enrique Florescano ; illustrations by
Raúl Velázquez ; translation by Lysa Hochroth.

      p. cm.

    Translation of: El mito de Quetzalcóatl.

    Includes bibliographical references (p.   ) and index

    ISBN 0-8018-5999-9 (acid-free paper)

    1. Quetzalcoatl (Aztec deity)   2. Aztecs—Religion.   3. Aztec art.
4. Indians of Mexico—Religion.   5. Indian art—Mexico.   I. Title.

F1219.76R45F613   1999

299'.72—dc21   98-8733

                                                   CIP